Ex Libris

William J. Fay

THE LAST GOSPEL

THE LAST GOSPEL

*Doctrinal and spiritual conferences on the
opening verses of St John's Gospel*

by

FRANCIS J. RIPLEY

SHEED & WARD · NEW YORK

NIHIL OBSTAT : JOANNES M. T. BARTON, S.T.D., L.S.S.

CENSOR DEPUTATUS

IMPRIMATUR : E. MORROGH BERNARD

VICARIUS GENERALIS

WESTMONASTERII : DIE 8a SEPTEMBRIS 1961

The Nihil obstat and Imprimatur are a declaration that a book or pamphlet is considered to be free from doctrinal or moral error. It is not implied that those who have granted the Nihil obstat and Imprimatur agree with the contents. opinions or statements expressed.

Library of Congress Catalog Card Number: 62-11095

CONTENTS

CHAP.   PAGE

1. "IN THE BEGINNING WAS THE WORD"   1

2. "THE WORD WAS WITH GOD AND THE WORD WAS GOD; THE SAME WAS IN THE BEGINNING WITH GOD"   9

3. "ALL THINGS WERE MADE BY HIM; AND WITHOUT HIM WAS MADE NOTHING THAT WAS MADE"   20

4. "IN HIM WAS LIFE, AND THE LIFE WAS THE LIGHT OF MEN"   28

5. "THE LIGHT SHINETH IN DARKNESS, AND THE DARKNESS DID NOT COMPREHEND IT"   38

6. "THERE WAS A MAN SENT FROM GOD, WHOSE NAME WAS JOHN"   47

7. "WHOSE NAME WAS JOHN"   57

8. "THIS MAN CAME FOR A WITNESS"   67

9. "TO GIVE TESTIMONY OF THE LIGHT"   76

10. "THAT ALL MEN MIGHT BELIEVE THROUGH HIM"   88

11. "HE WAS NOT THE LIGHT, BUT WAS TO GIVE TESTIMONY OF THE LIGHT" (I)   98

12. "HE WAS NOT THE LIGHT, BUT WAS TO GIVE TESTIMONY OF THE LIGHT" (II)   107

13. "THAT WAS THE TRUE LIGHT" (I)   119

14. "THAT WAS THE TRUE LIGHT" (II)   132

15. "WHICH ENLIGHTENETH EVERY MAN THAT COMETH INTO THIS WORLD"   139

16. "HE WAS IN THE WORLD, AND THE WORLD WAS MADE BY HIM, AND THE WORLD KNEW HIM NOT"   150

17. "HE CAME UNTO HIS OWN, AND HIS OWN RECEIVED HIM NOT"   161

18. "BUT AS MANY AS RECEIVED HIM, HE GAVE THEM POWER TO BE MADE THE SONS OF GOD, TO THEM THAT BELIEVE IN HIS NAME"   174

CHAP.   PAGE

19. "WHO ARE BORN, NOT OF BLOOD, NOR OF THE WILL
    OF THE FLESH, NOR OF THE WILL OF MAN, BUT OF
    GOD"   187

20. "AND THE WORD WAS MADE FLESH AND DWELT
    AMONG US"   199

21. "WE SAW HIS GLORY, THE GLORY AS IT WERE OF THE
    ONLY BEGOTTEN OF THE FATHER, FULL OF GRACE
    AND TRUTH"   211

    INDEX   223

1

"IN THE BEGINNING WAS THE WORD"

(John 1. 1)

"SUBLIME" has become a cliché when applied to the prologue to St John's Gospel. It *is* sublime in every sense—high, lofty, majestic, noble, exalted, dignified, magnificent, superb, august, none of these adjectives do justice to it. From the opening phrase it takes us far from time and creation into eternity.

"In the beginning"—the beloved disciple begins as the Holy Spirit began the Book of Genesis and his meaning is the same, "at the beginning of all created things" or "when time began". It is true that St Cyril and some of the other Fathers thought of "the beginning" as being the eternal Father; but that is not what St John wrote. Had he meant it, he would have written it.

"Beginning" does not mean eternity; there is no *direct* statement here of our Lord's eternity. At the same time we may reason as follows: when time began, in the beginning of everything else which had a beginning, the Word *was*. When everything else began he was already existing with the Father and the Holy Spirit.

What do we mean by eternity? St Augustine used to call the thought of it "the great thought". Yet it is not an easy thought. If you think of eternity as time doing a two-way stretch, backward but never beginning and forward but never ending, your notion is very inadequate. Time has really nothing to do with eternity. If you want to think of eternity as adequately as possible, you must forget time. It is only a nuisance when you try to realize what eternity means.

There is a famous definition made by Boethius, who died about A.D. 524. Here it is: *vitae interminabilis tota simul et perfecta possessio*, "the whole, perfect possession in one act of life without end". So eternity includes four essential notions: it is life; it has neither end nor beginning; it has no succession of moment to moment; it is most perfect.

When we think of life we always have the idea of a before and an after, what are we going to be, what we are, what we have

been. We should never think of God like that. With him there
is no question of before and after, or of what he was or will be
as implying change.

We can hardly think of life apart from day following day and
year succeeding year; but that implies life made of time, of part
succeeding part. It is very hard to keep the idea of life in one's
mind, and at the same time strip it of any idea of embracing
time or the succession of periods or parts. Yet, if we want to
appreciate God's eternity that is precisely what we must try to
do. No human words are adequate to describe God; no human
comparison, analogy or idea is worthy of him. All fall
short not by measurable distance but by infinity. The best
we can do is to choose the highest and most spiritual terms of
which we have any knowledge and say: "God must be like
that." For example, we talk about the existence of God.
Possibly we fail to realize that God does more than exist; he
lives. A loaf of bread exists but it does not live. Life implies
something higher than existence. God is alive. His essence is not
only his existence but his life.

We think of human life as beginning; that is an imperfection
—and God has no imperfections. He never began. Similarly, we
are familiar with the idea of life ending; that, too, is an imperfection which God cannot have. He never ends. But that is not
the principal notion of eternity. A poet once wrote:

> Little drops of water, little grains of sand
> Make the mighty ocean and the pleasant land;
> So the little minutes, humble though they be,
> Make the mighty ages of eternity.

That, strictly speaking, is untrue. The good lady might have
meant that what we do in the minutes that are ours on earth
results in eternal life—but that is not the obvious meaning. She
seems to be saying that if you string along minutes one after
another and go on and on and on, never beginning and never
ending, you have eternity. But that is precisely what you have
not got. Eternity has no minutes, no past nor future; it is
simply a never changing "now".

We will get a clearer idea of it all by thinking of another of
God's attributes, his immensity. Any material thing can be

divided into parts—a human body, for example, can be cut up. Spiritual things cannot be divided like that—a human soul, for example. All of my body is not in every part of me; my brain is not in my little toe. But all my soul is in every part of me. It has no parts. A bit of it does not operate in my arm and another bit in my ear. Wherever it operates it is present, whole and entire. It is just as wholly in my eye as it is in the tip of my finger.

Apply this to God; just as my soul is entire and whole in every fraction of the space my body occupies, so God is present, entire and whole, in every fraction of the space he has created. He has no limit in any direction but is yet entire and whole in the smallest conceivable point. Even this comparison with a human soul is inadequate to bring home the idea of God's immensity, for the soul does move and change. My soul now, to put it rather crudely, informs a larger body than it did when I was newly born; it moves about with me wherever I go. Not so with God; in him there is neither change nor shadow of alteration, neither growth nor movement (James 1. 17). He is the same here, there, everywhere—infinitely immense, yet infinitely present everywhere in his creation.

Transfer these ideas from immensity to eternity. Instead of thinking of God infinitely and immensely present in every point of space so that his immensity is not made up by adding point to point, think of him infinitely present in every "now". His immensity is an infinite, unchangeable point; his eternity is an infinite unchangeable "now". There is no question of duration or interruption, past or future, change or movement, beginning or end—simply an absolutely unchangeable, living "now".

In God, therefore, there is no advance knowledge of events nor any looking back on them. It is we who think of him seeing things in advance but he does not. It is always "now" with him. He does not foresee; he sees "now", is always present "now", helps his creatures "now". *We* do things at particular moments in particular places; in God there are neither moments nor places.

When you understand these concepts of immensity and eternity you see how futile it is to ask where God was before time and space began. There is no "before" with God. His life does not stretch back infinitely before he began to create things. To think of it in that way implies that God lasted or endured, that there was in him a succession of aeon after aeon; it contradicts the truth that he is simply the unchangeable "now", eternal. Even the *per omnia saecula saeculorum* of the liturgy could be interpreted in a wrong way, as implying succession of ages. It is a heritage from the primitive Church which took it from Holy Writ (Apoc. 1. 6; 5. 13; Heb. 7. 24). The English versions "World without end" or "For ever and ever" mean "through all eternity".

You and I exist only in stages. When I was four I did not possess the life I had at fourteen, and when I was forty-four I did not possess what I had when I was twenty-four. Not for one single moment do I possess the whole of my life; I experience it second after second. I have not now the life I had when I began to type this paragraph; I shall, so to speak, only be complete when this life is over. I have my life in successive moments; what I had yesterday I have not today; what I have today I shall not have tomorrow. God is quite different. The fact that I must go through my life second by second is an imperfection, a limitation; God has no imperfections or limitations. In one act of being, in one unchangeable "now" he is his infinite limitless self. Eternity, then, is not time with a two-way stretch; it is not time at all. To come back to our definition, it is the whole, perfect possession in one act of life without end, *vitae interminabilis tota simul et perfecta possessio*. The crucial words are *tota simul*, whole in one act or, if you like, all at once. So it is misleading to think of eternity just flowing by like a brook and creation happening at some time in it.

I once heard some children being taught how God waited until the right time before he decided to create; now we see how wrong that is. Perhaps that is why artists depict him as an old man with a beard. I suppose they must depict him in some way, but we have become so accustomed to these human images that we find ourselves out of our depth when we try to dispense with them. God isn't an old man; he isn't even an old God. There is no time, and so no age, with him. Our universe was made by God to possess its being bit by bit; but God himself is not like that—he possesses his being in one, single act. That is eternity. His act of creation was in eternity, but the result of it was time.

St John says that "the Word" existed before all creation. He possessed the eternity of God. Said St Basil: " If he was in the beginning, when was he not?"

By the "Word" St John means the Second Person of the Blessed Trinity. Outside his writings there is no certain instance in either Old or New Testament of this term being used in this way. Some scholars, but a minority, think St Paul was referring to Christ when he wrote about the "word" in Hebrews 4. 12.

Why did St John prefer to write "the Word" rather than simply "the Son"? We must not forget that he was the instrument of the Holy Ghost, who might well have required the use of such an important and such a significant term. It may be that St John used it because the Gnostic heretics of the time were using it in a wrong sense. It has been suggested, too, that, like all the Apostles, St John had a special power to understand the Sacred Scriptures, as St Luke said: "He (Christ) opened their understanding, that they might understand the scriptures" (Luke 24. 45). Therefore, may he not have seen clearly, as we do not, that certain phrases in the Old Testament referred to the Son of God? For example, "By the word of the Lord the heavens were established" (Ps. 32. 6).

The suggestion that St John borrowed his term from Plato, Philo or the school of Alexandria has been so often refuted that we need not concern ourselves with it here.

What is more to our point is to suggest that St John was inspired to use the term because it is so very appropriate. We must believe that the Son is *begotten* by the Father—not made nor created. How could he be begotten? Amongst ourselves *word* means something we produce with our vocal chords. God is a pure spirit; so his *Word* must be in the mind—an idea, a thought. With us an idea is the image, the mental double, of what we are thinking about. The more of the object it expresses, the more perfect it is. God is infinite perfection; when he has an idea of himself, that idea is perfect; it perfectly represents himself, is in no way less than himself, lacks nothing of himself but contains all his infinite perfection. It is equal to himself, an eternal living Person; God.

A thought has the same nature as him who thinks it; it is in the thinker's nature. So God's thought of himself, his Word, is wholly in the one, same divine nature. Everything the Word has he receives from the Father; everything the Father has he gives to the Word; each has the same divine nature in all its fullness; the Father has it as unreceived, the Word has it as received; the only difference is that of relationship.

Think of this now in the context of God's eternity—the infinite, unchangeable "now". Human language is our difficulty again. If I say that the Father has begotten the Son it seems to imply that something has happened and been finished. If I say the Father is begetting the Son it seems to indicate an action which is still going on but is not yet complete. Yet we have seen that in God there is no succession and no duration because there is no time. God did not become a Father at some time after he began to exist. He never began to exist; by the very act of being God he begot the Word. Both, Father and Word, have the one, same, infinite nature with all its limitless attributes. They have the same infinite knowledge. It is not separate knowledge in the Father that begets the Word; the same infinite knowledge is wholly possessed by Father, Word and Holy Spirit. Because the Father generated the Son, it does not mean that he has something the Son has not, namely that he has generated the Son. The difference is merely one of relationship. The whole, infinite Godhead is possessed by the Father and the Word each in his own way. As St Anselm put it and the Council of Florence defined it: in God all is one except for the opposition of relations.

So we see perhaps more clearly how appropriately St John referred to the second divine Person as the Word. He was implying the procession of the Son from the Father through the intellect. In us our word follows from our thought; it is the reflex of our thought; it takes nothing from our thought; it is begotten without passion or any imperfection of the flesh; it faithfully represents our thought. So in God, but in a way that is infinitely more perfect. The Son proceeds through the Father's intellect (which is common to all three Persons), taking nothing from the Father but being his perfect image, the "brightness of his glory and the figure of his substance" (Heb. 1. 3). Thus St Thomas is able to write: "'Word', said of God in its proper sense, is used personally, and is the proper name of the person of the Son. For it signifies an emanation of the intellect: and the person who proceeds in God, by way of emanation of the

intellect, is called the Son: and this procession is called generation."

Throughout Holy Writ there are allusions to the eternity of
the Messias. In the second Psalm the sacred scribe puts into
God's mouth an edict in which he proclaims that he has set up
his king, his anointed; the latter then declares his power: "The
Lord hath said to me: 'Thou art my Son; this day I have
begotten thee. Ask of me, and I will give thee the nations as thy
inheritance and the ends of the earth as thy possession' "
(Ps. 2. 7). The Messias has the fullness of the splendour due to
him as God's Son. There is no question of mere adoption here
but of making clear to all that the Messias is God's true Son. St
Paul later used this verse. Preaching at Antioch in Pisidia he
told how God had raised Christ from the dead thus endorsing
what was written in the second psalm (Acts 13. 33). The same
is gathered from the letter to the Hebrews (5. 5).

There is, too, the famous passage from the familiar 109th
psalm: "Thou art my Son, born like dew before the day-star
rises" (v. 3). The meaning is obscure but modern scholars are
agreed that the most satisfactory sense is that the Messias was
begotten before the stars were created. The prophet Micheas
was inspired to describe him as coming "from the first beginning, from ages untold" (Mich. 5. 2). The literal meaning is
"from the days of eternity" but Hebrew authors use the phrase
so loosely that it would be rash to attach certain theological
meaning to it.

Our Lord, of course, told the Jews of his eternal existence:
"Before ever Abraham came to be, I am" (John 8. 58). The
Jews understood the claim; they did not believe it; in their ears
it was a horrible blasphemy. So they tried to stone him for
making it. In his priestly prayer, our Lord asked his Father to
glorify his human nature in the glory that he as God had with
the Father before the world was: "Father, do thou exalt me at
thy own side, in that glory which I had with thee before the
world began" (John 17. 5). In the Apocalypse Christ reveals
himself as "before all . . . and the end of all", living, and to
the Hebrews: "What Jesus Christ was yesterday, and is today,
he remains for ever" (Apoc. 1. 17; 2. 8; 22. 13; Heb. 13. 8).

In principio erat verbum—only four words, and we are already
prostrate in adoration before Christ our Lord. He is God; his

life is that incomprehensible, unchangeable "now"—yet look at him—the Infinite confined within his mother's womb, the Measureless lying like any other human baby prattling in the straw, the Timeless living for only thirty-three years amongst us in human form, the Indivisible present in every consecrated Host everywhere in the world. The thought of Christ's eternity makes us realize how limitless his love is and what unfathomable depths are hidden by that most personal of all the phrases of St Paul: "He loved me and delivered himself for me" (Gal. 2. 20).

2

"THE WORD WAS WITH GOD AND THE WORD WAS GOD; THE SAME WAS IN THE BEGINNING WITH GOD"

(John 1. 1-2)

S<small>T</small> J<small>OHN</small>, inspired by the Holy Spirit, is not content with stating that God the Son is begotten by the Father in the everpresent, ceaseless, infinite "now" of eternity; he has to repeat and emphasize it. In the first place he would have us acknowledge that the Second Person lives in intimate union with the First. In his first epistle he is even more explicit: "That which was from the beginning, that which we have heard, that which we have seen with our eyes, that which we beheld, and our hands handled, in regard of the Word of life— and the life was manifested, and we have seen and bear witness and declare to you that everlasting Life which was with the Father and was manifested to us—that which we have seen and heard we declare to you also" (I John 1. 1-3). What sublime words those are! Perhaps it is significant that the Apostle omits the words of greeting customary at the beginning of letters; either it was unnecessary or he was so preoccupied with his message. Life, divine, eternal, infinite, the source of all life, God the Son has shown himself; John has seen and heard and handled him. He must pass on the vital message.

The beloved disciple wrote at the end of the first century. Even more remarkable is it that some forty years before another was writing ecstatically about the heavenly pre-existence of him whom the Jews had nailed as a criminal to a cross and whom he, Saul of Tarsus, had thought it a privilege to revile and refute. For him now, after his sensational conversion on the road to Damascus, Christ is higher than the highest heaven, vaster than the vastest space, more powerful than death, sole conqueror of sin, the fullness of the life of God, existing before all ages. "He is the image of the unseen God, firstborn of all creation. For in him were created all things in heaven and on

9

earth, things seen and things unseen, whether thrones or dominations or principalities or powers—all creation is through him
and unto him. And himself is prior to all, and in him all things
hold together" (Col. 1. 15-17). In this passage is inexhaustible
wealth of doctrine. Not only is Christ the Second Person of the
Blessed Trinity, above all creatures, existing from all eternity, he
is the efficient and final cause, the beginning and the end, the very
centre of everything created, corporeal or incorporeal. Through
his agency all came to be; in him they have their permanence,
for him they are. In him "lie hidden all the treasures of wisdom
and knowledge"; in him dwells "all the fullness of the Godhead
corporally . . . . who is the head of every principality and
power" (Col. 2. 3, 10).

What a picture of Christ this was to present to the world that
had crucified him only thirty-three years before! We find it
again in that famous passage from the Apostle's letter to the
Philippians; Christ possessed equality of being with God so that
every knee is to bend before him in heaven, on earth and in hell
(Phil. 2. 9-11). There was no gradual growth in St Paul's conception of Christ; it was complete from the moment of his
conversion. Christ was for him the incomparable, the one and
only, above whom or beside whom was nothing. Yet, our Lord
was only slightly older than Paul; they could be thought of as
contemporaries; they might have passed one another in Jerusalem's streets or the Temple's courts. The Apostle was converted at most only six or seven years after the crucifixion—
some say there was no interval of note—his preaching began
only ten years after it, his writings only another ten years later—
yet here is he proclaiming that the man who had cried out on
the cross, "My God, my God, why hast thou forsaken me"
(Matt. 27. 46), existed eternally before creation began and is
identical with the one, true God of Israel, "who is over all, God
blessed for ever" (Rom. 9. 5).

Let us glance in further detail at this picture of the divine
Christ which the New Testament presents to us. He is:

"our great God and Saviour" (Titus 2. 13) whose
"throne is for ever" (Heb. 1. 8), who is
"the true God and everlasting life" (I John 5. 19).
His origin is divine;

He "hath come down from heaven, from above, is above all, went forth from God" (John 3. 13, 31; 6. 38, 51; 8. 23, 42; 16. 5 ff.).
He is equal to the eternal Father, for "all things have been delivered to me by my Father; and no one knoweth the Son except the Father nor doth anyone know the Father except the Son and he to whom the Son may choose to reveal him" (Matt. 11. 27).

The Jews wished to kill him for "calling God his Father, making himself equal with God" (John 5. 17 ff.). When Philip begged to be shown the Father, Christ replied: "Believest thou not that I am in the Father, and the Father in me? . . . The Father abiding in me doth his works. Believe me, that I am in the Father and the Father in me" (John 14. 10 ff.). "I and the Father are one. . . . The Father is in me and I in the Father" (John 10. 30, 38).

He is eternal: "Before Abraham came to be, I am" (John 8. 58). Before the world came into existence he possessed the Father's glory (John 17. 5). He is unchangeable, "the same yesterday and today, yea, and for ever" (Heb. 13. 8). He is omnipotent, for all things have been delivered to him by his Father (Matt. 11. 27; Luke 10. 22) and all power is given to him in heaven and on earth (Matt. 28. 18). He gives life to whom he wills (John 5. 21).

He has divine pre-eminence over the angels who came and ministered to him (Matt. 4. 11), whom he sends forth as his (Matt. 13. 41), who will escort him to judge mankind (Matt. 16. 27) and on whom he can call at any time (Matt. 26. 53), they being "made subject to him" (I Peter 3. 22). "Believe in God and believe in me", he says (John 14. 1), asserting that because he goes to the Father he will do whatever we ask in his name (John 14. 13 ff.). He loves us with divine love; we must love him by doing his, God's, will (John 15. 9). Divine names are given him, Alpha and Omega (Apoc. 1. 8, etc.), Emmanuel (Matt. 1. 23), God (John 20. 28), Lord (Acts 2. 36; 7. 59 ff.; 10. 36; Rom. 10.9; I Cor. 8. 6; 16. 22 ff.; Phil. 2. 11; Jas. 1. 1; I Peter 1. 3; Jude 4. 17) and, as we have seen, Word (John 1; I John 1. 1; 5. 7; Apoc. 19. 13).

A brief summary like this not only reminds us of the supreme

dignity of our Blessed Lord, but it reveals the importance of a
right outlook towards him. The more we ponder the Godhead
of Christ, the more we will realize how his coming amongst us is
such a telling proof of God's love. We cannot really understand
devotion to his Sacred Heart unless we think of it in terms of the
hypostatic union.

Nor can we understand the epistle chosen for the feast of the
Sacred Heart unless we ponder it in the light of the eternal
Word. It is one of the most moving passages of the Apostle's
writings: "That Christ may dwell in your hearts through faith,
so that, rooted and founded in charity, ye may be able to comprehend with all the saints what is the breadth and length and
height and depth—to know the charity of Christ that surpasseth
knowledge, that ye may be filled unto all the fullness of God"
(Eph. 3. 17-19). The comment of Pope Pius XII on this passage
was: "The clearest reflection of this fullness of God, which
embraces all things, is precisely the Heart of Christ Jesus."*
He goes on: "It is blasphemous to assert that the contemplation
of the physical Heart of Christ is an obstacle to our reaching the
innermost love of God." When we honour the Sacred Heart we
honour the Person of the Word Incarnate, who, St John says,
was "in the beginning"

In the Person of Christ are united human and divine natures;
therefore, the loves of Christ are similarly united. His human
love reflects divine love. The created Heart of Christ can never
be a formal image or perfectly adequate symbol of subsistent
divine love; at the same time, we should adore the Sacred
Heart, as the Pope wrote, as "a token and as it were a footprint
of that Divine Charity which did not stop short of loving the
sin-stained race of men with the Heart of the Word Incarnate".†
The foundation of devotion to the Sacred Heart is the truth of
the hypostatic union, that is, the very truth which St John
enunciates at the beginning of his Gospel. The Heart of Jesus
is the heart of a Person who is divine, of the Word, who existed
from all eternity. It brings before us his infinite love as he
reaches out to embrace us. For this reason, and here I quote
Pius XII, "it is impossible to exaggerate the excellence of devotion to the Sacred Heart. If we consider the external practice

---

* Encyclical, *Haurietis Aquas*, C.T.S. translation, p. 36.
† *Ib.*, p. 38.

of the devotion, we must admit that it is a most perfect way of professing the Christian Religion. It is indeed, no more, nor less, the Religion of Jesus . . . . We cannot reach the Heart of God save through the Heart of Christ."

We do not pay separate homage to the divine nature and the human nature in Christ. Such a practice is condemned by the Council of the Lateran. We adore Christ's humanity, because it is the humanity of the eternal Word, and in that humanity the symbol of love is the object of special veneration, as our Lord told St Margaret Mary. All the desires, affections and inclinations of the Heart of Christ are divine; it is holy with the holiness of God himself. Thus we invoke the Sacred Heart as "infinite in majesty", the majesty of God.

What effect has all this on our spiritual lives? The lessons to be derived from the contemplation of Christ's Godhead are endless—the life of Jesus is a human life lived as God lived it and therefore the supreme example for every man; the teaching of Jesus is the revelation which God in his infinite love wanted us to know to guide us through this valley of tears, therefore we must appreciate it and use it as God intended; everything Jesus has meant to humanity is the gift of infinite love and should be valued as such; the more we try to understand the infinite majesty of his Godhead, the more we will appreciate the dignity of his Mother, and so on. But there is one lesson on which we might well concentrate here; it is the duty of adoration.

St John Eudes recommends us to adore the Sacred Heart for many reasons—the eternal Father, the divine Word and the Holy Spirit live within it; it is stamped with the impress of all the divine perfections which subsist and reign within it and it is the temple, the altar and the censor of divine love.

What is adoration? It is the self-surrender of one's whole being in prayer before God. St Bernard called it the highest form of human worship. It is the prayer of humble truth: we see ourselves as we are before God—he, infinite in all his perfections, we absolutely nothing apart from him. We acknowledge that truth; more—we express our joy that it is so; we tell God that we would not have it otherwise; we wish God all the glory that is his.

The basis of all prayer is our relationship to God, a relationship of absolute dependence. That relationship can be cultivated, no relationship has more right to cultivation nor will the cultivation of any other yield such great rewards. So often our prayer is dry or hard or unfruitful just because we forget its basis; we build on a false foundation; we do not approach God, whether as existing eternally or as incarnate amongst us, with the due spirit of reverence, subjection and surrender. The force of prayer, its life-energy so to speak, is this implicit acknowledgement of what God is in relation to ourselves; it is the source of reverence which God's majesty demands; it is the spring of the awe which should transfix our minds as we gaze upon God. Lack of reverence and awe in prayer—be it in the liturgical prayer said publicly in choir or recited in private or purely personal prayer—rather suggests that one who is guilty of it does not appreciate the nature of this relationship with God.

I have heard it said that Anglicans are far more reverent in prayer than we Catholics are. I have heard Anglican clergymen complaining bitterly about the conduct of Catholics in church, especially, say, in Italy, even in St Peter's in Rome when they are assembled for a Papal audience. I have heard the excuse made that the church is, after all, our Father's house, in it we are children at home, and therefore we are quite justified in behaving in that way. Excuses like that are even more scandalizing than the behaviour itself. Many converts find the lack of reverence to be seen in Catholic churches quite scandalous— and even sacristans are sometimes guilty. It is the old story of familiarity and what it is supposed to breed. At the same time, the fact that God is our Father, and bade us address him as such, does not mean that he is willing to deny himself the reverence which is his due. Every item of our worship and everything connected with it—ceremonies, observance of rubrics, cleanliness of the church, decoration of the altar, the quality of the vestments and sacred vessels, to name only a few—should all be stamped with reverence which shows that we appreciate the relationship between ourselves and God—even though that God be reduced to the shape of a baby in the straw, a village carpenter or a disc of unleavened bread.

Prayer should always be marked by a certain grandeur. I do not mean that we should address God in archaic language or

employ the piosities of some books of devotion. Simplicity is
often grandeur because it is integrity and sincerity. God is not a
public servant but some manuals of devotion give the impres-
sion that he is. It is we who are the servants, the slaves, with no
rights or claims against God. A child and a slave pray simply
but reverently. Before all else our prayer should be our reaching
out towards God. "Out of the depths" we pray—the depths of
our own nothingness, surrender, dependence and submission.

The prayer God-made-Man taught us must necessarily be
the model of all prayer. Here is what St Thomas wrote about it:

> The Lord's prayer is the most perfect of all prayers, for, as
> St Augustine says to Proba: "If we pray rightly and fittingly
> we can say nothing else but what is set down in the Lord's
> prayer." And since prayer is, in a sort, the interpreter of our
> desires before God, we can only rightly ask in prayer for
> those things which we can rightly desire. But in the Lord's
> prayer, not only do we have petitions for all those things which
> we can rightly desire, but they are set forth in the order in
> which they are to be desired. Hence this prayer not only
> teaches us how to pray, but serves as the norm for all dis-
> positions of mind.

So, the saint says, the first petition is for God's glory, the second
for the coming of his kingdom and the third for the triumph of
his will—all are adoration.

The Church teaches that the four purposes of the Mass are
adoration, thanksgiving, petition and propitiation. All prayer
can be included under those four headings. Therefore, every
prayer which is not thanksgiving, petition or contrition comes
under the heading of adoration; indeed, the other purposes of
prayer are inextricably bound with adoration and necessarily
imply it, because they suppose the acknowledgement of the
pray-er's due relationship to God. Adoration, then, includes
praise, admiration, abandonment, consecration, surrender,
resignation and any other act which springs from the acknowledgement of our true relationship with God. The adorer, too,
sees in God infinite perfection, unlimited power, boundless
goodness, the inexhaustible source of all good. Everything that
we are, everything we have, all we can do, whether in the order

of grace or the order of nature, is the overflowing of God's infinite love. So from adoration necessarily spring thanksgiving and petition. When we think of infinite goodness insulted by sin reverence itself demands that we make atonement; so from adoration comes contrition too.

In prayer we look on Christ the divine Person. We do not say merely: "O Christ, I believe that thou art God; I believe that thou art greater than I; I have no choice but to submit wholly to thee." That is an unworthy prayer. The true adorer prostrates himself before Christ simply because of what Christ is—the infinite, eternal Word of God, limitless in every perfection. From his act of faith, *Ex Patre natum ante omnia saecula; Deum de Deo, lumen de lumine, Deum verum de Deo vero; genitum non factum; consubstantialem Patri* comes his act of adoration: *Tu solus Sanctus, Tu solus Dominus, Tu solus Altissimus, Jesu Christe.*

We might find it helpful to go through the psalms seeking those of adoration and praise and in our prayers applying them particularly to our Blessed Lord. For example, kneeling before the Christmas crib we will help ourselves to understand something of the love we see there if we recall the words of Psalm 92: "The Lord reigns, he is clothed with majesty; the Lord is clothed with strength, he has girded himself. For in truth he has established the world, it shall not be moved. Your throne has been established from of old. You are from eternity." In the presence of the Blessed Sacrament, along with the *Adoro te devote*, the *Lauda Sion* and the other liturgical hymns, which, incidentally, all concentrate on adoration, we might recite many of the psalms of praise and longing: "As the deer longs for the water brooks, so does my soul long for you, O God; my soul thirsts for God, for the living God. How long till I come and see your face, O God?"*

Adoration is the essential act of prayer. It should be predominant in our relationship with Christ; it is a necessary outpouring of love. His presence should, so to speak, mesmerize us by the knowledge of what his human and eucharistic appearance conceals. That thought alone should be a powerful aid in our efforts to forget the world about us and to fight the constant worry of distractions in prayer. It confronts us with the indescribable richness of infinitely perfect being, with the transcen-

* Ps. 41; from *Praying the Psalms* by Mgr R. J. Foster.

dence of limitless beauty, with subsistent goodness, who alone can satisfy the yearnings of the human spirit.

The acts of the theological virtues, faith, hope and charity, are three aspects of the act of adoration. As soon as we appreciate how we stand with God we are moved to express to him our belief, our trust and our love. We kneel before Christ as we see him during any incident of his earthly life described in the Gospels—we tell him that we believe every word he speaks because it is the word of God, that we trust him to do for us in spirit and body what he did for those he met during his sojourn amongst us, that we wish to love him with all the ardour of a beloved disciple or a penitent Magdalen.

Wherever we are we can make our own simple acts of adoration or we can use those which have been consecrated by the tradition of the Church or the use of the saints: "Thou art the Christ, the Son of the living God"; "My Lord and my God"; "My God and my All"; "Jesus, my Lord, my God, my All", or simply "I adore thee", which embraces everything.

In our prayer we might care to gaze simply upon Christ as the human repository of God's infinite attributes. As we have seen, they are all manifested during his years on earth; the search for their manifestation is highly rewarding. Everything leads to adoration; it is the culmination of prayer. Contemplate Christ how you will—as the eternal Word, the Son of God, the Lord and Master, as God in the flesh, as the final Judge, as the one High Priest and Mediator of Salvation, as the Babe of Bethlehem, as Saviour, as King, as the Lamb of God, as the Life of men and Light of the world, as the Way to the essence of the Godhead and eternal glory—you are forced to your knees in reverence and awe.

With the Shepherds and the Magi we adore him in Bethlehem, with the leper we can draw near, worship and say, "Lord, if thou wilt thou canst make me clean" (Matt. 8. 2), with Jairus we can adore and beg healing for those we love (Matt. 9. 18); with the Canaanite woman we can adore, saying, "Lord, help me; have pity on me" (Matt. 15. 22, 25), with the demoniac in Gerasa we can adore and beg for the spirit of cleanness (Mark 5. 7), with the man born blind we can adore and give thanks for the true sight of faith (John 9. 38).

In a famous sermon Bossuet likened man to the pontiff of

creation, who must adore God not only for himself but on behalf of all creatures. Inanimate nature lacks an intellect to grasp God and a heart to love him. Before our eyes it displays its beauty, its harmony, its grandeur, its activities.

It cannot see—it reveals itself; it cannot adore—it brings us to our knees, loath to have us ignore the God it cannot comprehend. But man, a breath divine within a body of clay, possessed of reason and intelligence and capable of knowing God, both through his natural powers and the agency of creation, is urged by his own self and by all creatures to bow before God in humble adoration. For this reason is man, himself a microcosm, placed in this world, that contemplating this universe and, as it were, gathering it all up in himself, he may refer himself and all things to God alone. So much so, that man is made to contemplate the visible things of this creation only in order that he may adore the invisible Being who brought them out of nothing by the omnipotence of his power.

Thus the French orator.

In that spirit Father Olier used to pray:

My God, I adore thee in all thy creatures, thou the real, the sole strength that bears this mighty world. Without thee, nothing would be; nothing does subsist outside of thee. I love thee, O my God, and praise thy majesty shown forth in all creation. All that I behold, O God, but reveals to me the mystery of thy beauty unknown to mortal eyes. I adore the splendour of thy glory, the grandeur of thy majesty that outshines the noonday sun a thousand times. I adore the fecundity of thy power, more wonderful by far than that disclosed by the starry skies.

All that is true and very beautiful—but how much more it applies to the human nature of Christ our Lord and the mystery of the Incarnation!

So the opening words of St John's prologue have led us to the first act of all prayer, its foundation and its consummation, adoration, the prostration of ourselves before Christ, the eternal Word, acknowledging his absolutely supreme dominion over us and our utter nothingness before him. For the soul of deep faith no prayer should be easier and none more rewarding than simple adoration.

I heard of a young man who lay on the operating table in the theatre of a New York hospital. The surgeon bent over him and said: "I must tell you frankly that you have cancer of the tongue. You cannot live unless your tongue is removed. That is what we are preparing to do now." He paused. Then he said, "You realize that for the rest of your life you will be speechless; is there anything you wish to say before we give you the anaesthetic?" The young man, a devout Catholic, was silent for a moment; he shuddered a little as the full realization of what it meant penetrated his mind, which had already been rendered comatose by drugs. Then he smiled. "Yes," he said, "I want my last words to be: Praised be the sacred name of Jesus!"

It is not without immense significance that when the Holy Spirit records for all mankind a prayer of the Mother of God it is a prayer of adoration and praise, her *Magnificat*. In those beautiful words, in which she shows how familiar she was with the Old Testament, the canticle of Anna (I Kings 2. 1-10) and the psalms, she praises God for his mercy in the Incarnation, especially for elevating her from her lowliness to become the object of veneration for all times, for his power in shaping the destinies of the chosen people, humbling the proud and exalting the humble, and for his fidelity to his promises concerning the Messias. May she obtain for us a practical devotion to the prayer of adoration, which will unite us with the Heart of her divine Son.

3

"ALL THINGS WERE MADE BY HIM; AND WITHOUT HIM WAS MADE NOTHING THAT WAS MADE"

(John 1. 3)

THE beloved Apostle is prostrate in adoration before the eternal Word. He has spoken of his existence before anything was created; now he tells us that he is the Creator of everything. In the customary Hebrew way he repeats negatively what he has said so clearly positively. There are age-old controversies about the punctuation of this passage. Many prefer, for example, "Without him was made nothing. What was made in him was life." But such differing translations do not change the meaning: the Word of God, because he is God, is the Creator of all that exists outside God.

One suspects that St John had in mind the beautiful words of the Book of Proverbs:

> The Lord made me his when first he went about his work, at the birth of time, before his creation began.
> Long, long ago, before earth was fashioned, I held my course.
> Already I lay in the womb, when the depths were not yet in being, when no springs of water had yet broken;
> when I was born, the mountains had not yet sunk on their firm foundations, and there were no hills;
> not yet had he made the earth, or the rivers, or the solid framework of the world.
> I was there when he built the heavens,
> when he fenced in the waters with a wall inviolable,
> when he fixed the sky overhead,
> and levelled the fountain-springs of the deep.
> I was there when he enclosed the sea within its confines, forbidding the waters to transgress their assigned limits,
> when he poised the foundations of the world.

I was at his side, a master-workman, my delight increasing with each day, as I made play before him all the while. . . . (Prov. 8. 22-30).

What a marvellously prophetic passage this is! Wisdom is the master-workman whom God uses to create his marvellous universe and to imprint his wondrous order upon it. Wisdom is a real being, alive and working at God's side—not a creature, but existing eternally and concurring in the creation of everything; intrinsic to God, his essential wisdom, yet coming from God by way of generation. From wisdom so personified here it was but a step to the doctrine of the Holy Trinity and the prologue of St John.

We shall never quite know, this side of the grave, what St John means exactly by this reference to the Word as Creator. St Paul has something very similar: "Yet to us there is but one God, the Father, of whom are all things, and we unto him; and one Lord Jesus Christ, by whom are all things, and we by him" (I Cor. 8. 6). He writes of the Son, "the image of the unseen God, first born of all creation. For in him were created all things in heaven and on earth, things seen and unseen, whether thrones or dominations or principalities or powers—all creation is through him and unto him. And himself is prior to all, and in him all things hold together" (Col. 1. 15-17). Here are three precious points made by the Apostle:

1. All things were created in Christ; therefore he is not only superior to all of them but before them all;
2. He is pre-eminent because he existed before all else;
3. This applies not only to creation in general but to every individual creature.

Note the three terms St Paul uses for the Word: he is the Son, the Image and the First-born. All refer to his eternal life in the Godhead and each is an aspect of his eternal generation.

All things, St Paul tells us as well as St John, were created *by* the Word. He is their efficient cause, that is, by his activity all things came into existence. They were created also *in* the Son, that is, he is their exemplary cause because he is subsistent divine Wisdom. They were created also *for* the Son. How? Because God alone can be the ultimate reason for his act of

creation. He is its final cause. The example of an artist falls
short, infinitely short of the reality. He is the cause of his
picture; so the three divine Persons of the Trinity are the one,
common principle of creation. It is usually thought of as the
work of the Father because it seems to be appropriate to his
personal character; but Father, Son and Holy Ghost together
as one principle bring creation into being. So it is perfectly
correct to think of the Son as the Creator, too. Think again of
the artist; what compels him to paint? It might be one of many
motives. With God there can be only one reason and that is
himself. Nothing existed outside himself. So God's glory must
be the final purpose; it flows from the manifestation of his
perfections in creation. What is the model or example of
creation? Only divine wisdom; the created world is the
realization of the eternal, unchangeable thought of God. So
St Paul holds Christ before us as the agent, the purpose and
the exemplar of the Trinity's act of creation.

Is it any wonder that this passage from the letter to the
Colossians is chosen as the epistle for the feast of Christ the
King? His Godhead is the basis of his kingship. Seven centuries
before the fullness of time when God was to send his Word
amongst us, Isaias proclaimed his majesty: "A child is born to
us and a son is given to us, and the government is upon his
shoulder; and his name shall be called Wonderful, Counsellor,
God the Mighty, the Father of the world to come, the Prince
of Peace. His empire shall be multiplied and there shall be no
end of peace. He shall sit upon the throne of David and upon
his kingdom" (Is. 9. 6-7). More than a century later Daniel
took up the theme: "Power was given. him, and glory and
sovereignty; obey him all must, men of every race and tribe
and tongue; such a reign as his lasts for ever, such power as his
the ages cannot diminish" (Dan. 7. 14).

To Mary the announcing angel proclaimed the kingship of
her Son: "The Lord God shall give unto him the throne of
David his Father and he shall reign in the house of Jacob for
ever. And of his kingdom there shall be no end" (Luke 1. 32).
At his birth mysterious men of learning came from the east
asking to be taken to adore him who had been born king of
the Jews (Matt. 2. 2). St John relates how Nathanael (was he
St Bartholomew?) hailed our Lord as King of Israel (John

1. 49). After five thousand of them had been fed from five loaves and two fishes the Jews wanted to make Christ their king, but he fled into the mountains alone (John 6. 15). James and John looked forward to high places in his kingdom (Matt. 20. 20-23; Mark 10. 35-40). In the same chapter in which he describes our Lord's entry as a king into Jerusalem, St Luke records the parable of the nobleman who went into a far country to receive for himself a kingdom. St Matthew, too, as the climax of his earthly life is approaching reported the king's marriage feast parable and the description of the last judgment when "the Son of man shall come in his majesty, and all the angels with him; then shall he sit on the seat of his majesty. And all nations shall be gathered before him" (Matt. 25). To Pilate the Jews alleged that Christ had declared his kingship (Luke 23. 2); before Pilate he proclaimed it majestically: "My kingdom is not of this world. . . . Thou sayest that I am a king. For this was I born, and for this came I into the world" (John 18. 36-37). His kingly title hung over him as he died on the cross, having first been crowned with thorns in mockery. Before he ascended to heaven, he proclaimed that "all power was given to him in heaven and on earth" (Matt. 28. 18).

It was in the Holy Year 1925 that Pope Pius XI instituted the new feast of Christ the King. To mark the occasion he wrote an encyclical letter in which he pointed out the lesson we have already learned from St John and St Paul, that Christ is King because he is the second Person of the Blessed Trinity. He is King by natural right, as well as by the right he acquired by redeeming us. "We are no longer our own, for Christ has purchased us 'with a great price' " (I Cor. 6. 20).

When we look back over the centuries we may be surprised to discover that when the Church emerged from the catacombs and began to build and adorn new temples of worship Christ was usually represented, as in the marvellous mosaics of the apses of the ancient basilicas, as the majestic Ruler. Even the crucifix as we know it now was a late development; originally the cross was a royal standard and the Conqueror was often depicted as enthroned.

If we glance at the liturgy we shall see how Mother Church never allows us to forget that Christ is our supreme Ruler. Advent is the time when we await the coming of the King.

"Lift up your eyes, Jerusalem, and see the power of the King," we sing; "Behold there shall come the Lord and King of the earth; every knee shall bow to Me and every tongue shall confess to God." The great "O" antiphons repeat the same theme: "O Emmanuel, our King and Lawgiver, the Expected of nations." At Matins we sing: "The Lord, the King who is to come, come let us adore" or "Now the Lord is nigh, come, let us adore." And: "Behold, the Most High King shall come with great power to save the nations." At Christmas, the Church greets not so much the Babe in the straw as "the King of peace".

> O Jesus, Redeemer of all men,
> Who ere created light began
> Didst from the sovereign Father spring,
> His power and glory equalling.

The Epiphany is, of course, a feast of the kingship of Christ. The liturgy at once proclaims his eternal dominion: "Begotten before the day-star and before all ages the Lord our Saviour has appeared this day to the world. Like a flame of fire that star pointed out God, the King of kings; the Magi saw it and offered gifts to the great King."

The Christmas liturgy ends with the feast of our Lady's Purification and further reminders of the regal glory of her Son: "Behold, the Lord and Ruler is come to his holy temple: rejoice and be glad in meeting your God, O Son. . . . Adorn your bridal chamber, O Sion, and receive Christ the King."

Even the sombre liturgy of Passiontide at its very climax cannot forget that the sufferings of Christ are his weapon of kingly conquest.

> Abroad the royal banners fly,
> Now shines the Cross's mystery;
> Upon it Life did death endure,
> And yet by death did life procure.

And

> Sing, my tongue, the Saviour's glory,
> Tell his triumph far and wide;
> Tell aloud the famous story
> Of his body crucified;

How upon the cross a Victim
Vanquishing in death he died.

Throughout the last three days of Holy Week we prepare for
the climax of the liturgy by the antiphon proclaiming the
exaltation of Christ as King after his Passion: "God also hath
exalted him and has bestowed upon him the name that is
above every name."

On the high solemnity of the Holy Eucharist we cannot
escape the kingly theme. "Let us adore Christ the King, the
Lord of nations, who gives marrow for the spirit to those who
eat him," we sing at Matins. Even the antiphons for the Sacred
Heart begin with an acclamation of Christ's gentle kingship:
"Rule, O Lord, with your sweet yoke in the midst of your
enemies." The Transfiguration is in a special way a feast of
Christ's kingship, as we proclaim at Matins: "Christ, the most
high King of glory, let us adore."

How often, too, in the ordinary offices of the year do we not
turn to him as King—of angels, apostles, martyrs, confessors and
virgins. Every new day is ushered in with the words of St Paul
to Timothy: "To the King of ages, who is immortal and
invisible, the one only God, be honour and glory forever and
ever. Amen." Every prayer ends with a reminder of his kingship, "who lives and reigns for ever".

A glance at the liturgy for the feast of Christ the King shows
much emphasis on its social aspect, as the Pope stressed in his
encyclical: "Nations will be reminded by the annual celebration of this feast that not only private individuals but also
rulers and princes are bound to give public honour and
obedience to Christ." It is significant that all the world over
on this day Catholics are bidden to recite publicly the act of
consecration of the human race to the Sacred Heart of Jesus.
We should often pray for the poor, blind rulers of the nations
which show no respect for the reign of Christ. The Pope's
warning is very grave: The feast "will call to their minds the
thought of the last judgment, wherein Christ, who has been
cast out of public life, despised, neglected and ignored, will
most severely avenge these insults". In this spirit is the prayer
of the office of the feast: "Almighty and everlasting God, who
in thy beloved Son, the King of the whole world, hast willed

to restore all things anew, grant in thy mercy that all the
families of nations rent asunder by the wound of sin may be
subjected to his most gentle rule."

The application to ourselves is made also by Pope Pius XI.
Christ must reign in our minds, he tells us. That means deep
faith; it can never be deep enough. In fact, it would be
practically impossible to overemphasize the importance of faith
and, therefore, of prayer for it. Once we are supernaturally,
wholly and effectively convinced of Christ's universal dominion,
flowing from his Godhead, we are well on the way to an intense
spiritual life. From such faith every other virtue will spring,
especially absolute abandonment; Christ's feelings and thoughts
will replace ours; he will live fully in us; our horizon will
become as infinite as our human capacity will permit; we will
begin to embrace the secrets of the Godhead; holiness will be
unified and stabilized; we will live in God's presence, see by
God's light, be directed by God's goodness, strengthened by
God's power and surrendered to God's providence. "Whosoever believeth that Jesus is the Christ is born of God," says
St John (I John 5. 1). To receive Christ by faith, to acknowledge
him without reserve as Lord and King of our minds, means
that we prostrate our whole being before him. By faith it is that
Christ reigns in our minds; if we develop it by prayer and
practice and constantly exercise it by love, it makes our own the
substance of the joys that are to come and results in unshakable
trust.

Without deep faith Christ cannot reign in our wills, for his
reign there demands obedience. There can be no true religious
obedience in one who is lacking faith to see Christ making his
will known through the Church, through every superior and
through countless happenings of daily life. If we have faith to
see God's will where it is to be seen, love should compel us to
accept it and cheerfully obey. If Christ reigns in our minds by
faith and in our will by obedience, he will surely reign in our
hearts by love. From his kingdom there he will urge us on
always to love him more and to spread the kingdom of his love
amongst others. Every lover of Christ the King, even the most
cloistered religious, must necessarily be an apostle, sacrificing
self and everything one may have to bring more souls beneath
the stream of the Saviour's royal blood.

So the words of St John, "All things were made by him; and without him was made nothing that was made," have led us logically to the contemplation of the kingship, the regal dignity and dominion of the Word of God. He made everything; everything is his to rule. The liturgy has revealed the mind of the Church; Christ's kingship is the back-cloth, the scene, as it were, the context of all his mysteries. Whether we think of him at Bethlehem or Nazareth, during his hidden life or his public life, preaching or suffering, present in the Eucharist or by his Father's side in heaven, he is always King, demanding our complete subjection. Nevertheless, the eternal King is our Brother, our closest Friend—more, he becomes our very own in Holy Communion. He does not demand our submission without first giving himself completely. The infinite Creator, "without whom was made nothing that was made", begs that we try to show towards him something of the generous surrender of self he never ceases to display for us.

4

"IN HIM WAS LIFE, AND THE LIFE WAS THE LIGHT OF MEN"

(John 1. 4)

IN the opening verses of his Gospel the beloved disciple has taken us to the heart of the Godhead. There we contemplate the infinite, eternal activity of the most holy Trinity, the unchangeable "now" when the divine Word is begotten. Apart from the Word not one creature has come to be. He is the infinite King of all.

After a word about creatures in general, St John writes about men. Most of the commentators see in this phrase the simple assertion that the Word is the source of man's supernatural life. Others, adopting a different punctuation, say with St Cyril of Alexandria that the Apostle is here teaching that the Word, the essential Life, is present in all things, conserving them in existence; in the case of men, he is also their Light, that is the Source and Author of their faith. The supporters of this second interpretation make the text read like this: "All things were made by (or through) him, and without him was made nothing. In that which was made was the Life, and the Life was the Light of men." It is impossible to decide which of these interpretations is correct. For our purpose we will adopt the first and the meaning that the spiritual life of men comes through the Word. He is the source of our life of grace here and of glory hereafter.

The question we have to discuss now is this: How can the life of the Word of God be the light of men? The answer will be clearer when we have thought about other passages of this mighty prologue; we must not anticipate too much. For the present we shall try to find an answer from other sources. Thus, at the offertory of the Mass the Church bids us put a drop of water into the wine we are about to consecrate, praying that we "may be made partakers of his divinity who condescended to become partaker of our humanity". Humanity is represented by the drop of water, divinity by the wine. The water, we might say, is completely absorbed by the wine to such an extent that it forms part of the whole which will soon be changed into the substance of Christ. How can this take place between ourselves and Christ? How can we share his eternal, indivisible life?

This is not a solitary quotation from the Church's prayer. In the preface for the Ascension we sing of Christ going up to heaven *ut nos divinitatis suae tribueret esse participes*, "so that he might make us partakers of his Godhead". Incidentally, how weak is the translation given in a modern Latin-English missal: "so that he might grant us fellowship in his Godhead." "Fellowship " hardly indicates the real sharing we are going to describe.

Some of the collects have similar passages. Thus, on the feast of St Cyril of Jerusalem we pray after Holy Communion: "O Lord Jesus Christ, may the sacrament of thine own body and blood which we have received, sanctify our minds and hearts, through the prayers of the holy bishop Cyril, and thereby make us worthy to become partakers of the divine nature." There is a very beautiful secret prayer in the Mass for the fourth Sunday after Easter: *Deus, qui nos per hujus sacrificii veneranda commercia, unius summae divinitatis participes effecisti. . . .* To translate this, as has been done, "O God, who in this sacrifice hast given us a worshipful pledge of fellowship with the one sovereign God-head," is somewhat inadequate. Our prayer is surely that "through the sacred exchange proper to this sacrifice we become sharers in God's own nature". "Fellowship with the one sovereign Godhead" hardly indicates an actual sharing in the nature of God.

It is interesting to recall that when some of the early Christian writers wanted to demonstrate that the Second and Third Persons were divine, they began with the truth that men share in the divine nature. That was common to all; not even the heretics denied it. Thus St Cyril of Alexandria, who died in A.D. 444, argued that we are called children of God because we share in the divine nature; thus the Spirit is God by nature because it is by participating in him that we participate in the divine nature. And elsewhere: "The Spirit is God and transforms into God . . . those who are worthy of it, by communicating the divine nature to them himself." Similarly, St Athanasius reasoned that "the Son is he through whom the

Father deifies. From which it follows that if he were God only by sharing and not having the same substance, he could not deify others. The true Son became man in order to make us gods."

Quotations like these could be made from the writings of many of the Fathers. They simply took it for granted that grace does deify men. This was an unquestioned fact in the first centuries of the Church's life; more, it was a fact closely related to daily spiritual living.

How did these doctors and saints come to be so insistent on this truth? Because they found it in the Scriptures. Here are three important texts:

Love ye one another earnestly from your heart, now that ye have been begotten anew, not from perishable but from imperishable seed (I Peter 1. 23);

Whoso is born of God doth no sin, because the seed of God abideth in him; and he cannot sin, because he is born of God (I John 3. 9);

He hath bestowed upon us the precious and very great promises, so that in consequence of these ye may become partakers of the divine nature (II Peter 1. 4).

In the first two of these the Holy Spirit uses the metaphor of the seed. Think about it. Plants and animals produce their seeds; those seeds pass on to another plant or animal the nature and characteristics of that from which it comes. Seeds are cells which become separated from living bodies by division; they become the embryos of new living bodies of the same nature. How can there be a seed of God when there can be absolutely no division in God? God cannot detach anything from himself; there are no parts in him. Nevertheless, is there anything to prevent God creating a something which reproduces his nature in some way and introducing that new creation into creatures? Such a process could be described by the seed metaphor because the new creation comes from the divine parent and it reproduces his own nature and characteristics in the one who receives it. St John uses the expression "born of God" seven times.

The use of a metaphor like this would be invalid if the new creature did not share the nature of the parent. Birth means the transmission by a living being to another of a life like its own. The purpose of generation is to preserve and increase the species by transmitting it unchanged. So the seed of the oak grows into another oak tree; dogs beget dogs, birds beget birds, fishes beget fishes and men beget men. That is a universal law. So, if the Holy Spirit inspires sacred writers to speak over and over again of our being begotten by God, born of God and the seed of God he can only mean that we are given the divine nature in some way. The process by which this takes place is, for the moment, not important; we are concerned with the fact. The first two texts quoted above lead inexorably to the phrase found in the third, "partakers of the divine nature" and used so often by the saints and doctors and in the liturgy.

St Peter's wonderful phrase has led to considerable discussion. Some writers have asked whether it should be understood as only referring to the life of glory when we share in the divine nature. After all, in the context St Peter does refer to "promises", apparently indicating a reality as yet unfulfilled. The weight of opinion is strongly in favour of regarding our sharing in the divine nature as something which takes place here and now by grace. St Ambrose, St Cyril of Alexandria and St Leo interpret it in this sense. So does the Church in the liturgy, as we have seen.

The fact that after death we shall be capable of enjoying the direct vision of God demands that we have the capacity for it. Grace gives that capacity; it is not only the condition for glory but its principle and its cause as well. No one can be admitted to heaven without grace, but those who have it have the right to and aptitude for heaven. A little baby shares in his father's human nature long before he is capable of performing his father's intellectual operations. Grace, which gives us the capacity for the beatific vision, also makes us partakers in the divine nature.

We will, perhaps, understand something of this mystery if we think of the life we receive from the Word as a created miniature of the essential activity of God. Aristotle defined nature as the intrinsic principle of motion and action. Grace is the model of his own activity which God has created in our souls. It is important to notice that St Peter wrote of our sharing in the divine *nature*; we could not share in the divine essence, which is the being of the Godhead; but by nature we understand the essence of God considered as the principle of his own operations.

We can think of nature as that which includes whatever distinguishes a being from those inferior to it; thus man is a *rational* animal; the ability to reason distinguishes him from the rest of the animal kingdom; it is his nature to reason. What, then, is the nature of God; what does he have which distinguishes him from the angels and from men? One thing—the direct vision of himself, without any intermediary. It is natural to him alone and infinitely surpasses the capacities of all creatures.

Now we are beginning to see what partaking in the divine nature means. If the direct vision of himself is that which distinguishes God from everything else, it is his nature; therefore, it is in that that we share in some way. So the life which the Word gives to men, to enable them to share in the divine nature, must endow us with the ability to share in God's direct vision of himself. That is what sanctifying grace means. It is, as St John and St Peter say, a seed or a germ which enables us to share in God's essential activity.

This does not mean that we are "bits of God" or that grace abolishes the distinction between God and us; it does not mean a pantheistic fusion or union of Godhead and humanity. God's essential activity is infinite, uncreated and indivisible; the created reproduction, called grace, which enables us to share in that essential activity is finite, limited and, of course, over and above what is natural to us as men. God is necessary and unchangeable; our sharing in his nature is neither; we can lose it and it can change in its intensity. Nor is this sharing of ours comprehensive; if it were, it would be infinite, for only the infinite can fully grasp the Godhead. It allows us to see God *in the way* he sees himself; the procedure is the same; it is by intuition but imperfectly. The way is the same, the degree is different.

So, grace, the life the Word of God gives us, makes us similar to God in a very real way. It transposes us from the natural to the supernatural order; it enables us to share in God's nature by adding to our human nature perfections which are really proper to God. It raises us to God's level of

activity; it communicates God's life to us; it gives us the
capacity for the essential operation of God, the knowledge, the
vision, the "light" of himself. So grace gives us something of
God's dignity.

How can we grasp it? We cannot—for God is infinite,
utterly beyond our grasp. That certainty, though, enables us
to see that our dignity is, in a sense, incomprehensible; so is
the responsibility that goes with it.

I have read stories when I was a child in which animals have
been endowed with human faculties. You may remember the
legend of St Kevin. He went to live in that remote cave in
Glendalough to escape the attentions of an amorous young
woman. There he used to pray with his arms extended in the
form of the cross. Something happened which, one feels, could
take place only in the lovely land of St Patrick. A bird came
and laid her egg in St Kevin's palm. Being a saint, he did not
remove the egg nor tip it into the water below; he held his
hand there until the bird hatched her egg! Now, suppose that
when all was complete, mother and child had turned to
St Kevin, flapped their wings and said: "Thank you so much
for your patience." Yes, it would have been extraordinary;
those birds would have acted as human beings; they would
have been endowed with the power of reason, the essential
human activity.

Grace is something like that. It permits us to do things which
are completely beyond us as humans and which are natural
only to God. But note where the comparison with St Kevin's
birds falls short: both the saint and the birds are finite; the
gap between them is measurable and limited. In the realm of
grace, the distance between man and God is immeasurable,
infinite, without any limit.

If we think of the Incarnation we see the process reversed.
When God became man he so emptied himself, to use St Paul's
expression, that it became possible for God to perform human
acts. Grace makes the opposite happen. It makes it possible
for men to do things which are divine. How? By causing a
created reproduction of God's nature, that is of his essential
activity, to inhere in a created person, man, as an accident is
united to a substance. The Word came down; man is raised up;
God humbled himself to elevate man, or, as St Athanasius put

it, "the true Son of God became man in order to make us gods." Is it surprising that the first antiphon for the second Vespers of the octave of Christmas fixes upon this marvellous exchange: "O wondrous exchange! the Creator of man, having assumed a living body, deigned to be born of a virgin and having become man without man's aid, enriched us with his divinity?"

"The life was the light of men", said St John. Man comes to his true life only when his earthly pilgrimage is ended; death is birth to the true life—and that life consists in light, the light of the vision of God. *Lumen de lumine*, light from light, we sing of Christ in the *Gloria in excelsis*. God's bliss is light—the knowledge and love of himself. Grace is a sharing in the divine nature, the seed of and capacity for the life of light which shall be ours after death; the life is God, the light is God. We share his life and his light because we see him face to face immediately, in the way he sees and loves himself. Grace gives us the capacity for that.

Let it be repeated that of ourselves we are no more capable of seeing and loving God in the way he loves himself than a dog is of using rational language. Indeed, it is not finitely but infinitely beyond us. Yet, St John has written: "Beloved, now we are children of God, and it hath not yet been manifested what we shall be. We know that if he be manifested, we shall be like to him, because we shall see him even as he is" (I John 3. 2). St Paul contrasts this direct vision with the indirect light of faith: "For now we see in a mirror, obscurely; but then face to face. Now I know in part; then shall I know fully, even as I have been fully known" (I Cor. 13. 12). In the same sense we should understand our Lord's promises to the Apostles that they are to share his glory.

Now let us take our enquiry just a little further. There is always a danger that we regard the spiritual life as being simply the effort to love God, acquire virtue, hate evil and eliminate our faults. That would be only a partial definition. It ignores God's part—and it is he who plays the principal role. God lives within us; although the Blessed Trinity is present we refer to the indwelling as being of the Holy Ghost. Faith reveals to us that, dwelling within us, the most holy Trinity performs its ceaseless, eternal operation, carries on the essential life of the Godhead. Therefore within us the Word is begotten and the Holy Spirit is breathed forth. Living within us, God enables us to share his own nature; the three divine Persons give us a life like theirs, a Godlike life in the strictest sense of the word.

In heaven we see God in such a sense that he unites himself, his very essence, to the soul so that we will be able to contemplate him directly. Grace, our partaking in the divine nature during our life on earth, is the seed or even the bud of the beatific vision. So by grace God lives within us; we possess him; he is ours truly, physically and substantially. The Holy Ghost is in us by grace. In him we see God. St Paul tells us so: "The things of God none hath come to know save the Spirit of God. Now we have not received the Spirit of the world, but the Spirit which is from God, that we may realise the graces God hath given us" (I Cor. 2. 12). God dwells in the souls of the blessed in heaven. Strengthened by the light of glory, which he infuses into their souls, they grasp God by their acts of knowledge and love. So, here on earth, in virtue of our sharing in the divine nature, we grasp God by our acts of faith and love so that he comes to live in us. Faith is certainly an imperfect vision, as St Paul says; nevertheless, it is a vision of God himself.

Unaided human reason would never know anything of the inner life of the holy Trinity. Faith is given us by God to enable us to know him in his inner nature and life. When we know God by reason from nature, our ideas are always of created things; when we know through faith we form our ideas *from* created things but they are not *of* creatures; we know God in his own reality, even though darkly and inadequately.

So the deification of man, of which the Fathers spoke so often, has two elements, one created and one uncreated. The uncreated element is God himself, living in us. The created element is sanctifying grace, which confers capacity for the direct vision of God. Its purpose is to bring about union between ourselves and God. In heaven that union will be perfect; here it is incomplete—but nevertheless real because God does live in us. Grace makes that indwelling possible. That which gives grace its indescribable value is its power of putting us in possession of God. It is something given to us over and above our human nature; it changes us, transfigures us, lifts us up above ourselves by endowing us with energies of a divine character. In virtue of those energies we make our acts of faith, hope and charity; by them we know God and love God in the way he knows and loves himself and bring him to live within us.

What practical help can be drawn from all these ideas? In the first place, we can ponder in our prayers the effects of grace in our souls. What a privilege it is to see God as he sees himself, "as" meaning in the same way! This act, the most intimate and essential of all the acts of God, that by which he is Three in One, has its created image within us; we are the privileged monstrances of it. How close it brings us to God! How it assimilates us to him! How it enables us to commune abundantly in his divine nature! Theologians tell us how the character of certain sacraments impresses a uniform, as it were, on our souls, the uniforms of a child of God, a soldier of Christ and of a priest. Grace seals us with God's most personal characteristic: "Ye have been sealed with the Holy Spirit of the promise, who is the earnest of our inheritance, unto redemption as the chosen people" (Eph. 1. 13). Children resemble their parents; our resemblance to God is deeper than any earthly likeness; it is more extensive, more perfect. The supreme privilege of souls in grace is to carry within them the supernatural likeness to God. An artist impresses his ideas on the materials with which he works; God impresses his sign on all his creatures, but he does more for the soul in grace; he communicates to it a divine character which makes us living images of the very substance of God.

The more we resemble God, the more we possess true beauty. We may contemplate the beauty of creation, the lines of the landscape, the tints of the countryside in autumn, the loveliness of all the flowers, the royal blue of the sunlit ocean, the majesty of the highest peaks, the limpid purity of the mountain streams, the masterpieces of human achievement in painting, sculpture, architecture and music—yes, put together all natural beauty wherever it is found whether on our planet or far away in the universe and you have not begun to see beauty like that of a soul that shares in the nature of God. "A divine picture" is what St Ambrose calls it; "a golden statue" says St John

Chrysostom; "a streaming light" wrote St Basil. So great is the beauty of the really saintly soul that one sees a reflection of it even in the physical features of some of the saints. After all, it is the dawn of glory—and glory will transform the body after the final resurrection. Is it not logical to expect to see something of that transformation even now? St John Chrysostom wrote: "It is as if God had taken a young man disfigured by illness and suddenly made him a marvel of beauty exceeding all others. In this way he has adorned our soul with a beauty that makes it attractive and lovable." One of the joys of heaven will be to behold the beauty of all the souls who share in God's nature. *Tota pulchra es, Maria*, we sing of Mary; she who is fullest of grace shares God's life to the utmost and so bears the stamp of the beauty of the Godhead. Surely the practical consequences of this are to avoid as worse than the plague anything which diminishes grace, and so beauty, within us, and, on the other hand, to make the most of all the means of grace, that our beauty will be increased before God and the whole court of heaven.

Here is what St Augustine wrote: "God's grace surpasses in dignity the stars and the heavens. Far more, it leaves the most sublime angelic natures far below it." Even Mary's divine motherhood, of itself, does not bring with it a sharing in the divine nature. Perhaps that is what Our Lord meant when he said: "Nay, rather, blessed are they that hear the word of God and keep it!" (Luke 11. 28). It is more glorious for Mary to be God's daughter by grace than his mother by nature.

St Leo makes our final conclusion: "Let us become aware of our dignity, and having become partakers of the divine nature let us not fall back into our former lowliness." We can never sing our *Magnificat* often enough or fervently enough. Indeed, he that is mighty hath done great things to us—and the more he has done, the greater is our responsibility to respond to it. The surest way is to contemplate often these great realities— God, eternity, the joy of the blessed and the seed of glory, which is the life of grace. Then, indeed, the light of the Word will guide us finally to the throne where dwells the "blessed and only Sovereign, the King of kings and Lord of lords in light inaccessible" (I Tim. 6. 16).

5

"THE LIGHT SHINETH IN DARKNESS, AND THE DARKNESS DID NOT COMPREHEND IT"

(John 1. 5)

THE life-light theme of St John is so characteristic that it will help our spiritual lives if we search the New Testament in an effort to understand more about it.

Let us take "light" first. The ancients thought of light as containing materially very little; it was, therefore, a fitting symbol of the pure, holy, spiritual God. Translating the familiar language of the New Testament into rather more modern terms we may sum up as follows:

The message Christ gave was this: God is light; not the faintest shadow of darkness can exist in him (I John 1. 5); which is to say that he possesses infinite truth and holiness;

God dwells in unapproachable light (I Tim. 6. 16).

He will shed his light on the saints in heaven and they will reign like kings for eternal ages; they live in the light (Apoc. 22. 5; Col. 1. 12).

The Gospel message seems veiled to some; it is because they are spiritually dying, so blinded by the spirit of the world, that the Gospel cannot dawn on them and bring them light (II Cor. 4. 3).

The Jews converted to Christianity, with all the Christian people, have a right to all the titles of God's people of the Old Testament; they must demonstrate God's goodness; he has called them from darkness into his amazing light (I Peter 2. 9).

Christ's message is the true light now shining in the world; it has entered the world but men prefer darkness to it (I John 2. 8; John 3. 19).

The light of the Gospel produces in men the opposite of evil; if they live as children of the light the results will be all that is wholesome, good and true (Eph. 5. 9).

Immortality is light; the Gospel opens up the shining possibilities of eternal life (II Tim. 2. 10).

Paganism is darkness; Christianity is light; essentially they are opposed as evil and good, as the devil and Christ (II Cor. 6. 14); so a missionary's work is to turn souls from the darkness to the light (Acts 26. 18). Converts must fling away the things people do in the dark, arm themselves for the light of day and live cleanly in that light (Rom. 13. 12).

Light is, of course, used as a symbol of Christ outside the writings of St John. So the author of the letter to the Jewish Christians calls him the radiance of God's glory, his "flashing-forth", his brightness, his effulgence. In his canticle, Zachary, re-echoing the prophecy of Isaias, spoke of the Messias's mission as bringing light to shine on those who lie in darkness; he was the first light of heaven (Luke 1. 79). Similarly, holy Simeon saw the Christ-Child as a light to show truth to the Gentiles (Luke 2. 32). St Matthew reports our Lord as saying that his disciples are the light of the world; they are to let their light shine in the sight of men like a light in the home, which is put on a stand so that it will give light to everybody in the house (Matt. 5. 14-16).

Now let us see what we can discover in the same way about the theme of life, applied especially to sanctifying grace. It is quite clear that the inspired writers regard grace and glory as being fundamentally the same supernatural life; death is no break but just the passage from one to the other. Those who keep Christ's word will never see death; they will rise again to life. That is what our Lord told Martha at her brother's tomb, words which the Church uses in the Mass on the days of death and burial (John 8. 51-53; 11. 21-26). Eternal life has already begun for us; we are living in the prelude, the prologue before the raising of the curtain; the charity God pours into our souls now is the same charity with which we shall love him forever, when faith and hope have given way to reality. St John uses life and eternal life with the same meaning. Thus: "He that believeth in the Son hath everlasting life" (John 3. 36). He has passed from death to life; when we receive Holy Communion we have everlasting life—St John uses the present tense, indicating that the life is already ours (John 5. 24; 6. 53). "God hath given us everlasting life; and this everlasting life is in his Son.

He that hath the Son, hath the life" (I John 5. 12). One who believes and loves, the Apostle is saying, already possesses eternal life, for grace is the seed of glory.

God is infinite, limitless, eternal life. He has life in himself, St John says (5. 26). He is the *living* Father (John 6. 57). In this verse St John writes that Christ possesses the Father's life and that Holy Communion passes on that life by uniting the recipient with Christ. When our Lord said "I live because of the Father" (v. 58), he was probably referring to both his life throughout eternity and his incarnation in time. As we read this we can hardly help ourselves recalling those other words of his: "Abide in me and I in you. As the branch cannot bear fruit of itself, unless it abide in the vine; so neither can ye, unless ye abide in me. I am the vine, ye the branches; he that abideth in me and I in him, the same beareth much fruit, for apart from me you can do nothing" (John 15. 5-6). This idea of abiding in God or in Christ and they dwelling in the soul returns again in the Apostle's epistles. Thus: "He that keepeth his commandments abideth in God and God in him; and hereby we know that he abideth in us, by the Spirit which he hath given us. . . . Whosoever confesseth that Jesus is the Son of God, God abideth in him and he in God" (I John 3. 24; 4. 16).

Like the Father, God the Son, Christ our Lord, is eternal life. "As the Father hath life in himself, so he hath given to the Son also to have life in himself " (John 5. 26). The thought is in St John's mind as he begins his first epistle. He writes, he says, about something which has always existed but which he has himself actually seen and heard, watched closely and even touched; that something was "everlasting Life, which was with the Father" (I John 1. 1-2). The letter ends on the same thought: "His Son, Jesus Christ. He is the true God and everlasting life" (I John 5. 20). In the opening passage St John writes that he passes on his message that the Christians "may have fellowship" with him. In a sense that word *fellowship* is the key to understanding his doctrine. It means communion, a joint-sharing, intimacy, intercourse—something much stronger than the words often mean today. We possess certain good things in common with Christ and his Father; we must increase our treasures—our fellowship—by growing in faith and increasing the grace within us.

Thus we see something of what our Lord means when he declares: "I am the resurrection and the life; he that believeth in me, even if he die shall live" (John 11. 25). And the inner significance of that famous saying, "I am the way and the truth and *the life*" (John 14. 6). Here is a compendium of the New Testament itself. Christ is the way because he is the one mediator between God and man, the door through which all must pass; he is the truth, the revelation of truth in both word and person, and the life, the source of all spiritual life; apart from him nobody can go to the Father.

The source of our spiritual life is undoubtedly this divine life in Christ. Recall that phrase of St Paul: "The first man Adam became a 'living soul'; the last Adam became a life-giving spirit" (I Cor. 15. 45). Here "spirit" is used to indicate man elevated by the grace, which is the seed of glory. Adam is said to be living; Christ is life-giving. His spirit, that is his grace, is life-giving; it never ceases to beget the life of grace within us. Similar doctrine is contained in a passage written to the Christians of Colossae: "Ye have died, and your life is hidden with Christ in God; when Christ, our life, shall appear, then also shall ye appear with him in glory" (Col. 3. 4). Our spiritual lives are hidden now; God alone knows them. One day they will be manifest to all.

When our Lord speaks of himself as the Good Shepherd he is still teaching the same lesson. He came that his sheep "may have life and have it abundantly" (John 10. 10). To bring this about he will lay down his life. That is his Father's design; redemption is consummated only in his death, which he freely accepts in obedience to his Father for love of men. But he will resume his life again because he *is* life; his death proves that he is really man; his resurrection will prove that he is God. This exalted doctrine was not well received. "He hath a devil" said many of his audience (John 10. 17 ff.).

After his last meal, our blessed Lord prayed to his Father: "Glorify thy Son, in order that the Son may glorify thee; even as thou hast given him power over all flesh" (John 17. 2). Why is this? The answer follows: "In order that to all thou hast given him, he should give to them everlasting life" (John 17. 3). What is this eternal life? "That they know thee, the only true God and him whom thou hast sent" (v. 3). So we learn that our Lord is the divine agent of grace to men. What is this knowledge which is eternal life? It implies practical acquaintance with Christ, recognition of him; then accepting him and all he is and means, and finally, it means service. Such knowledge is, of course, God's gift; only faith and love can make it effective. The implication is clearly that eternal life is the glorification of God; here on earth we can share in it by "knowing", that is by faith.

In view of all this we are not surprised to find our Saviour called "the author of life" (Acts 3. 15), "the author of eternal salvation" (Heb. 5. 9), "the bread of life" (John 6. 35), "the Word of life" (I John 1. 1) and the fountain of life (John 7. 37 ff.). It was by dying on the cross that our Lord merited this wonderful life for us: "So must the Son of Man be raised up, that whosoever believeth in him may have everlasting life" (John 3. 15). Or, as St Paul expresses it: "Through a single justifying act there cometh to all men life-giving justification" (Rom. 5. 18).

What does the New Testament tell us about the nature of spiritual life? Firstly, that it is a gift or a grace offered to all men; God makes the first approach, for without him we can do nothing. We have already quoted St John as saying that God has given men eternal life and this real life is to be found only in his Son. Without real contact with Christ nobody can possess it. St Peter writes that husbands and wives are equally heirs of the grace of eternal life (I Peter 3. 7). St Luke implies that conversion is God's gift when he writes of those who heard St Paul's words at Antioch in Pisidia: "As many believed as were appointed to everlasting life" (Acts 13. 48).

It is through baptism that the spiritual life comes to us. Here is what St Paul says: "As many of us as were baptized unto Christ Jesus, we were baptized unto his death. We were buried therefore with him through this baptism unto death, that as Christ was raised from the dead through the glory of the Father, so we also should walk in newness of life" (Rom. 6. 3-5). He is saying that baptism means intimate union with our Lord, being made one Body with him. This union is so close that as Christ really died on the cross to satisfy for sin, we die mystically to sin. The Apostle is referring to the way baptism was usually administered in the primitive Church—by immersion. Naked, the catechumen went down into the font, symbolizing the body's descent into the grave. Coming out again symbolizes rising again to a new life. It is very obvious that St Paul sees more than a symbol in the rite; as a result of it we are incorporated into Christ's mystical Body to live a new life.

This life, received when we are baptized, is a new manhood for us. St Paul describes it quite vividly to the Christians at Ephesus. They had to fling away the dirty clothes of the old way of living; they were rotted through and through with the illusions of lust. Remade mentally and spiritually, they were to put on the fresh clean clothes of the new life. Now they were intimately related to one another in Christ. "Ye are to put off the old man who falleth to corruption through deceitful lures of lust, to be renewed in the spirit of your mind, and to put on the new man, who is created according to God in justness and holiness of truth" (Eph. 4. 22-24). The new man is one who is under the influence of the Holy Spirit; he shares in the life of God. St Paul clearly implies this when he writes that those who refuse to believe are alienated from the life of God (Eph. 4. 18). The life in question is that which God lives and communicates to men.

It is always with Christ, as members of his mystical Body, that God brings us to life. "God . . . brought us to life with Christ—by grace ye are saved—and raised us up and seated us in Christ Jesus in the heavenly places, to show in the ages to come the surpassing riches of his grace through his kindness to us in Christ Jesus. For by grace ye are saved; through faith; and that not of yourselves, it is the gift of God" (Eph. 2. 5-8). Note how St Paul is saying that those with grace in their souls "sit in heavenly places"; that is, their glorification has already begun.

This glorification, this life, is the gift Christ came to give to all of us, as we have seen. It is union with Christ, a fact which he emphasized as he was walking with his Apostles to his agony (John 15. 1-17). What an apt comparison that is! In the Old Testament Israel was compared to a vineyard. Its people rejected the true husbandman; the vineyard did not produce the fruit God had willed. So Christ proclaimed himself to be the true vine; his disciples were as branches united with him. He, the vine, was to bring life and fruit to the whole world. That life would circulate from him through all the branches of the vine, the members of his body. So, as long as we remain attached to Christ his life flows in us. Only mortal sin kills it. Where there is life there is fruit; the stronger the life, the fairer the fruit. Recall what Mgr Benson wrote on this comparison: "The branches are not an imitation of the vine or representation of the vine; they are not merely attached to it, as candles to a Christmas tree; they are its expression, its results and sharers of its life. The two are in the most direct sense identical. The vine gives unity to the branches, the branches give expression and effectiveness to the energy of the vine; they are nothing without it; it remains merely a Divine Idea without them."

So the life St John is describing from the beginning of his Gospel means that we are bodily, really, physically and vitally united with Christ. From him we draw life and nourishment. As St Paul tells us, if Christ dwells in us by his spirit, our body is indeed subject to death as a punishment of sin, but our soul enjoys the life of grace, which is the life of glory hereafter (Rom. 8. 10).

What has this excursion of ours discovered in the inspired words about the life the Word came to give? We are created by God for himself; our destiny is to live with him for ever, knowing and loving him directly. Grace is the beginning of that eternal glory; the life of the blessed has already begun for us; it is within us as a seed—faith is the beginning of the direct vision of God, charity is of the same nature as the love that will be ours in heaven. Holy Communion brings that life to us because it is the Word, life itself, the life of the Godhead. The life of grace means that God abides in us and we in God. By faith, hope and charity we are raised far above our natural selves to know God in the way he knows himself and to love him as he loves himself; God puts these new powers in us. By them we share in the intimate family life of the most Holy Trinity. Through the Word, the Second Person, Jesus Christ our Lord, that life is our life; it endows us with the capacity to grasp God when, as the preface for the requiem Mass says, our earthly life is changed, not taken away. It is the Spirit of Christ which is continually begetting this new life within us. We have it only because the eternal Word of God became man and laid down his life for men. The purpose of the Incarnation was that all men might enjoy everlasting life, which is the perfect knowledge and love of God. This is the reward reserved for those who preserve the seed of life during their sojourn on earth, for those, that is, who per-

severe in knowing and loving Christ. The more they know and
love by faith, hope and charity, and the more they increase
their capacity to know and love by frequent, fervent reception
of the sacraments, especially Holy Communion, the greater
becomes their capacity for knowledge and love after death.
Through baptism the marvellous seed is placed within us; we
are born to union with God. It is a new manhood for us, a life
in which we are under the influence of the Holy Spirit, sharing
in God's own life. By it God communicates to us something of
his own life. Through Christ that life always comes to us; by
it we are united with him, forming the one vine and the one
body; he is the parent stem, he is the head.

When we think of the terms of this union we are aghast at the
vision of what God has done for us. He the infinite, he who is
absolute perfection, he the unknowable, intangible, inappre-
hensible, incomprehensible, he the wisdom who has ordered the
minutest detail of his mighty universe, he the power who has
brought everything that is from nothing, he the eternal who
never began and will never end, whose existence is beyond the
power to time to span, he who is love and goodness immeasur-
ably surpassing our holiest visions—he has not only made us
from less than the dust, from nothing, but he has put within us
this miniature of himself by which the unbridgeable is in some
respect bridged, the unfathomable fathomed, the finite raised to
share the life of the infinite, sinners admitted to life with Justness, flesh exalted to partake of the life of the one, pure Spirit.
How can we ever thank God enough for all this? How can our
love be ardent enough to prove that we appreciate all he has
done for us? Everything turns on faith—our trust depends on it,
our love is proportionate to it, our prayer hinges upon it.

As for the rest, what matters but our eternal destiny? We
are drawing nearer to it with every beat of our heart, to that
final consummation that is far beyond the power of the keenest
spiritual vision to discern and infinitely above the yearnings of
the greatest saint to love. It is there, waiting for us; already its
seed is in us. Just how far we shall grasp it depends on our
spiritual lives now; that is, eternity depends upon every moment
now. Of course, it is a question of practising all the religious
virtues—but, in a sense, that is a consequence of the intensity
of our conception of the ultimate reality and its embryo which

is in us now. In other words, all depends on faith—and faith is given us by God with the seed of glory. Exercise it and we know God in the way he knows himself; we reach out to him; we bring him to live within us. He then nurtures us in the supernatural conviction that we are God's children. We "have received the spirit of adoption, whereby we cry, 'Abba! Father!'" (Rom. 8. 15). Our daily spiritual lives—our humility, our obedience, our community spirit, our chastity, our poverty and the rest—will be just what our conviction of these great doctrinal realities makes them. Therefore, it is in our interests here and hereafter to ponder them in prayer and thereby increase our conviction of their reality.

Finally, let us not forget that all graces come through Mary. God willed to come through her. She is the channel of all graces. Her faith is the model of ours. Is it not highly significant that Elizabeth told her she was blessed, not because she loved, or was humble, or obeyed, or even because she was at that moment carrying her Creator incarnate within her, but because she believed? After her Son's Ascension she was in the Cenacle, the Queen and teacher of the Apostles. Could she be doing anything more precious than nurturing their faith by her words and her prayers? We know the result. Pentecost, the birth of the Church and its glorious life to the present day. We should try to live with Mary and the Apostles in spirit, never resting satisfied that we believe enough or love enough—but, by the help that always comes from God through Mary, trying to deepen and enliven our conviction of these truths than which none could be more vital. Let it never be said that we were in the smallest possible way deliberately allied with that darkness which refused to accept the Life that was Light.

6

"THERE WAS A MAN SENT FROM GOD, WHOSE NAME WAS JOHN"

(John 1. 6)

Is it not strange that in the middle of his sublime prologue St John should refer to John the Baptist? Doctors and saints have thought so and have tried to find an explanation. Perhaps the Evangelist, having spoken of eternity and the Word, knew that he was going to write principally of his Incarnation and wishes this mention of the Precursor to be an appropriate transition. More likely is the explanation that there were still some who thought that the Baptist was the Messias and the beloved disciple wished to refute them at once. The fact that God sent a great saint like the Baptist to prepare the way for Christ at once stresses the supremacy of the Redeemer.

Most commentators point out that a better translation of this sentence would be "there came" or "there arrived" rather than simply "there was a man". He had come on a prophetic mission indicated by his name, for John means "Yahweh has had mercy", a name supremely fitting the herald of him who was to bring about the at-one-ment of God and man.

St Luke tells us that John's father was Zachary "of the course of Abia". He was a priest but not High Priest. "The course" means, if the Greek is to be taken literally, the service in the Temple for a day. As this daily service of the priests was continued by each division for a week, from Sabbath to Sabbath, the word came to mean the class by which the daily services were performed in turn. The descendants of Aaron, who were the divinely appointed priests in Israel (Exod. 28. 1; 29. 44), were so numerous that there could have been much confusion about their service in the Temple. Therefore King David divided the descendants of Aaron's two sons, Eleazar and Ithamar, into twenty-four priestly classes or ranks. They were each to carry out the priestly functions under the guidance of the chief from whom each family took its name for a week in the Temple. The order of precedence was determined by lot and the eighth lot

fell on Abia. You can read all about it in Chapter 24 of the First
Book of Paralipomenon or Chronicles. The long word, we
might mention incidentally, comes from the Greek and means
"things missed out". The Chronicler wanted to give the Jews
who had returned from the Babylonian exile a religious history
of Juda and to stress in particular the rights of the Davidic
dynasty. He therefore recapitulated all their sacred history.
Only four of the priestly "courses" returned after the captivity
but the original division into twenty-four classes was retained.

St Luke depicts Zachary and Elizabeth, his wife, as the ideal,
pious Jewish couple, a complete contrast with the types who had
been so roundly denounced by the prophet Malachy. He tells
us that Elizabeth was of the daughters of Aaron, which raises a
difficulty because a few verses further on he refers to our Lady
as being her cousin, and Mary belonged to the tribe of Juda and
the house of David. Without going into details of how he
worked it out, we may satisfy ourselves with the explanation of
St Hippolytus that Elizabeth was of the daughters of Aaron on
her father's side and a cousin of our Lady on her mother's.
Why does St Luke mention such details? Evidently he wants us
to understand that even the Precursor of Christ was nobly
descended from a holy priestly race—and that was the only
source of nobility amongst the Jews. The more you enhance the
herald, the more you dignify him whom he announces.

John was not only dignified by his heredity but also by the
great personal holiness of his parents. They were both "just
before God" (Luke i. 6). The inspired writer wants us to
understand justice here in the strict sense: they possessed sanctifying grace and all the virtues. "Before God" implies more than
external goodness. They "walked in all the commandments and
justifications of the Lord without blame". By keeping God's law
they preserved, strengthened and increased their holiness; they
were "just" before God and "without blame" before men,
completely irreproachable in every respect.

This devout couple had no son. St Luke gives two reasons for
this. Elizabeth was naturally sterile and now they were both
elderly, beyond the age when, in the natural course of things,
they might have expected children. St Luke notes this because
he wants to make it quite clear that the herald of the Messias
was conceived miraculously by a special grace of God. We read

the same of Isaac (Gen. 18. 11 ff.). From the words of the angel we gather that Zachary and Elizabeth had being praying for a child, even when it seemed naturally out of the question. It is just one of the many reminders we find in Scripture that we should never hesitate to beg such favours of God. He wants us to ask them of him.

Now we visit the Temple. The week had come round for the priestly family of Abia, Zachary's family, to minister there before God. The Temple was his dwelling place. Zachary had drawn the lot of offering incense in the sanctuary before the lamb was sacrificed. It was such an honourable office that no priest exercised it twice. The altar was in the Holy Place, which opened into the Holy of Holies so that the incense could penetrate thither; a veil separated the two. Once a year on the feast of Expiation the High Priest alone could offer incense in the Holy of Holies. Zachary was not the High Priest but merely performing an office which could be discharged by any of the priestly family to whom the lot fell. So now Zachary, who had waited until old age for this privilege, sprinkles incense on the fire in the Holy Place and bows to the Holy of Holies before retiring.

"All the multitude of the people were praying together without," St Luke tells us. They cannot see Zachary; they are in the Outer Court, but they are united with him in their prayer. Possibly it is the Sabbath or a festival, bringing particularly large numbers to worship. Time passes and Zachary does not appear. As Moses and Aaron have done, the duty priest blessed the people when incense had been offered. So they wait; they want to hear from Zachary the prayer God dictated to Moses: "The Lord bless thee, and keep thee. The Lord show his face to thee, and have mercy on thee. The Lord turn his countenance to thee and give thee peace" (Num. 6. 23-26). Now there is movement; he is coming; necks are strained to look at him; they sense that something extraordinary has happened.

He looks strange; he walks as if he is unaware of his surroundings; he makes a sign; they see that he cannot speak. Soon they begin to murmur that he has had a vision; excitedly they gossip about it. Zachary indicates that he will continue like this for the rest of the week. There is one question now in the air of Jerusalem; what has happened to the priest on duty in the Temple?

We know. Standing on the right side of the altar of incense an angel had appeared to Zachary. Like Daniel and others before him, who had had heavenly visitations, he was afraid. Probably the appearance of the angel was majestic enough to indicate whence he had come; in any case, such an experience was completely unexpected and dramatic in its suddenness. The Jews believed that to see an angel was a certain sign that death was near.

Little wonder that Zachary was afraid. "Fear not, Zachary, for thy prayer is heard; and thy wife Elizabeth shall bear thee a son, and thou shalt call his name John", the angel said. What was this prayer? Most probably it was the priestly prayer of Zachary for the redemption of Israel and the coming of the Messias. But the fact that the angel added the news that his wife would conceive rather seems to imply that Zachary and she had prayed for that also. On the other hand there are those who argue that, even though he was assured by an angel, Zachary doubted that his wife could yet become a mother; therefore, he was hardly likely to have asked for this in his prayers. We do not know for certain—but we may gather from this the certain lesson that God does hear our prayers. Possibly Zachary had prayed for a child long ago, and only now does God will that his prayer should be answered. It is far safer for us in practice to learn the lesson that no prayer is ever unheard when it is humble, confident, sincere, persevering and according to God's will.

There is no case, apart from our Lord and his Precursor, in the New Testament, of a name being given from heaven to a child before birth. The spiritual writers remind us that Zachary means "Yahweh has remembered" and Elizabeth "my God is my oath"; so God's oath and its memory brought forth his mercy, for John means "Yahweh has had mercy". We can well apply that to ourselves and resolve to think often about the many promises God has made concerning our salvation, his burning love of us and his desire that we should all be saved and live with him for ever. Nothing should ever keep us from his merciful love. Did not the little Saint of Lisieux plead with him to raise up a legion of victims of his merciful love?

"Thou shalt have joy and gladness, and many shall rejoice in his nativity", the angel told Zachary. How true those words have proved to be! Of course Zachary, Elizabeth, their relatives and their friends rejoiced when their child was born, but their joy was only the beginning of the joy the coming of the God-man was to bring to men.

Why should the birth of Zachary's child be the cause of so much joy? The messenger from heaven explains. "He shall be great before the Lord. And 'he shall take no wine or strong drink', and shall be filled with the Holy Spirit even from his mother's womb; and many of the children of Israel shall he turn to the Lord their God. And himself shall go before him in the spirit and power of Elias, 'to turn the hearts of fathers to their children' and the disobedient to the wisdom of the just, to prepare for the Lord a ready people."

"He shall be great"; Christ himself was to confirm this: "For I say to you: Amongst those that are born of women, there is not a greater prophet than John the Baptist. But he that is lesser in the Kingdom of heaven is greater than he" (Luke 7. 28). Greatness here refers specifically to John's mission as the last of the Prophets; it by no means follows that his holiness exceeded that of all those in the Old Testament or in the New, St Joseph, for example. Our Lord is saying that in this man we have the culmination of Old Testament prophecy; but even at its highest point the Old Dispensation is lower than even the least who has reached and entered the New. John, of course, personally did enter the New Dispensation but his prophetic mission belonged essentially to the Old. He will be essentially holy in his threefold dignity as Prophet, Priest and Precursor. More, his virtues will correspond with this essential sanctity. The angel said so.

."He shall take no wine or strong drink." Here is a reference to the book of Numbers in which we read about the Nazarites, the Jews who bound themselves by vow to serve God for a limited period or even for life. As ascetics they renounced wine, which was a symbol of a pleasant life. Normally the vow was taken for thirty days. The holiness of John the Baptist is emphasized because he took this very strict vow for life. More, the angel proclaimed that he would be filled with the Holy Ghost even from his mother's womb. The phrase "filled with the Holy Ghost" or its equivalent occurs no less than fifty-three times in St Luke's Gospel and his Acts of the Apostles. "Even" indicates that John's sanctification would begin before his birth; thus the tradition of the Church has been that it took place when his mother was visited by our Blessed Lady bearing Christ within her.

We can well imagine how staggered Zachary must have been at receiving a message like this at such a time under such sensational circumstances. He knew well the words of Jeremias: "The word of the Lord came to me, and his message was: I claimed thee for my own before ever I fashioned thee in thy mother's womb; before ever thou camest to the birth, I set thee apart for myself; I have a prophet's errand for thee among the nations" (Jer. 1. 5). He knew also that the prophet Malachy had said that a precursor would appear before the long-awaited Messias: "I am sending an angel of mine to make the way ready for my coming!. . . . I will send Elias to be your prophet; he it is shall reconcile heart of father to son, heart of son to father" (Mal. 3. 1; 4. 5).

Zachary recognizes in the angel's words allusions to these words of the last of the prophets. Is he dreaming? Is this really an angel of God speaking to him? Is his son going to be another Jeremias and another Elias? The message seems clear enough. This child of his will lead such a holy and penitential life and preach so efficaciously that he will turn many of the Jews from sinful lives to God. It is hardly likely that there and then Zachary grasped the revelation that he whom his son was to herald was to be God himself. Yet that is what the angel says. He will turn many to the Lord their God before whom he will go: therefore, the one who is to be announced is the Lord and God of the Israelites.

His mission is to be in the spirit and power of Elias. Jewish tradition had believed that Elias would come again to anoint the Messias; no doubt Zachary believed it, too. But the angel does not say that. He intimates that his son will be another Elias in his courage, zeal, fortitude, resistance to wicked men in the high places of the world and in living in the desert on what God sends him. The words of Malachy refer directly to the return of Elias before our Lord's second coming. We recall how he himself explained it. When his Transfiguration had made it clear that he was indeed the Messias, "the disciples asked him saying, 'Why, then, do the Scribes say that Elias must come first'? And he answered and said, 'Elias is indeed to come, and he shall restore all things; but I tell you, Elias hath already come, and they have not recognized him, but have done to him all they could. Even so is the Son of Man about to suffer at their hands.' Then the disciples understood that it was of John the Baptist he had spoken to them" (Matt. 17. 10-13). Already he had told them: "He [John], if ye will receive it, is the Elias who is to come" (Matt. 11. 14). Perhaps it was to dispel all possible doubt that John might be Elias that the latter appeared with our Lord as he was transfigured.

The mission of this new Elias is summarized by the angelic messenger. He is to reconcile father to son. The Jews have led such scandalous lives that their fathers, the patriarchs, have turned away from them. The Precursor is to restore the right order. Through his example and words many of the Jews will return to a way of life worthy of the traditions of Israel, the way taught by their fathers of old. He will turn the "disobedient to the wisdom of the just, to prepare for the Lord a ready people". Ready for what? The coming of God himself. That is the meaning of the angel's message.

This startling event is essentially joyous. It is the first message of the coming of God amongst us. Yet God is to mark it by a sign of his displeasure. Zachary must have received enough grace to know that this was in truth a heavenly message; he should have accepted at once. Instead of humbling himself, as Mary was to do later, he remained obstinate: "Whereby shall I know this?" he said. "For I am an old man; and my wife is advanced in years" (Luke 1. 18). The spirit before him then made himself known: "I am Gabriel who stand before God", he said; "and am sent to speak to thee, and to bring thee these good tidings. And behold, thou shalt be dumb, and shall not be able to speak until the day wherein these things shall come to pass; because thou hast not believed my words, which shall be fulfilled in their time" (*ibid.* vv. 19-20).

Let us pause here to glance at the practical lessons we might gather from this first annunciation of the imminence of God's coming amongst us. Perhaps it is significant that it took place in the Temple at the most solemn of all moments in the life of the priest; God spoke through his angel to a priest, in the Temple at the hour of sacrifice. We know that those who built the Temple and worshipped in it were deliberately and culpably to reject the Lord of the Temple; but until they did, God recognized it and them. So it is today; his voice on earth is the Church speaking through the priesthood, which finds its fullness in the episcopacy. If we are faithful followers of Christ we anxiously look for every manifestation of his will in the Church; we neither doubt nor hesitate; once it is clear that the Church wants this or that we obey, even though it may mean setting aside well-established traditions. A topical example is the liturgical reforms of the present day. Privately we may prefer the old form of the celebration of Easter, for example; we may be quite unreconciled to the idea of the dialogue Mass; we may have anticipated Lauds for decades; *Dominus vobiscum* might have become almost part of ourselves in the private recitation of the divine office. Yet, when the Church speaks, Christ speaks. Our love of him compels us to obey.

John's birth was announced at the moment of sacrifice. Our daily sacrifice infinitely surpasses those of the Old Law. The moments of the Mass are the most precious of our day. It is then that the eternal High Priest, our God and our Creator, intercedes particularly for us. Therefore, the Mass is surely the most suitable time for our prayer. If we want gifts from God, if we need graces to make us holy, if we desire the conversion of sinners or anything at all which is according to God's will, there can be no more suitable time of asking than the time of Mass.

Another lesson for us is that God grants his favours in response to goodness of life shown by faithfulness to his will. The inspired writer stresses the virtues of Zachary and Elizabeth. They were free to love God or to reject him, to love him more or to love him less. We are the same. Zachary certainly did not know that by living a holy life amidst the corruption about him he was preparing himself to be the father of Christ's great herald. Precisely the same is true of us: we do not know what God wills to accomplish through our virtue nor do we know how, absolutely speaking, we are frustrating God by our mediocrity. The holiness of each of us is a contribution to the treasury of Christ's mystical Body; thence it is dispensed through Mary according to the divine will. Suppose our contribution is deficient? Only God knows the consequences, what he might have wrought through us if only we had loved him more.

As we have already hinted, it seems clear enough that Zachary did not hesitate to demand of God what would have been beyond the power of nature. When it happened he could not believe it. How like and unlike us that is. Unlike, in that we do not ask God enough. Every petition is an implicit act of adoration. God wants to be asked, and he wants to be asked for favours which show our faith in him, that he can do things which seem to surpass the ordinary or expected, be they temporal or spiritual favours. Zachary was like us in that when God grants our prayers we tend to doubt or to attribute the favour to natural causes or we omit to thank him for it. Devotional writers, evidently having beginners in the spiritual life in mind, tend to deprecate the prayer of petition because, they say, when we think of prayer we always think of asking. Maybe, but how much time does the average person devote to begging favours of God? Our needs are as numerous as the sands of the seas, for they are not only personal. As members of the mystical Body the Church's needs are our needs. As members of society, the needs of everyone of God's children are our needs, too. Moreover, let us not forget that when we pray, Christ prays in us. When we ask, he asks; what we ask, he asks, for we are "members of his body, of his flesh and of his bones" (Eph. 5. 30).

We can apply this particularly to a theme which runs all through the story of Christ—his mercy. Gabriel's messages to Zachary and to Mary were of God's mercy; John's very name meant mercy. So, as far as we are concerned, we must never fail to trust in his mercy, that is in his goodness towards us in our sorrows and trials; in particular, we should offer ourselves to him as victims of his merciful love for all the designs of his Sacred Heart, uppermost amongst which is surely the conversion of sinners. If we do that and, by God's grace, live in the spirit of absolute surrender to his will, we will be by the side of all in the Church who are actively working for the salvation of souls. Every detail of the events we have been considering and of the whole of the Bible, particularly the New Testament, is a voice proclaiming God's infinite mercy and yearning for the salvation of all men.

The angel's words about the holiness of the Precursor have two important lessons for us. Firstly, we must always show due reverence for holiness of state. John was officially holy because of his mission. So it is in the Church: God chooses some of his Son's members for special likeness to himself—the Pope, bishops, priests, and in their measure also, all who hold office in the Church, because theirs is the authority of Christ. It carries with it the grace of state. Similarly, we are bidden to show reverence for holy places and things dedicated to God's service. Familiarity should never be allowed to lessen the spirit of sacred awe for everything concerned closely with the Christian mysteries. Secondly, St John the Baptist's virtues corresponded to his dignity. His vocation is, to some extent, that of every Christian, and especially of priests and religious: we must bring Christ to the world by example and by word. He already stood by Calvary's cross by his life of mortification, renunciation and self-denial; he left the world completely to prepare himself for his mission. There is no other way. "The wisdom of this world is foolishness with God"; "Love not the world nor the things that are in the world; if any man love the world, the charity of the Lord is not in him"; "The friendship of this world is the enemy of God" (I Cor. 3. 19; I John 2. 15; James 4. 4). We must renounce self in order to be filled with Christ's spirit. That is a lesson of the Baptist's austerity. There were no half-measures with him. Let us beg of him that our passing through this vale of tears will mean in God's providence that our race will be brought nearer to Christ in the degree he wills. Let us pray, too, that our yearning for Christ may be comparable to St John's. It was through Mary that he was sanctified; so will it be with us; every grace comes through her. To acknowledge it by a life of dedication and union is to ensure that we are in the richest stream of grace. So, in the words of the hymn at Lauds on the Baptist's birthday, we may pray:

> Oh, then on us a tender, pitying gaze
> Cast from thy glory's throne;
> Straighten our crooked, smooth our rugged ways
> And break our hearts of stone.

7

"WHOSE NAME WAS JOHN"

(John 1. 6)

"HE shall be called John", said Elizabeth. "John is his name", wrote Zachary. A century later another John repeated that John was the name of the herald sent to prepare the way for the Messias.

What mysteriously sacred moments are concealed in the text of St Luke's first chapter. We are neither worthy nor holy enough to be told of the conversation between the two mothers-to-be in their intimate moments together. The evangelist leaves us to imagine it, how they talked together over the messages the angel had brought to each of them, compared them, looked backward through the prophecies and forward to their fulfil-ment. Only in heaven shall we know whether Mary remained with her cousin for the birth of her child. From the actual text some scholars argue that she did not, for St Luke says that "Mary abode with her about three months; and she returned to her own house." On the other hand, it seems hard to imagine that she should remain so long and leave just when the heaven-announced child was to be born. Surely God's Mother would wish to see and embrace the Precursor who had been sanctified as she brought his God to him within her.

The name seems to have been conferred at the time of circumcision. St Luke reports that they were going to call the child Zachary. His mother heard this and, because she knew all about the angel's message to her husband, said "No; he shall be called John." Relatives and friends objected. Why depart from the custom of calling the child after its father or other member of the family? In the end they appealed to Zachary. It seems that he was deaf, because they made signs to him. He could not speak because of the punishment he was suffering for his doubt of the angel's word. So he took a tablet and with the stylus or iron pen wrote his decision: "John is his name."

For over nine months Zachary had been dumb. No doubt
during that time he had been turning over prayerfully in his
mind the significance of the angel's message and the mission of
his child. Now he found himself able to express the thoughts
that had accumulated within him. Filled with the Holy Ghost
he recited the prophetic hymn which we know as the *Benedictus*.
Every day the Church sings it as the solemn climax of her
morning prayer, the office of Lauds. It is appointed to be said,
too, at the graveside during the funeral ceremony. It will be
much to our advantage to think about its meaning now.

We will understand it best if we divide it into five stanzas,
each of them indicated by a name. The first might be translated:

> Blessed be the Lord, the God of the people of Israel,
> because he has specially intervened to deliver us, his people,
> and has raised up a powerful Saviour for us
> in the house of David, his servant.

The key words here are "powerful Saviour", indicating the
name *Jesus*. This stanza marks the theme of the canticle; its
phrases recur later on. It is noteworthy that Zachary seems to
leap over the immediate events, the birth and circumcision of
his own divinely announced boy, to the far more important
reality, the imminent coming of the Saviour. The Jewish
expression, which is translated as *cornu salutis*, literally "an horn
of salvation", alludes to the animals, like the bull, whose power
is symbolized by the horns which they use to attack others or
defend themselves. The same thought occurs several times in
the Apocalypse of St John, where the fullness of strength and
power is emphasized when the Lamb is described as having
seven and the dragon ten horns. The metaphor is used frequently in the Old Testament to denote strength. So "horn of
salvation" means a powerful Saviour; the holy name, *Jesus*,
means Saviour; therefore it is not fanciful to see *Jesus* as the
appropriate name in this stanza of Zachary's canticle. The
special intervention for which he thanks God is nothing less
than the Incarnation.

During those months when he was dumb Zachary was
Mary's pupil. She could not have lived under his roof without
passing on to him something of her own faith in the mystery
that was even then being enacted within her. Perhaps it is not

unlawful to believe that it was from Mary herself that St Luke learned this canticle of praise and prophecy. Certainly the events preceding it are described very much in the way of an eye-witness.

Why does the New Testament refer so often to David? Gabriel from heaven told our Lady that her Son would sit on David's throne. St Peter in his first Pentecostal sermon proclaimed that Christ's resurrection had fulfilled David's prophecies. St Paul wrote to the Romans stating the meaning of God's plan that Christ's human birth should be from the line of David. Why is all this? Why does Zachary emphasize the same fact? Because the prophet Nathan had foretold that the Messias would be a descendant of David (2 Sam. 7. 8-16). So the New Testament makes it clear that hope for the Messias was focussed on David's house. For that reason Christ's enemies were angry when the people acclaimed him as David's son (Matt. 21. 15). Our Lord himself emphasized the title by reminding the Pharisees that the Messias was to be David's Lord. In many passages of Scripture the Saviour is himself called David (Jer. 30. 9; Ezech. 34. 24; 37. 24). These three texts emphasize that Christ will be, like David, king and shepherd, matters also emphasized in the New Testament.

So when we recite the *Benedictus* we will be helped by the thought of the holy name of Jesus who saved his people in a far more real sense than did David of old. By dying on the cross he became for ever and by a new right the king and shepherd of souls. Saviour embraces all his titles, so Jesus is his most fitting name. It is surely most appropriate at the beginning of each day when the *Benedictus* is begun to think even momentarily of God incarnate precisely as our Saviour. God has brought me to another dawn; he has given me yet another opportunity of returning love to him for the infinite love he showed in becoming one of us to save us; another day lies before me in which he permits me to gain merit for heaven, to walk before him and be perfect, to try to save souls. *Benedictus Jesus Salvator.* "May every heart confess thy name And ever thee adore; And seeking thee, itself inflame To seek thee more and more. Thee may our tongues forever bless, Thee may we love alone, And ever in our lives express The image of thine own. O Jesus, most desired and dear, The hope of longing spirits here, To thee my earnest tears shall turn, For thee my inmost heart shall yearn." So did St Bernard express his longing to grow daily in love of his Saviour, Jesus.

Here is the second stanza:

As he promised through the mouth of his holy ones,
his prophets from of old:
to save us from our enemies
and from the hand of all that hate us:
thus to show mercy towards our fathers,
and to be mindful of his holy covenant.

The important words here are the last: "to be mindful of his holy covenant". Long ago God had made covenants or agreements with Abraham and his children, with the Jews through Moses, too, and with the house of David. He added to them the promise of the Messias. So salvation through the Messias is the fulfilment of God's promise made in those covenants. It is to this that Zachary is alluding here; St Peter was later to remind the Jews of the same fact in his sermon which followed the curing of the lame man at the Beautiful Gate of the Temple. All that God agreed with Abraham, Isaac, Jacob, Moses and David is fulfilled now in the coming of the Redeemer; so God has been faithful to his promises; he has indeed saved his people from their enemies. All this is expressed in Zachary's name which means "God remembers".

How appropriate that is for our morning prayer! "God remembers"—yes, he remembers me at the beginning of another day. Not a hair of my head will perish without his knowing it (Luke 21. 18). The tiniest detail of my life is permitted by God; every incident is the gift of a Father who loves me with tenderness and mercy, a gift to be used to prepare myself for eternal life. So my daily *Benedictus* is a reminder of my morning offering; every second of my day is God's, to be used to promote his honour and glory and to grow in his love.

Zachary, "God remembers"—but do I remember God as I should? Our conferences on the prologue to St John's Gospel have revealed a little of the mysteries of the life of grace. More is to come. Are we thinking as deeply and as prayerfully as we are able, seriously trying to penetrate the riches God has placed within us? God lives in us; he could not have brought himself any nearer. If we penetrate a truth like this we will find it becoming stimulating, gripping, burning, purifying. It will drive us on to seek more enthusiastically after our infinite Lover. The world's motto is often, "Forget and be happy; eat, drink, be merry; get away from the realities of life". The motto of a good religious is precisely the opposite: "Remember and be happy; familiarize yourself, be penetrated, saturated with the ultimate realities; enjoy God living in you; imitate Mary and Elizabeth during their months of waiting; Christ is coming—daily in Holy Communion, continually by grace, finally as judge." In the words of the *Imitation* we should call the divine Guest and then close the door on ourselves. It was when the doors were shut that our Lord appeared to the trembling Apostles and reassured them with the words "Peace be to you".

So it will be with us if we entertain as we should the Holy Trinity, the Guests of our souls. St Teresa once wrote that all our troubles come from not gazing on God. He could hardly have made it easier for us to gaze on him. He lets us see him in human form in the Gospels; his cloak of flesh and blood becomes bread and wine in the Eucharist; he begs us to see him in every one we meet, in the Church and in our souls. His presence is our supreme reality. "Oh that I might be a sower of solitude", prayed Claudel—yes, we mean the solitude of ourselves with our God. Even in a monastery that solitude can be disrupted. It is particularly easy with those who have contact with seculars. It is hard to be with them and not talk to them; it is difficult to keep the conversation always on a worthy level; it is even easy to give scandal by falling into worldly faults of the tongue, gossiping about others, displaying irritableness and so forth. The soul of a religious should be a secret, silent dwelling place of God—not a public house, a club or a market-square where all kinds of thoughts jostle for a place.

"God remembers"; do we remember God? Here is what St John Chrysostom had to say about recollection: "Look at St Paul; did he have at his disposal a church in which to pray? No, only a prison. The King Ezechias had but his room and a bed; the good thief, a cross. Jeremias was plunged into a mire, Daniel into a lake, Jonas into a whale; and Job was stretched on a dung heap. Pray in any place you may be. You are the Temples of God; do not seek temples other than yourself." So the canticle at Lauds should be a daily stimulus to perfect our spirit of recollection, practise silence, avoid all unnecessary conversation with seculars, mortify our curiosity, guard our eyes and other senses, banish desires for worldly news and gossip—and all for a positive aim, to remember God.

The third stanza of Zachary's hymn goes thus:

[He is mindful] of the oath which he swore to Abraham our father,
to grant us that, delivered from our enemies, without fear we would serve him in holiness and justice
in his sight all our days.

We see at once that this is simply a more emphatic repetition of the preceding stanza. The crucial word, which differentiates this section, is "oath", and so the appropriate name is Elizabeth, which means "my God is my oath". Is it not, then, appropriate to recall each morning that God has bound himself in our regard in many respects by solemn agreement? For example, read the eight beatitudes; each of them is a promise made by Christ; throughout the Gospels you find other promises too numerous to mention in detail. They can all be summarized in the saying that nothing done for God goes without its appropriate rewards, that he denies help to nobody, that he gives every individual enough grace to get to heaven and that eternal life with him is the ultimate destiny of all of us.

In particular religious might recall at the saying of the *Benedictus* Christ's special promise to them: "Everyone that hath left houses or brothers or sisters or father or mother or children or lands for my name's sake, shall receive a hundredfold now in this time . . . and in the world to come life everlasting" (Matt. 19. 29; Mark 10. 30). There can hardly be a more consoling thought than that with which to embark on a new day. It is the certain promise of infinite Truth, and we know from experience how he fulfils it in practice in so far as the hundredfold now is concerned. Only infidelity brings unhappiness.

Might we not also use our daily *Benedictus* to think of our agreement with God, of our vows to him? The divine office is a main element in the monastic vocation; it is the precious setting of the infinite treasure of the Mass, the sacrifical spirit of which must be evident at every moment of every day. Our work, like the office, should be an appropriate setting for our Mass. Our life is like the monstrance. At the centre is the Host, the Mass; around it is the first highly decorated, most worthy halo, the official liturgical prayer of the Church; beyond that extends the nimbus of our other prayers and religious exercises; that, in turn, blends into our daily work, and the strong support of all is our life solemnly consecrated to God by our vows. At the moment we are not concerned with the details of the vows, but simply with the fact of consecration, which implies the solemnly sealed desire to aspire after total union with God. So as we sing the morning canticle we may very appropriately recall our solemn covenant and rededicate ourselves to spend another day in the task of perfecting our union with him. That implies effort; union with God is not floating around in the air to be breathed in by all and sundry; nor will it come from a merely mechanical, routine observance of rule, constitutions and customs. There must always be the continuous, ceaseless effort after union—negative in the sense that we never relax our exertions to banish every attachment that comes between self and God, and positive in that we relentlessly pursue him, especially in desire and prayer for perfect oneness of spirit with the Heart of Christ.

The fourth stanza follows:

And thou, little child,
thou shalt be called the prophet of the Most High,
for thou shalt go before the Saviour to prepare his ways,
to give his people knowledge of salvation
through remission of their sins.

There is no doubt that the important words here are the first, "And thou, little child", and that therefore the appropriate name on which to meditate is John, which means "the Lord is gracious". The contrast between this stanza and the preceding three is like that between the New Testament and the Old. Gone are ambiguity and obscurity; deliverance from enemies is now clearly stated as forgiveness of sins, and that comes through God's graciousness or mercy, that is his love especially in so far as it helps us in our sorrows and afflictions.

Here is another highly pertinent thought for the beginning of the day. It was the main support of the little Saint of Lisieux. As a small child she lost her mother; then the sister who had taken her mother's place entered Carmel; she was herself afflicted with serious illness; even after following her sister into the cloister she had to suffer from lack of understanding on the part of some of the other nuns; then came her father's insanity and her own death-dealing tuberculosis. In all these sufferings she saw the gifts of God's mercy. With the beloved Apostle she cried through her tears: "We have come to know and have believed the love which God hath in us. God is love" (I John 4. 16-17).

The basis of holiness is faith; its heart is love; and the surest way to it is faith in love—real, living belief in the fact that God is infinite Love and loves us with that same infinite love. What a difference it makes to life if we never, under even the most trying conditions, forget that we are loved. There is no escape from the truth that unfaltering, complete divine faith in God's love for us is the first, necessary, indispensable condition for all real communion between ourselves and him. Teresa of Lisieux was a saint because she perfectly realized this. She never thought of God except as her Father, as the tenderest, kindest and most affectionate of Fathers. Saints grow in that atmosphere, in the simple realization of their true relationship with God; they are saints because they live in it, breathe it in, mature, develop and expand in it. From faith in infinite merciful Love spring humility, trust, abandonment and joy. So the *Benedictus* is a dawn summons to go out to face another day in the living faith that we are infinitely loved and to love our Lover to capacity in return. Even when our Lover leads us along dark ways, when the consolations of prayer elude us, when illness afflicts us, when others hurt us, when the spiritual heavens seem darkest our faith in his merciful love must never waver. Behind the dark clouds the divine Sun is always shining.

This stanza of the *Benedictus* emphasizes mercy. So St Teresa of Lisieux, whom the Popes say has been raised up as a model of holiness for all the faithful, not only believed in God's love, but she emphasized especially her devotion to his compassionate

or merciful love. It is one thing to understand it theologically;
that may be a purely natural thing; it is quite another to
believe in it effectively, to such an extent that it makes us
gallop along to road to complete union. It will not avail us
before God to have had a splendid metaphysical understanding
of the Incarnation, Redemption, the Mass or the Eucharist and
to be able to discourse about them with brilliance and defend
them with subtlety. Perfection demands that our natural knowledge be accompanied by complete surrender in utter simplicity. We can be too fond of trying to explain everything,
understand everything, rationalize everything. God does not
make holiness proportionate to or dependent on human
intelligence. It is faith that counts, and the simplest soul can
have the deepest living faith in God's compassionate love. We
have to dare to be a little child, to love as a child loves because
we know we are loved as little children are loved by infinite
Love. What galvanizing thoughts these are with which to begin
the day!

So we come to the final stanza:

A work of our God's merciful tenderness;
he brings to us from on high the visit of the rising Sun
in order to enlighten those who sit in the darkness and
    shadow of death
to guide our feet into the path of peace.

The theme of merciful love continues but the vital words are
"the visit of the rising Sun" or, as some translate it, "the first
light of heaven" or "like a dawning from on high". It is a
visitation comparable to sunrise after the darkness of night.
Now, who was it that first brought consolation to Zachary
when he was bearing his punishment of dumbness? Surely it
was Mary, who changed his darkness into light; her visit,
bringing with it the sanctification of Zachary's son, was a
prefiguring of what God's visit incarnate would be to the
world. What the coming of Jesus within Mary did for Zachary
and Elizabeth, he would do for the whole race of men. Through
Mary he came, like the dawning of the morning, bringing
light and peace to men.

Oriens ex alto is a picturesque phrase which has aroused no
little speculation amongst scholars. The corresponding Hebrew

word, *Tzemah*, was translated by St Jerome from the original Hebrew as "a bud" in some places (Is. 4. 2; Jer. 23. 5; 33. 15) and as "orient" in others (Zach. 3. 8; 6. 12). Both meanings apply to Christ. We may think of him as the bud, the new life of men springing forth, or as the rising sun darting forth its rays of light. So we have here the light and life theme so common in St John.

It is fitting that the name of Mary should characterize this final stanza, excelling all the others in its warmth of feeling, the beauty of its poetry, the richness of its imagery and the consolation of its message. Christ still comes to men. Redemption continues as long as grace is given to souls. Grace is life; life's channel is the mother; the mother who transmits supernatural life is she who willingly allowed herself to be the channel of life to men. She is the mediatrix, the channel of every grace. Christ still comes through her, infinitely merciful and tender, bringing life to souls, enlightening minds, inflaming hearts and leading men into the path of peace, which is his way.

So, as we come to the end of our morning *Benedictus* it is fitting that we should renew the consecration of ourselves to Christ through Mary, surrendering all we have to her to be embellished by her and offered to her Son as her gift and ours to be disposed of according to his will, which is also hers. As we look forward to the day that is dawning we rightly have confidence for we intend it to be spent in union with Mary, who is so completely united with the holy Trinity. Everything we do or say or think must be our gift to her for her Son; therefore it will be as perfect as the grace that comes through her permits us to make it. The surest way to keep our feet in the path of peace, which is the way of Christ, is to say to Mary, "Lead us" and to walk through life united in mind and heart and will with her.

8

"THIS MAN CAME FOR A WITNESS"

(John 1. 7)

IMMEDIATELY after recording the *Benedictus* St Luke writes: "And the child grew, and was strengthened in spirit; and was in the deserts until the day of his manifestation to Israel" (Luke 1. 80). Possibly when God had taken Zachary and Elizabeth to himself their son went out into the lonely places south-west of Jerusalem to prepare for his vital mission. The Holy Spirit draws a veil over those years, but we are justified in pausing to draw inspiration from two things—the intense faith which must have dominated John's life to force him to leave the Temple, renounce his priesthood and live alone in austerity, and the prayer and penance to which he devoted himself.

Very few spiritual books treat of faith in anything but an intellectual way. Many of them take it for granted, as if the authors say to themselves, "Only people with the faith would read a book like this"; so they write of every virtue but the fundamental one. There is, of course, a treatise on faith in the manuals of theology. As he studies it the student examines every aspect of faith; he analyses, dissects and vindicates the Church's teaching about it; he studies its development, its relation to reason, the part grace plays in it, and so on. Yet it is possible to know more than St Thomas Aquinas about faith and yet to be wanting in it. The difference between the saints and the rest of us lies precisely in faith; we all have it; the saints lived it. They saw God and hardly anything else; at least, whatever else they saw, they saw in God. He was life for them.

St Paul told us that charity is the greatest virtue. Of course it is. The Holy Eucharist is the greatest sacrament; but you cannot have it without baptism. So you cannot have charity unless you have faith first, and the intensity and merit of your love will depend on the strength of your faith. From childhood we have learnt that God made us to know him, love him and serve him. That is life, the whole of life. Many people, I am afraid, fail to appreciate that. They divide life into the holy

67

part and the secular part. Or if they do not go as far as that they are still not ready to allow faith to be dominant. They are prepared to take their rules of behaviour from Christ's teaching but they fear to give him all; they will not take him literally, when he means to be taken literally; they try to hang on to just a tiny bit of self-will; they still make some little concessions to the world. They do not admit that life is indivisible; that every moment is valuable only in so far as it contributes to the whole purpose of knowing, loving and serving God. We are never off duty; we can never regard any thought or word or deed or omission as being "off the record".

It is possible to be externally perfect in regular observance in a monastery or convent and yet be gravely defective in faith. There are some who are able to concentrate immediately on what they think of as serving God. They say to themselves: "I only know in order to love; I show my love by service; so, if my service is perfect there is not much wrong with either my knowledge or my love." So you find in communities the sisters who abhor the slightest unpunctuality, the tiniest deviation from the ceremonial in choir or the most insignificant departure from tradition—yet they are strangely lacking in warmth. They are like blocks of granite. Often they are critical, usually lacking in charity. What matters most for them is "their work", whatever it is, in the community or out of it; nothing must interfere with that. Priests or religious like this are not interested in spiritual perfection as such; they do not think about it or talk about it. They are models of efficiency; desk work, accounts, records—everything is just as precise as it could be. Yet one feels that this type is an official rather than a genuine servant of God. Such will never do great work for souls because their spiritual life will never rise above mediocrity; they will never be consulted by many of those in trouble; they will never be called upon to direct souls to holiness, because others recognize that they are not interested in holiness as something they are intent on attaining. Service is their watchword—and by it they are ruled.

One result of an attitude like this is that the work becomes one's own rather than God's. Many a work that has promised well has been put in jeopardy by such a spirit. Those in charge of it have had their own ideas of how it was to be done; no methods but theirs would work; other people did not understand it and suggestions from them were bound to be useless; superiors had no experience of it, either; under the circumstances, it was argued, disobedience was excusable; at all costs this work of God had to be safeguarded; if those in charge of it, by divine providence, resigned, the whole thing would fold up and the Church would suffer irreparable harm. So they went on, dominated by self-interest, fighting against authority, causing untold worry around them until the final crash came. When one experiences such cases one realizes the immense harm that results from concentration on work at the expense of spiritual growth. People who are otherwise capable and zealous deprive themselves of the one thing necessary, God's blessing, by putting service before knowledge and love, work before the life of the spirit, selfishness before obedience and submission. The cardinal mistake is to regard work for souls as one's own rather than as God's.

Defective faith often culminates in war with God's will. Those who are guilty of it fix their gaze on time rather than eternity; they think *their* vision is all important—the souls *they* are working for, *their* method of apostolate, *their* organization, *their* way of doing things; they forget that the vision of God is what superiors see or what God in his providence sends. The good religious gazes beyond time; whatever is being done transcends time; it is a contribution to eternity; it is God's work, done for God, by God's power and grace. More, it is a contribution to the formation of oneself in faith, hope and charity. There is something seriously wanting in the person who is more interested in effecting something than in being affected for the better by what is done. Through faith alone we can adopt this outlook; only faith centres us in God, his providence and his love.

The things that happen to us in life, even the smallest of them, are more important in making our souls than the things we do. It is through them that we weld together into unity our faith, love and service. Happenings which are absolutely of our own choosing are few; circumstances we did not choose outnumber them by far. The time in which we live, the place, our parents, our school, our teachers, our physical make-up, our brains, the people and things which surround us, events in the world near to us and far away, those under whom we find ourselves, the weather—literally thousands of details of life are offered us by

God. Each of them, from the smallest to that which influences us most, is meant to mould us for eternity. It is through each that we are not only to serve God, but to know him and love him. Deep faith sees in everything the gentle hammer of God's love, the appointed channel of his providence, the mould of his wisdom.

Service can exist without love or with inadequate love. Service, of a sort, can outstrip love. That is true of all the fanatics of history. Many of them have been well-intentioned; they have been patriotic in a wrong kind of way; they may have been inspired by a genuine concern for men's material welfare—but how soon fanaticism leads to cruelty, bloodshed and inhumanity. Something similar can happen in God's case. One can exaggerate the element of service, until it becomes service for the sake of service rather than for the sake of God. Genuine faith leads to love and genuine love leads to service—and the quality of the service, especially the humility and obedience with which it is done, gives some idea of the intensity of love. But when one clings to a particular work or to anything else against the will of superiors—that is a certain sign that faith is weak.

It is possible to be wedded to God's service without being wedded to God. One feels that occasionally about those who are excessively devoted to the externals of the liturgy. The ceremonies must be perfect; why? Not because they are part of our service of God but because the reputation of an individual or a community is at stake. I once heard it remarked that the ceremonies at a certain religious house were so perfect as to be inhuman! The attainment and maintenance of such perfection can be a serious distraction and an impediment to union with God. The same is always true when what are essentially means are promoted to be ends in themselves. Our daily tasks are means and nothing more than means to godliness. They are particularly valuable means because they are not usually of our own or of even human choosing; they are the divinely appointed instruments for the fashioning of the soul. It requires much faith to see that.

Every item of the daily round should be impregnated with a sense of intimacy with and affection for God. If that is our aim we will not fall into the trap of seeking to serve God without seeking God. We must realize that it is possible to spend years in God's service, even in the cloister, and yet amass very little merit for eternity. Our work is valuable only in so far as it is done with charity. I am thinking all the time of the enclosed religious who is excessively concerned about her work—her particular job in the community, her sewing, her printing, her gardening, her altar-bread making, her choir, her sacristy, her dairy, her kitchen; about the active religious whose vision seems to end with her speciality; of the order which promotes a certain way of life simply because it belongs to that order—it may be a Third Order, a Confraternity or a Sodality; of the priest on parish work who is immersed in the pools or bingo or clubs or in even visiting—all of them are making a colossal mistake if interest in the work or love for the work or absorption in the work supplant interest in, love for or absorption in God. The thing done may be first-class; it may seem to promote God's glory; it may win praise and plaudits on all sides but, unless it springs from the love of God, is inspired by the love of God and is accompanied by intimacy with God it will frustrate God's work in the soul of the worker.

It is sometimes suggested that all will be well if we pause from time to time during our work to direct our attention to God and to purify our intention. We must be on our guard against thinking that this will put everything right; it will not. It may be pure imagination. Merely to recite a formula from time to time to the effect that we are doing everything for God does not of itself make everything be done for God. More is necessary—that the dominant force in directing life should be God's good pleasure. Our aim should be to remember it all the time; the will must be firmly anchored in that direction. That cannot happen unless the will is rightly informed, and the informing is the work of faith.

We hope to enjoy eternity in God's presence. As we have seen, the activity of the blessed is essentially to know and love God. These two, knowledge and love, are intrinsically, inseparably bound together. Love comes from knowledge; if you want to love a thing or a person you must know it or him or her first. Then your love will be in the measure of your knowledge. If your knowledge is inadequate your love may be misplaced. The most attractive object of knowledge is God; in the supernatural order we know him only by faith. After death faith gives way to vision to such an extent that we are irresistibly drawn to God. So, during life, we should aim at such intensity of faith that nothing will divert us from God. That means putting everything in its right place as an instrument leading to God, as a tool designed to fashion our souls to love God more. The more perfect knowledge is, the more complete is the love that springs from it—and the more perfect is the love, the more perfect is the service. And service which genuinely springs from love will have a warmth, an intimacy and an affection about it which will stamp it indelibly as being God's work. So it follows that the absorbing pursuit, the dominant aim, the essential business of life is to get to know God, not by natural, speculative knowledge, but by supernatural faith.

Little wonder that it was the one thing our Lord demanded before everything else. Remember how he praised the centurion for his faith: "I have not found so great faith in Israel" (Matt. 8. 11). St Matthew tells us that when they brought a paralytic to him, "Jesus, seeing their faith" cured him (Matt. 9. 2). To the possessed boy's father he said: "If thou canst believe, all things are possible to him who believes." And the man made that unforgettable act of faith: "I do believe; help my unbelief." When the Apostles came to him afterwards privately asking "Why could not we cast it out?" our Lord told them: "Because of your unbelief" (Mark 9. 13-28; Matt. 17. 14-20). When he had cursed the fig-tree and it had withered the astonished Apostles asked, "How did it come to wither up immediately?" Our Lord answered: "Amen I say to you, if you have faith and do not waver, not only will you do what I have done to the fig-tree, but even if you shall say to this mountain, 'Arise, and hurl thyself into the sea', it shall be done. And all things whatever you ask for in prayer, believing, you shall receive" (Matt. 21. 21-22).

The Scribes and Pharisees were condemned by our Lord precisely because they emphasized external observance, the work if you like, at the expense of the faith that makes it God's. "Woe to you, Scribes and Pharisees, hypocrites! because you pay tithes on mint and anise and cummin, and have left undone the weightier matters of the Law, right judgment and mercy and faith" (Matt. 23. 23). And, very significantly, Christ added: "These things you ought to have done, while not leaving the others undone." We know the result: those who concentrated on works without faith, intimacy and love eventually plotted their Saviour's death.

Twice during storms on the sea of Galilee the Apostles were rebuked for their lack of faith. On the first occasion our Lord was asleep in the boat with them. They awoke him; he stilled the storm and said to them: "Why are you fearful? Are you still without faith?" (Matt. 4. 40). The other time was when he came to them walking on the water and St Peter went out to meet him. All was well as long as he could see his Master, but when a huge wave hid him, Peter cried: "Lord, save me!" We might have expected him to blame the Apostle for being so foolish as to try to walk on such a stormy sea. On the contrary, he was blamed for his want of faith: "O thou of little faith, why didst thou doubt?" (Matt. 14. 31).

So we could go on and on right through the Gospels, the Acts and the epistles always finding evidence for the same lesson. It was faith that Christ looked for; it was faith that attracted him and lack of faith that repelled him. But the faith he wanted was not just an intellectual assent to a set of theses or creeds or dogmas. It was a life: "He who is just lives by faith" (Hab. 2. 4; Gal. 3. 11; Rom. 1. 17; Heb. 10. 38). It must be our life, too. It is not the life of faith merely to assent speculatively to Christ's teaching, to admire it, to study it, to meditate on it. His teaching is not like mathematics, geography, art or science; it is to be lived as well as learned. So it must saturate us; it must be the real force behind our spiritual lives.

Think of John the Baptist again, there in the desert during all those waiting years. He never faltered; he never hesitated. He just waited until the appropriate time and then he startled the country by proclaiming his message. God's will kept him there praying and fasting; that was the light which guided him. So we should look for the same light in everything that betides us. God is acting in everything that befalls in his creation; he is acting on me and for me in everything that happens to me. If we live by faith we will place no limits to the way he works in us. We will see far more than Shakespeare's Duke, who described some of the picture in the second Act of *As You Like It*:

Sweet are the uses of adversity;
Which, like the toad, ugly and venomous

Wears yet a precious jewel on his head;
And this our life, exempt from public haunt,
Finds tongues in trees, books in the running brooks,
Sermons in stones, and good in everything.

We will see God in everything and Christ in everyone. "If the providence of God does not preside over human affairs," St Augustine wrote, "there is no point in busying oneself about religion." We all believe that; but real faith means that we live it down to the tiniest detail. It means putting into practice what St Gregory wrote: "The acts of our Maker ought always to be reverenced without examining, for they can never be unjust." How can we recognize the acts of our Maker? Only by faith, and that will see them everywhere. One of the maxims of St Teresa of Avila was this: "Discern the providence and wisdom of God in all created things, and in all give him thanks."

One day our Lord was talking to the Jews. He knew all about their fanatical adherence to the Law, of how they apparently treasured divine truth and displayed their religion in the magnificent worship of the Temple; yet he said to them: "It is my Father who glorifies me, of whom you say that he is your God. And *you do not know him*" (John 8. 54). Could our Lord condemn us in the same way? Could he speak to us like this: "I came to you in that illness, that frustration, that change of office, that disappointment, that bereavement but you did not recognize me. I was with you in that inconvenience, in that storm, in that sunshine, in that rebuke, in that separation, in that difficulty, in every tiny thing that has ever happened to you, but you have eyes and see me not"?

Nor is it enough that we see God; we must love him wherever he is. Maybe we try to create a God of our own. We are prepared to see God in some things and not in others, Christ in some people but not in everyone. It may be easier to see God in a severe illness than to see him in a petty frustration; it may be easier to see Christ in a major superior than in a minor one. But the life of faith brooks no exceptions; God hems us in completely; "in him we live and move and have our being" (Acts 17. 28). There is no end to the disguises in which God appears to us. Faith penetrates them all. Not only does it see him in the Church, in the Eucharist, in superiors, in every individual, but—and let it be repeated—in every occurence of life.

Our infinitely loving Father has a plan; we are part of that plan. With boundless longing he wants us to be holy; the smallest detail of life is his agent for our fashioning. He is the divine smith; we are the precious metal; life is the anvil and everything that happens is the hammer. If we twist and squirm and resist; if we fail to see that there is a master-plan; if we try to jump away to another anvil the heavenly craftsman is frustrated. Faith is the gift he has placed in us; he gives us grace to nourish and strengthen it so that it will grow sturdy and strong. By prayer, obedience, humility, resignation, abandonment and constant efforts to see God everywhere we merit increase of faith; we co-operate with the divine worker.

Faith sustained John the Baptist during the years of waiting. Faith compelled him, when the time came, to go out and proclaim a message which was very contrary to the spirit of his day. Likewise, it was faith which made Mary blessed. "Blessed is she who has believed", Elizabeth said (Luke 1. 45). So if we believe, God will be in us; we need fear nothing; we can dare everything for him: "Amen I say to you, if you have faith . . . nothing will be impossible to you; things that are impossible with men are possible with God" (Matt. 17. 19; Luke 18. 27). Those are the words of infinite Truth; faith accepts them at their face value and dares to live by them. But first of all they must be applied to the task of sanctifying ourselves. "I can do all things in him who strengtheneth me" (Phil. 4. 13).

9

"TO GIVE TESTIMONY OF THE LIGHT"

(John 1. 7)

JOHN the Evangelist recalls how his namesake, the Precursor, came as a witness. His purpose was to proclaim the coming of our race's Saviour. So deep was his faith, so profound his conviction that for all the years of his young manhood he lived, prayed and did penance in lonely places to prepare himself worthily for his mission. That mission is, says St John, to give testimony of the light, to be a witness, to give evidence. It seems legitimate to assume that John the Baptist must have been the greatest preacher of all time, next to Christ himself. In him Old Testament preaching and prophecy reached its apex; he was specially announced by a heavenly messenger as the Messias's herald; he had to be in all things worthy. John was himself so conscious of this that we cannot doubt that those years in the desert were spent in prayer. The mouth speaks only from the heart's abundance, our Lord told the Pharisees (Matt. 12. 34). John knew that; his task was to fill himself with the genuine love that would flame forth as converting zeal. Prayer was the only way.

It is unfortunate that so many religious congregations have adopted the custom of speaking of mental prayer as meditation. It might be a good thing if that word were forbidden in this context. So long as prayer is envisaged, even subconsciously, as meditation untold harm may be done. Those who should advance to higher forms of prayer will be retarded, they will suffer much internal strife, prayer will become a burden for them, despair may set in and one who might well have progressed to outstanding holiness remains on the common level.

Discursive prayer, commonly called meditation, is the prayer of beginners, of those who wish to turn to God from ways of sin, of those who have never taken prayer seriously, of those who are still doing battle with attachments to rather serious bad habits. In a word it is the prayer of the purgative way. By it one tries to understand ·the mysteries of revelation and

76

instruct himself in them by various considerations, at the same time applying what is learned to life, making resolutions and praying for the grace to keep them. It has been set out in methodical form by St Ignatius of Loyola, St Peter of Alcantara, St Francis de Sales and others. In many cases, possibly the majority, discursive prayer of this kind—preparation, consideration, personal application, petition, resolutions—is a necessary apprenticeship to the life of prayer. But it is only an apprenticeship, not the life itself. It should not last longer than is necessary.

For many centuries we find barely a mention of discursive prayer in the spiritual literature of the Church or in the rules of religious orders. In fact, these rules did not consider mental prayer of any kind as a separate exercise. Life was meant to be an act of faith. One who lives in the spirit of faith, seeing God in everything and everybody, always conscious of his infinite love, necessarily tries to turn to him always. He is never far from the mind; he is like the pole to which the compass needle always turns. So the life of the first religious, alternating between the recitation or singing of the Psalms, study and manual work, was one of union with God. It was full of prayer. Some might ask: Did not those religious in the early centuries need considerations and meditations like we do? How is it that fifteen centuries passed before the coming of systematized meditation? The answer is that they did indeed need the supernatural knowledge of faith to sustain their good-will and they found it in the Scriptures, the writings of the Fathers, in conferences and in sermons.

In many cases the same is true still. There are numerous people who for a variety of reasons, especially a devout home background, are able to practise affective prayer without the apprenticeship of discursive meditation. It is constantly said by experienced directors that these probably form the majority of our devout Catholic people. When, therefore, they go to a retreat house for a week-end and hear discourses on the familiar methods of meditation, they may suffer very grave harm if they try to force themselves to use such methods for they have already outgrown them. Precisely the same is true of seminarists and young religious. Directors should not regard discursive prayer as a necessity or as even the generally accepted rule for them. It may be prudent to suggest that each individual gives methods of meditation a trial to discover what stage has been reached; but as soon as it is clear that one has already been won over to the love of God and can talk to him in a loving way, formal point-by-point meditation should be abandoned in favour of affective prayer.

In this form of prayer one does not spend time presenting considerations to the intellect; rather one aims at getting the will into action. It is already sufficiently informed; faith has grown deep enough; the motive force is there. Such considerations as there are in affective prayer are short, preparatory and need very little development. Emphasis is all the time on the will and its acts.

Some find it easiest to concentrate on the four basic acts, which as an acrostic spell out the word a-c-t-s: adoration, contrition, thanksgiving and supplication. We are familiar with them as the four objects of the sacrifice of the Mass. Under each of them other acts may be grouped; they follow naturally and spontaneously from the act which is basic. Thus, when one adores God one is moved to praise, love, surrender, humility, desire, abandonment, conformity and so on. Contrition includes reparation, compassion for our Lord in his sufferings, repentance and the rest. Acts of thanksgiving and supplication are almost limitless in their possibilities. All these acts are, of course, made in formal meditation but then they come after only comparatively long concentration on considerations, thrashing out mentally the meaning of a doctrine or what is implied in a passage of Scripture or reading a meditation book. It is these acts that are the prayer; the thought or reading is only the preparation for it. So, if one can at once make the acts, at once get into touch with God, at once talk to our Lord, considerations are not only useless but positively harmful because they are occupying time in which the will might well be gathering the precious fruits of intimate conversation with God. Meditation is really for those whose love is not enough to launch forth at once into expressions of affection; they have to work hard to rouse and incite such acts.

My own personal experience is that very few people can satisfactorily use the traditional methods of prayer for any length of time but that the vast majority are grateful for the suggestion that they should abandon their attempts to use such methods and try at once to express their love. Religious or seminarists who are not anxious to converse with God and who, apart from dryness, are unable to do so are exceptional. They should be encouraged to follow their hearts to the Heart of Christ.

You will not find the term "affective prayer" in the writings of St Teresa, St John of the Cross or St Francis de Sales. None the less they do describe such prayer. For example, St Teresa in Chapters 28 and 29 of the *Way of Perfection* describes the prayer of recollection, which is a form of affective prayer. Others distinguish just two forms of prayer, meditation and contemplation; then affective prayer comes under contemplation because for such writers meditation is that in which reason plays the greater part and contemplation is that in which the will takes over. Those who practise affective prayer—and they are or ought to be the vast majority of the religious and seminarists who have not yet passed on to the prayer of union —are already so convinced of a truth, for example that God loves them with infinite love, that nothing is to be gained by going into it further; rather, they must pour out their thoughts and feelings in fervent aspirations, even though these be only half expressed.

St Teresa calls it the prayer of recollection because, she says, "the soul collects all its powers together; that is, it holds captive both the understanding, in which it permits no useless considerations, and the imagination, whose frivolous creations it dissipates. It enters into itself in company with its God." A good religious in whom faith occupies its rightful place is quickly able to turn to God as a merciful, loving Father, Christ as a fond Brother, the Holy Spirit as the comforting Guest of the soul, or Mary as a devoted Mother and at once pour out all the yearnings that are pent up within. We should try to do this often; if we perfect ourselves in it we may by God's good favour find ourselves in the vestibule of contemplation. We may know that our desires far outstrip our attainments; daily faults may be constant reminders that we have not yet attained union with our infinite Lover, yet at times or even constantly we are able to recollect ourselves without difficulty and to breathe forth our aspirations of love. If this ·is so, we must thank God for a consoling grace. At such precious times we should continue our fervent acts as long as grace permits.

We ought not to despise feelings in prayer. In fact, the thought that there is something unworthy in sensible consolation might well spring from pride. Once we have left the purgative way, once, that is, we find ourselves free from deliberate attachment to sin and are sincerely yet humbly convinced that the struggle against voluntary grave faults has been won, we may expect consolation. Pleasant, lively emotion, the feeling that we are at last on the way to God, is characteristic of affective prayer. These feelings themselves are an indication, especially when they are frequent, that we have passed beyond the stage of needing lengthy considerations in order to pray. We may judge, too, from our general outlook on the spiritual life. If we easily avoid mortal sin, if we are sincerely trying to draw nearer to God, even though we may fail in minor matters, we can be pretty certain that discursive prayer is no longer suitable for us. It would be a mistake under these circumstances to spurn the sweetness we find in prayer. If we are wise we will thank God for it and try to fix our gaze on him more and more.

Progress in prayer is not so clear cut that we are always able to say with certainty that a person has left the purgative way or has advanced even beyond the illuminative. But what is certain is that the surest way to progress is to gaze on God rather than on self, to bring home to ourselves the implications of his attributes. Our greatest desire should be to find ourselves really thrilled at the thought of God's perfections, enthusiastic for his honour and glory and peaceful in living his will, no matter what it brings to us. We should express these things whenever we feel them; tell God all about them. The oftener we repeat acts like that the more easily will they become part of ourselves and so much the more rapid will be our progress towards the life of union and contemplation.

Another sign that we have left behind the stage when our prayer should consist mainly of reasoning is that we are happy with and interested in spiritual books, especially the classics like the *Imitation of Christ*, the *Spiritual Combat*, the *Introduction to the Devout Life* and so on. The writers of these masterpieces presume that their readers have a sincere wish to love God more and have already detached themselves from mortal sin.

So the right prayer with which to accompany books like these —I am not writing now about the thought that is needed to discover the author's exact meaning—is that which uses the will rather than the intellect, acts rather than processes of reasoning.

We will be helped in our prayer-life by the thought of the mysteries of Christ's life and of the Church. The liturgical cycle of feasts will help us, and we can help ourselves by taking an interest in the life of Christ mirrored for us in the liturgy. Each feast should bring its own special happiness; so should ceremonies of special importance. The joy may be associated also with sorrow, especially sorrow for our own past sins or for the infidelity of the world at large or for our apparent inability to walk faster or further along the way of perfection. We will sorrow, too, in union with our Lord and his holy Mother during their sufferings. Joy and sorrow like this will help us towards perfection, the joy by fixing our gaze on divine realities and the sorrow by purifying us, increasing our hatred of sin and begetting a thirst for suffering in union with Christ.

Particularly important at this stage of the spiritual life is devotion to the Blessed Sacrament and our Lady. The Eucharist is the sacrament of sweetness; the Bread from heaven contains in itself all that is delicious. So we should long to grow in love of it; we should gaze upon it, love to adore it, to watch before it, to see it beautifully adorned and solemnly honoured, to prepare ardently before receiving it and give fervent thanks when it rests within us. Similarly in regard to Mary. Some feel ardently drawn to her; they wish to give themselves through her to her Son, with all that they are and all that they have; they long to live in union with her. Often, as at Lourdes, Mary leads souls to the eucharistic presence of her Son. Still, God seems to implant different attractions in each individual; it is his will that we should each follow our particular line, always provided that it is good and sanctifying. We should never try to lead souls from a good way along which they are progressing in favour of another which may appeal to us more, even though ours may seem to be more sanctifying. For example, I have known souls helped at the beginning of the spiritual life by great sensible devotion to the Blessed Sacrament; this has led to the desire to make reparation for all that is done against the

Eucharist and for all the lack of fervour in its regard; in turn the blessed Mother of God seemed to take over and finally to lead to the contemplation of the mysteries of the hidden life of the Trinity. If during this development an unwise director had intervened to try to impose, let us say, a devotion in which he or his order was particularly interested, immense harm might have resulted.

It is well known that at the beginning of the spiritual life one often experiences graces and even forms of prayer which seem strictly to belong to more advanced states. God gives graces like these to encourage the beginner. They are genuine graces; they are not to be despised; but those who experience them should not be surprised when God, so to speak, hides himself. Then he wants them to continue in the way of prayer and fervour for his sake rather than for the consolation they find in it. The testing times are trials, frustrations and dryness. If they persevere through these in the spirit of faith, trying to see the hidden God in everything, they will find themselves ultimately much better established in the life of the spirit.

Are there any practical rules to be followed by those who have advanced beyond the way of meditation? There are indeed. If God's grace is enabling us to live more or less in his presence; if we have genuinely succeeded in living by faith to such an extent that the thought of God is never very far away; if we are conscious of our efforts to surrender always to his will we may be tempted to think that we can dispense with all preparation for prayer. Not so. Before this prayer we should mentally recollect ourselves in God's presence, make an act against distractions, adore him and surrender ourselves to him. Sometimes we will find ourselves able to embark almost immediately after this preparation on the body of our prayer. If so, we should allow grace to work and make the affections as they come to us. At other times some brief considerations may be necessary according to circumstances. We can think of these as being rather like striking a match; once it is lit it is foolish to go on striking it; in fact, we could in that way extinguish the flame altogether. So it is in our prayer. Considerations at this time are not used for their own sake; they are simply the instrument which may or may not be necessary to fire the will.

As for the substance of our prayer, it should be our own; we should put ourselves into it. When all is said and done it is our personal communion with our infinite Lover, kind Father, devoted Friend, fondest Brother or tenderest Mother. Why should we be so formal and stilted with them? If in our ordinary daily life we were to produce a book to help us a every conversation we would rightly be considered quite mad. There is a difference, of course; we can see our earthly relatives and friends; those of heaven are invisible. Yes, true enough; they are invisible to the eye of the flesh but they should be seen with the eye of the spirit, faith. Custom has a lot to do with it and the unfortunate association of prayer with meditation. Priests, seminarists and religious should be sufficiently intimate with our Lord to be able to dispense with slavish subservience to a book. They should talk simply to him about fundamental matters, especially love, the virtues and the mysteries of the faith. If books are used it should be simply to suggest thoughts. To follow a book line by line during prayer time indicates that one has failed to understand the nature of prayer. How foolish it would be for a nun to talk to her family when they come to see her from a script prepared by somebody else possibly centuries ago! There is not the slightest reason why we should feel compelled to allow spiritual writers to force us to follow their line in prayer rather than our own. We will pray best if we converse about subjects which move us most, our special needs, our favourite devotions and our particular spiritual interests. Some holy people hardly ever leave the foundations of the spiritual life in their prayer; for years they commune about God's love or his mercy, the Sacred Heart of Jesus, reparation, apostolic zeal, abandonment, trust or some other basic principle. It is a mistake to try to cover ground in prayer or to regard prayer time as useful for probing problems of theology. The primary purpose is intimate conversation, communion, outpouring of the spirit. There is not the slightest detriment in limiting the subjects of prayer to those which appeal to us most; in fact, by setting such limits we will probably help ourselves to pray well.

We must not be afraid of asking much. God wants to be asked; begging spiritual favours is a sign of our good desires. Sometimes we find the prayer of petition almost derided by spiritual writers. One can see some point in chiding those who never pray except to ask for temporal favours. That does not concern us here. The first interest of people who are dedicated to God, whether in the active or the contemplative life, should be the intensity of their love. A whole hour of prayer in which one does nothing but beg for more love is·time excellently spent. So it is with any other petition for our spiritual growth or the extent of God's kingdom. God wants us to be daring in prayer; he is honoured when we remember that he is all-powerful, all-rich and all-loving. He wants to be asked to work spiritual miracles in our soul, to pour out those riches of his upon our poverty, to make us the special objects of his love.

We must not imagine that when we pass beyond discursive prayer we have no more need of resolutions. We always need them, but they will now be more intimate and prolonged. One resolution, frequently renewed, may last a lifetime. Like the body of our prayer they should correspond with our particular interest. For example, we may find something in our daily lives, possibly something about which a superior has admonished us, which is incompatible with our high desires. We could well make a resolution concerning it. It is a good sign if we find that we can persevere with the same resolution rather than be constantly changing it. We will find it all much easier if we gaze always upon God rather than upon self. It can hardly be emphasized too much that the way to successful, sanctifying prayer is to look outwards and upwards to God and his heavenly court. If our gaze is fixed there we will not only progress in the way of prayer but we will advance correspondingly along the road to virtue.

St Teresa wrote that for several years she grieved because she could not fix her mind upon one single truth during the hour of prayer. Then she discovered a method which helped her. It was to imagine that our Lord was by her side; he was instructing her, she was trying to please him. From prayer-time the habit extended to embrace all her life. She admonishes her readers: "If one year is not enough to attain this happiness, let us work on it for several, and not regret such well-spent time. I repeat, it is in our power to accustom ourselves to work in the presence of our Lord. Let us make generous efforts, and in the end we shall have the consolation of enjoying the company of this true Master of our souls."

She does not expect us to make long meditations upon our divine Companion. "Just look at him," she says. When everything else seems impossible gaze upon him for some moments. She reminds us that in spite of all our shortcomings he never takes his eye off us. Why, then, should we imagine we are doing something particularly noble when we manage to fix our eyes upon him for a few moments? When we are happy we should gaze upon him in his moments of joy and triumph; when we are sad we should comfort ourselves by looking at him in Gethsemani, throughout his Passion and upon the cross. "Away with all studied language", the Saint writes; "use only simple words and those dictated by your heart. They have the greatest value in his sight."

Our image of Christ, our daily Companion, should be a personal one. The simpler, the better. If it is over ornate it will become artificial and insincere. "You feel no embarrassment when you speak with his creatures", St Teresa wrote; "why should you want for words when you converse with your God." If we persevere in prayer of this kind the feeling of strangeness will soon disappear; friendliness, intimacy, simplicity and love will succeed it. Gradually we will find our prayer becoming less active on our part; God will take over. The process may cause us distress unless we realize what is happening. Yet, so long as we continue to gaze upon God, Christ, the Holy Spirit, Mary, the angels and the saints, all will be well.

We must not expect prayer of this description to banish all dryness. It will not. Sometimes our Lover will withdraw himself to make us seek him for himself alone and not for the joy we find in converse with him. Possibly the dryness arises from some infidelity on our part, some self-seeking, some lack of humility. If so we must discover the cause, lovingly tell God of our sorrow and submit ourselves anew to his will. On the other hand, it is wrong to presume that all dryness comes from some fault of ours. Far from it. It is often the divine way of training us in perfect detachment. God wants us to seek him more vehemently, to beg yet more graces, to surrender ourselves more completely to his will.

Dryness does not mean that grace is being withdrawn. It

may mean precisely the opposite. For grace is not something we can feel. Indeed, feelings are often thoroughly misleading in the life of the spirit. For example, we must not imagine that we are growing holy because we feel near to God in prayer. If we feel like that, we must thank God for his favour. But when that feeling goes, we must not despair and think that our love has grown cold. God is our supreme Director; he consoles us, he tries us, he frustrates us, he eludes us—but always to help us. So, in the harder moments of prayer we should tell him that our main concern is with him; that it is for him that we are praying, for his pleasure that we wish to surrender ourselves, and that if he wills that prayer should continue to be a burden, that the night should be prolonged—then his will be done.

When distractions persist we are advised to complain lovingly to our Lord about them. We should tell him of our inability to pray well, express our humility and beg his help. It will be useful at times like this to go back to some well-tried device which has proved useful in the past or to a favourite book which we know usually helps us. St Francis de Sales reminds us that when it seems that God is far away because of dryness or distractions, we should still frequently try to pay our respects to him. We may not succeed in seeing him at the first, second or hundredth attempt, but we must persevere nevertheless. In times of difficulty, writes the Saint, "we should come to holy prayer purely and simply to pay our respects and show our fidelity". He will speak to us again when it pleases him. We must never cease to try to gaze on him nor allow ourselves to turn even slightly away from him or become disquieted or worried. If we persevere in gazing upon his love he will infallibly reward our patience.

In the desert St John the Bapitist lived with austerity. He must have been a rather frightening figure for those who lived more comfortably. He is a reminder for us that mortification is absolutely necessary if we wish to pray well. The purpose of mortification is positive. We use it as an instrument to detach us from ourselves in order to become attached to our merciful Lover. St Vincent de Paul emphasized that mortification should cover not only our senses but also our memory, understanding and will. All must be turned towards God. That means continual watchfulness because not only will our eyes and ears gather worldly and sensual satisfactions with depressing ease, but these are picked up by the higher faculties of the soul. Intellectual achievements can become notorious distractions. When they are not aligned with the supreme objective of loving God more they can displace that love altogether. That is even true of intellectual interest in theology and the spiritual life. If we see everything from the standpoint of the supreme objective, which is the love of God, we will be able to direct our life of abnegation wisely to that end.

This is certain, that if we are always interested in praying well and anxious to pray better, understanding prayer aright— as intimate personal conversation with the King and the citizens of heaven—we will become by our lives what St John the Baptist was, "testimony to the Light".

10

"THAT ALL MEN MIGHT BELIEVE
THROUGH HIM"

(John 1. 7)

I N those words John the Evangelist expresses the immediate purpose of the Baptist's mission. Towards the end of his Gospel he designates something very similar as the purpose of his writing: "These are written that you may believe that Jesus is the Christ, the Son of God, and that believing you have life in his name" (John 20. 31). The Precursor proclaimed the Messias; the Evangelist hailed the Messias as God.

Before he returned to heaven God in the flesh told us he would not leave us orphans. He would send his divine Spirit to comfort, teach and guide us. He did more. He remained with us himself, living by grace in our souls, sacramentally under the appearances of bread and wine and in a mysterious way in his Church. The Church is himself; he does in and through the Church just what he did for men when they could see his human body walking amongst them. He teaches, works miracles, saves, sanctifies, prays, loves his Mother, suffers and is sacrificed. In the words of Bossuet, the Church is Jesus Christ "prolonged in space and time and communicated to men". It is not to my purpose here to demonstrate how or why the Church is Christ's Body; we believe it on the often repeated explicit statements of the inspired word of God.

We believe, too, that we are members of Christ. He lives in us. It is only through being incorporated into Christ that we return to God. There is the basis of the theology of the spiritual life. We are one with Christ; we must be other Christs; we live and move and have our being in Christ. Or, in the words of St Paul: "Whatsoever you do in word or in work, do all in the name of the Lord Jesus" (Col. 3. 17). And, "Let this mind be in you, which was also in Christ Jesus" (Phil. 2. 5). There is a Christ, God-man, because there was a human race to redeem: "Christ Jesus came into the world to save sinners; God sent not his Son into the world to judge the world; but that the world may be saved by him" (I Tim. 1. 15; John 3. 17). That was why he was called Jesus, "for he shall save his people from their sins" (Matt. 1. 21). So it follows that of all the virtues a member of Christ should be distinguished especially for that which epitomizes the purpose of God's coming amongst us— zeal for souls.

Zeal is not the most popular of virtues. It is unpopular with those who ought to practise it and fail to do so. They dislike anything which threatens to disturb their way of life, especially by detaching them from their smug self-satisfaction. There is a story, good but probably apocryphal, about Pope John XXIII. An eminent personage, wishing to make conversation during an audience, asked His Holiness: "How many people work in the Vatican?" "Oh, about ten per cent," came the reply. If one looks at the Church the situation is even more deplorable. The Catholics who actually take part in organized apostolic work form an infinitesimal minority. Is it because they are lazy or ill-instructed or unconscious of their obligation to have the mind of Christ or unencouraged or not given the opportunity? Whatever the reason Catholic lay inaction is one of the most serious wounds of Christ's Body in the world of our day.

Not everybody is bound to join an apostolic organization; but all are bound to be apostles simply because membership of the Church implies that all are to be other Christs. Yet there are those who deride apostleship as the sign of the fanatic. They class Catholic Evidence Guild speakers, Legionaries of Mary or Brothers of the St Vincent de Paul Society as cranks like the Salvation Army or Jehovah's Witnesses. Apostleship is not quite respectable. It is interference in something which is the private concern of the soul and its God. Such an outlook diametrically contradicts the mind, spirit and explicit commands of Christ. If the Apostles and the early Christians had thought like that the Church would never have spread beyond the upper room in Jerusalem.

True zeal is not fanaticism; it is gentle love. In the first place it is the love of God overflowing upon all whom God loves and whom he wills to respond to his love. Throughout eternity the Father begot his only-begotten Son; from all eternity redemption was present in the divine mind. The Father would send his Son; the Son would leap forth to embrace the cross, crying, "Behold I come to do thy will, O God" (Heb. 10. 9). And as the infinite love of Father and Son flashed forth eternally in the third divine Person, so he, infinite Love, burned with the desire to dwell in men's souls to transport them to heaven. Why did God create men? That they might live in his presence in limitless happiness for ever. For them he created the world and heaven and even hell as works of love—the world as an instrument, heaven as a reward and hell as a warning. Little wonder that St John Eudes could write: "The salvation of souls is the end and purpose of all the works of the power, wisdom and goodness of God. It is, therefore, the great work of his divine majesty."

The love of God—it is the first and greatest commandment. Yet look at our beloved country. There are over 45 million people living in England and Wales now; the Church of England claims 27 million of these as her baptized members and nearly 10 million as having been confirmed. Yet her parochial Easter Communions number only 2,248,229. The Methodists claim less than 800,000 members, the Presbyterians about 200,000 and the Congregationalists 212,000. So, in practice, there are something like forty million churchless people in England and Wales. Is it possible for one who sincerely loves God to remain indifferent to such a state of affairs? How often we pray, "Hallowed by thy name, thy kingdom come, thy will be done on earth"—and yet here, all around us, are those who never call on God's name, are not interested in his kingdom nor bothered about his will. Is our prayer sincere? Does it spring from a heart overflowing with love? If it is and does it should result in serious efforts to make God known and loved by his creatures. We should be beside ourselves at the thought that each of those churchless souls was made for God, is infinitely loved by God and yet cares so little about God. God loves them so much that when he taught us to pray his zeal found expression in the first petitions of his prayer.

With those millions in mind turn to the mind and heart of Christ. "As the Father knoweth me and I know the Father: and I lay down my life for my sheep," he said (John 10. 15). According to the Angelic Doctor God the Son is stressing that he knows his Father's mind; he knows especially his love for

souls; and so he sacrifices himself for them. For them he
emptied himself (Phil. 2. 7). See him hidden within the womb
of the mother he created for himself; look at the shivering child
lying lonely on the straw in a cattle's feeding trough; gaze on
him as he sheds his blood only eight days after his birth; recall
how he was forced to flee to a foreign land; visit him in the
poor cottage at Nazareth; sit by him as he learns his first letters
and figures; be there as he joins the grimy millions of the
workers of the world, goes out to a lonely place to fast and pray,
begins his life of preaching and wonders at a village wedding
and is at length designated to death. Witness the gift of himself
at his Last Supper; kneel by him as he sweats blood in
Gethsemani; watch them arrest, mock, strike and otherwise
ill-treat him; attend the travesties called his trials; feel the lash
of the scourges that tore his flesh in your own and the pricks of
the thorns that pierced his brow in yours. Carry the cross with
him to Calvary; imagine that you are nailed to it in place of
him and hang there in agony for those three dreadful hours;
listen to his seven last loving words. Join the Apostles at the
empty tomb; follow them to Galilee to meet their glorified
Saviour; gaze in awe as he ascends to his Father and kneel with
Mary and the Twelve as the Holy Spirit comes upon them.
Remember all the time that every tiniest incident is a proof of
his love for men and that each is the deed of God. Or, to quote
St John Eudes again, "The mysteries of the Incarnation, Birth,
Circumcision, Passion and Death are so many voices crying
out to us: 'Thus Jesus loved souls'." Indeed his heart was so
aflame with love that into that fire he cast everything he had—
wealth, possessions, comfort, happiness, even his good name—
that we might understand his love. If he could have prolonged
every incident from his conception to his ascension for an
entire eternity he would have been more than ready to do it
to demonstrate his love.

We are his members. His mind should be our mind. He has
willed to make himself dependent on us—to use our feet now
to visit the sick, our lips to pray and preach, our hands to do
good deeds, our eyes to search for souls, our heart to love him
in every soul. Is our love even a faint shadow of his? Does it
burst forth as his did into active zeal? Does it force us to seek
every chance to lead souls to him? Every community of

Catholics, and more especially of religious, should be aflame with the zeal of Christ. It should be obvious for all to see—the kindly, gentle, loving, humble zeal of the Good Shepherd. Every community—it does not matter where or under what circumstances it exists—reflects zeal according to its fervour. Wherever there is the Catholic faith there should be zeal for souls, the zeal of Christ; faith and zeal should be inseparable. The more truly contemplative a community becomes, the more should its zeal be evident, for zeal is simply ardent love, which springs from faith. Those who know Christ with the supernatural knowledge of faith try never to let their gaze stray from him; they penetrate his mind and heart; they know as he knows and love as he loves. The more perfect their knowledge the more fervent is their love. Fervent love cannot remain pent up within a soul; like that of St Thérèse of Lisieux it will blaze forth in prayer and all possible deeds of zeal. There can be no union with Christ without zeal for souls.

The second great commandment is the same as the first but it goes further. It tells us that our love of God must be such that it will pour itself out on all God's creatures. We must love them all for his sake. The more genuine our love is the more effective it will be. It will not remain in the mind and will; it will demand and be given practical expression in prayer, penance and conduct. Consider apostolic charity on the lowest level, as obligatory on those of Christ's followers who believe in him but make no claim to piety or fervour of life. If they believe, then they know that in Christ's teaching are to be found the solutions to most of the problems which are afflicting man today in every department of life—in industrial relations, in education, in international affairs, in politics. In all these and other departments men are failing mainly because they choose to ignore the justice and charity of Christ. Surely those who are convinced that Christ's message is the divine truth God wants men to apply to their daily life must, in charity, do everything they can to make that truth known! On a higher level we think of good people who, whether in the world, the religious life or the priesthood, appreciate the Church's treasures—the surety of her guidance, the wonders of divine grace, the beauty of the liturgy, the consolation of confession, the intimacy of the Eucharist, the tenderness of devotion to

Mary, the joy of being able to help the departed, the possession of all the wisdom of the doctors and fathers, the treasures of all the classics of spiritual writing, the example of countless saints, these are only some—have we not a duty in charity to share such things when those about us know little or nothing about them? On the highest level are those who are sincerely, perseveringly trying to grow in the life of faith and love. Fervent souls like these really appreciate these treasures, because they try to see them as Christ sees them; they understand, too, the need of those about them and the yearning of Christ for his treasures to be shared.

Conversely, the nearer we are to Christ in spirit, the more will we appreciate the malice of sin and the urgency of rescuing souls from the way of sin. From childhood Catholic children have been familiar with St Paul's grave warning, that those who commit mortal sin crucify Christ again and mock him. As faith grows so does the conviction that every mortal sin prevented is another crucifixion prevented. It is worth any sacrifice to bring that about, especially when it is remembered that the prevention of one mortal sin might mean the damming of a whole torrent of sin which might have engulfed all future generations.

Turn now to God's holy Mother. Her supreme work is the salvation of souls. Why did God make her? That he might take from her the body which, united to himself, was to bring about the world's redemption. Why did he preserve her immaculate? That she might be a worthy mother and sharer in the saving of men. For the same reason he filled her with graces and the fullness of every virtue. God wanted her to be as worthy a co-operator as possible. Just because she is the channel of every grace, just because she took such an intimate, vital part in God's plan for saving us, she must be interested with all the intensity of the love of her immaculate heart in the spiritual progress of every soul. Hers is the interest of the most loving of mothers. St John Eudes writes rather quaintly: "I hear our Lord and his Blessed Mother saying to St Brigid, whose revelations are approved by the Church, that Adam and Eve lost the world by eating an apple, but that they saved it by a heart: as if by one Heart we saved the world." Mary's heart was one with her Son's—one in feeling, mind, love and will.

The flame of zealous love in Mary's heart was as perfect a reflection as there could be in a creature of the furnace of love that was the Heart of Christ. He died to save souls; beneath the cross Mary immolated herself in union with him. To quote the French saint again: "The Blessed Virgin Mary so loves souls that she was and is ready to undergo every torment of earth to save even a single soul." It follows, does it not, that there can be no integral devotion to Mary without zeal for souls. If we love her sincerely we must wish what she wishes and, as far as possible, in the way she wishes; and there is nothing she wants more than that souls should be saved and love her Son, each according to capacity. We will be very dear to her if we pray, suffer and work to bring this about.

The Church has only one reason for its existence—the salvation of souls. Like its head, it is the way, the truth and the life of men. He came to save souls; the Church continues his mission for all time. Everything in the Church's life has the same objective—sacraments, ceremonies, liturgical cycle, sermons, pastoral work, councils, synods, laws—there is no exception; every item is designed to assist the Church in the one, supreme task. In our prayer we ought to consider all that membership of the Church has meant to us, all that we have received from the Church since baptism, all the Church offers, all that we may yet receive. What return are we making? How can we best prove that we are grateful and appreciative? There is no better way than to contribute as best we can to the Church's supreme task, the saving of souls and their sanctification.

Even the angels have a like interest. Some of the archangels have come from heaven as divine messengers; we believe that each human being has an angel as his special guardian; Christ has told us that the heavenly spirits rejoice every time a sinner repents; St Paul says they are spirits in God's service, commissioned to serve us "who shall receive the inheritance of salvation" (Heb. i. 14). St Jerome wrote: "How great is the value of the soul that every single person has from birth received an angel for his protection." Therefore we endear ourselves to the angelic courtiers by the practice of zeal. When we are trying to help individuals we should never forget to enlist the aid of their guardian angels.

What can we say of the saints in this matter? One and all they are saints because they loved God, and such love can never be separated from apostolic zeal. With St Paul every saint in heaven's high court could say: "I most gladly will spend and be spent myself for your souls" (II Cor. 12. 15). So great was the Apostle's zeal, says St John Chrysostom on Romans 9. 1-3 ("I wished myself to be anathema from Christ for my brethren"), that he "was ready to sacrifice even the happiness of heaven on behalf of his brethren". In transports of fervour saints, like Catherine of Siena, have offered to suffer the pains of hell if in that way they could save souls from being lost. Little need there is to recount the labours of the apostles who have enriched the Church by their zeal in every century. They want us to imitate them; they will join their prayers to ours for souls; they will assist all our efforts as far as they can from their places in glory. In particular, we should look to the example and beg the prayers of those who have special interest in the souls or places which are the objects of our zeal. If it is for the conversion of England, then we ensure the special aid of Mary, whose Dowry the country is, and of all the saints and martyrs who have lived and died in our land; if it is for certain souls, then in addition to praying to the guardian angels we should invoke the aid of their patron saints. Angels and saints will respond to our prayers in the degree in which they see that we are sincere, that is, to the extent to which our endeavours correspond to our words. Like their heavenly Queen the angels and saints wish above all else to fill the hungry with good things, the gifts of God's love.

"The salvation of one soul is far greater than fasts or vigils or the austerities of the hermits; it is greater than to give most generous alms to the poor," said St John Chrysostom. There are few subjects on which the saints have been so eloquent. St John Eudes tells us that there are five good works of paramount importance: works of mercy, prayer and contemplation, fasting and mortification, miracles and martyrdom, yet the saving of a soul is greater than even these works. "To ransom a soul from purgatory", he continues, "is a marvellous act, but to snatch a soul from mortal sin is greater, for theologians teach that the slightest sin is worse than all the evils of earth, purgatory and hell." All agree that to bring grace to a mortally sin-stained soul is more precious in God's eyes than to raise the dead to life. They go even further: to bring a soul in mortal sin to the life of grace excels the raising to life together of all those who have died. How the world publicizes the remarkable happenings about us—every new discovery, every fresh process, every novel achievement. Imagine the headlines if it was known that one of us created a new satellite from nothing. Yet, says St Augustine, it is far greater to bring a sinner back to God. St Paul told the Christians at Philippi that he was torn in two directions. On the one hand he longed to leave the world and to live with Christ. On the other, it was probably more necessary for them that he should stay on earth. Commenting on the passage (Phil. 1. 23-24), St John Chrysostom remarked that to forgo martyrdom in order to work for souls is more acceptable to God. "Of all divine works," St Denis wrote, "the most divine is to co-operate with God in saving souls."

As we kneel at the crib at Christmas we must not let the purpose of it all escape us. The divine Babe is there to bring salvation to men. At the end of his life he will send his Apostles out, fishers of men, to preach the Gospel to every creature: he will proclaim that he is the Good Shepherd who gives his life for his sheep; he will insist that no man has greater love for his friends than to do what he will do, lay down his life for them. Such thoughts will enkindle anew our zeal. From morning to night every thought, every prayer, every task, every tiniest item we are able to offer we will give to Mary to be disposed of as she wills. We know that her will is completely united with that of her Son. He came amongst us to save; he reigns now and she reigns with him to save. He is there always living to intercede on our behalf (Heb. 7. 25). If our wills are rightly directed we will seize every chance, no matter how remote it seems to be, of doing good. It is always that first step that matters. Take it, and a second will soon be possible, then a third, a fourth and more. We will soon discover that just as Christ once multiplied a child's five loaves to feed a huge crowd, so will he use even our smallest efforts to bring his light and life to souls.

Let it not be thought from what I have written that I am in the least critical of the enclosed, contemplative life. Far from

it. That life has a legitimate place in the Church. It is highly
fitting that there should be souls wholly dedicated to imitating
Christ's prayer-life in his mystical Body, just as there are
souls dedicated principally to imitating his preaching, his
poverty, his obedience or his suffering. But whatever facet of
Christ's life a congregation regards as its primary vocation to
reflect, all must aim at making their own the whole mind of
Christ. That is the essence of the spiritual life. As I have said
above, the highest contemplative is one who lives entirely by
faith. Such faith makes the mind and will of Christ the only
vital realities. At the very peak of his will, so to speak, was his
desire to sacrifice himself for souls, the purpose for which he
assumed a human nature. So it is not surprising that the most
active apostles in the Church's history, like St Paul and the
founders of the active Orders, have been at the same time true
contemplatives while those of strictly contemplative communities have been outstanding apostles, like St Bernard,
St Teresa of Avila and St Thérèse of Lisieux, who, with St
Francis Xavier, is patron of all the Church's missionary
activity.

Zeal is inseparable from holiness because it is essentially love
which must blaze forth. In an enclosed community it will show
itself especially as a motive for the practice of virtue, self-denial,
regular observance and the perfection of community life. Every
defection will be seen as harming Christ's body, as impeding
work for souls. In addition, in the most enclosed of communities there are many opportunities in letters and other
necessary, advisable or permitted contacts with those outside to do good with discretion and kindness. No chance
should be lost. If we think over the obligation and nature of
apostolic zeal, its relationship with Christ and the many
motives for practising it; if we pray about it; if we spare no
effort to keep its flame strongly burning in ourselves, it will be
of inestimable value in leading us to communion with the love
of the Heart of Christ.

11

"HE WAS NOT THE LIGHT, BUT WAS TO GIVE TESTIMONY OF THE LIGHT": I

(John 1. 8)

ST JOHN THE EVANGELIST here tells us what St John the Baptist had said of himself very emphatically. "There cometh after me one mightier than I, the latchet of whose shoes I am not worthy to stoop down and loose. I have baptized you with water: but he shall baptize you with the Holy Ghost" (Mark 1. 7-11). When they sent priests and Levites from Jerusalem saying to John, "Who art thou?" he told them: "I am not the Christ" (John 1. 19-21).

It seems to us unthinkable that John the Baptist could possibly have claimed to be Christ and we take for granted his humility in retiring from the scene as soon as our Lord appeared. Yet, is not history full of usurpers, rebels, upstarts and those who have seized power from those who exercised it legally? Even in the Church antipopes have tried to usurp the supreme authority, holy founders of Orders and Congregations have been deposed and humiliated by their spiritual children, and positions of influence, authority and glamour have always been the target of people filled with worldly ambition.

These few words of St John's prologue lead to the subject of humility. Spiritual progress is impossible without it. We cannot advance the smallest distance on the road to perfection without God's help. The Holy Spirit assures us that it is the humble and the humble alone who receive that help: "God resisteth the proud and giveth grace to the humble"—a saying which is repeated no less than three times in the inspired word (Prov. 3. 34; James 4. 6; I Peter 5. 5).

There is endless food for prayer in the many references to humility in the Word of God. Recall, for example, the prayer of Judith, the heroic widow of Bethulia, before her successful liberation of her city from the invading Assyrians. "Thy power, O Lord, is not in a multitude, nor is thy pleasure in the strength

98

of horses, nor from the beginning have the proud been accept-able to thee; but the prayer of the humble and the meek hath always pleased thee" (Judith 9. 16). As the psalmist avers God "hath had regard to the prayer of the humble" (Ps. 101. 18) and Ecclesiasticus: "The prayer of him that humbleth himself shall pierce the clouds" (Ecclus. 35. 21).

Every treatise on humility emphasizes that it is a virtue which comes from the right understanding of our relationship with God. That is that God is everything and we are nothing. But he is not an impersonal everything; he is a loving, merciful, infin-itely knowing and wise Father. Whatever happens to us is by his permission, even though it results from the sins of others. He knows us through and through because he made us. Therefore, the many humiliations we have all to endure during life—and often the little ones, the pinpricks, seem to hurt more than the big ones—are our kind Father's gifts. He stoops down to us in our weakness and sends us these humiliations to help us. They never come alone; they are packed in our Father's help, his actual graces.

That is surely why Holy Scripture insists so much on the high value to the soul of humiliations. "He that hath been humbled shall be in glory", says Job, "and he that shall bow down his eyes, he shall be saved" (Job 22. 29). "It is better to be humbled with the meek than to divide spoils with the proud", the book of Proverbs says (Prov. 16. 19). Friendship with the proud, ambitious and tyrannical, the Wise Man wants to remind us, may bring with it certain perquisites which seem to be emi-nently desirable from the worldly point of view, but it will not help us in God's judgment. With sadness we hear it said so often nowadays that it is not *what* you know but *who* you know that counts in life—even in the Church. Genuinely humble people have no time for a spirit like that. Their main concern is to know God and to know themselves; they have no time for the spirit of ambition, no desire for self-advancement, no longing to be in authority. They are interested only in how they can love God more and make him loved.

"Take all that shall be brought upon thee; and in thy sorrow endure, and in thy humiliation keep patience. For gold and silver are tried in the fire, but acceptable men in the furnace of humiliation" (Ecclus. 2. 4-5). So wrote the son of Sirach in the book which became known as Ecclesiasticus because it was read in the Church to instruct catechumens. Put his words into their context and you find him exhorting one who would serve God to wait in his presence with honesty of purpose and awe, ready to be tested and to bear everything with submission. "Wait for God, cling to God and wait for him; at the end of it, thy life shall blossom anew", the Wise Man exhorts us (*ibid.*, v. 3). "Trust in him, and he will lift thee to thy feet again; go straight on thy way and fix in him thy hope" (*ibid.*, v. 6). There are few more beautiful passages on humility and trust than this. Its message is that whatever comes to us from God is the gift of his mercy; we must be humble enough to see that and trust him. We must not worry about what may happen tomorrow, but live for today, remembering that we are always in his loving care. Our fear of God should never be without trust. "Fear him?" asks the Wise Man, "Ay, and trust him; you shall not miss your reward. Fear him? Ay, and fix your hope in him; his mercy you shall find, and have great joy of it. Fear him? Ay, and love him; your hearts shall be enlightened" (*ibid.*, vv. 8-10).

Humility is the golden thread which binds all the virtues together. It enables us to see ourselves just as we are in God's sight. From that knowledge springs the conviction that we must trust our loving Father as helpless children, knowing that he cannot permit anything to befall us except what is for our good. We love his will, therefore; we are patient when it seems to treat us harshly; we persevere when everything seems to be most difficult, because we know that our kind Father never deserts us nor gives us less grace than we need to make full use of all he permits to happen to us. Humility thrusts us upon the care of God; it makes us leap like little children into our Father's arms; it keeps us there; it makes us persevere always because we completely distrust ourselves and depend entirely on him.

The Psalms are full of thoughts about humility. Sometimes we must feel spiritually rather like the composer of the sixth psalm. Doers of evil and various enemies made him afraid and worried; his strength was failing, his whole system shaken. Suddenly his fear was changed into triumphant hope. Why? Because he threw himself and his weakness upon the power of God. "Be gracious unto me, O God, for I am weak", he prayed; "Heal me, O Lord, for my bones are shaken" (Ps. 6. 3). The psalmist knew that his sin had brought on his punishment; we may not know that so clearly. Perhaps we are not conscious of deliberate sin. But the remedy for depression and fear is always the same— to realize that alone we are weak and incapable of helping ourselves; we need God; he alone is adequate to help us.

The eighth psalm sings of the glory of God which nature and especially the heavens reveal and contrasts it with the littleness of man. We are so trifling, David seems to say, that it is strange that God should think of us at all. That is the kind of thought God likes: "What is man that thou shouldst remember him? Or the son of man that thou shouldst visit him? And yet thou hast set him but a little below the angels; with glory and with honour thou hast encompassed him; thou hast placed him over the works of thy hands . . . . O Lord, our Lord! How wonderful is thy name in all the earth!" (Psalm 8). We may well imagine King David singing those words as he gazed at the night sky, pouring out the praise of the God who made it all. And man —the literal meaning is "Thou hast made him to lack but little of a God", prophetic indeed of the glory of the life of grace by which we share in the divine nature. So David's humility referred everything to its right source—God. We must follow his example, as St Paul tells us: "What hast thou which thou hast not received? And if thou hast received it, why dost thou boast as if thou hadst not received it?" (I Cor. 4. 7). Yes, humility is indeed truth. It compels us to acknowledge our talents without exaggeration or diminution but to acknowledge also their source and to realize that all we have of our own is what we have gathered by the misuse of God's gift of free will and neglect of his grace—sin. That is why the greatest of the saints could recite the *Miserere* with absolute sincerity.

That model prayer we find in the twenty-fourth psalm again cries out in deep humility for God's aid: "Look thou upon me and have mercy on me, for I am lonely and poor. Allay the grief of my heart and set me free from my worries. Behold my woe and my anguish and forgive me all my sins" (Ps. 24. 16-18). In the same spirit the psalmist prays elsewhere when he is sick and needs God's help: "Lord, be gracious to me! Heal my soul for I have sinned against thee" (Ps. 40. 5). The conduct of a humble person is still the same. When trials and difficulties come one source of strength never fails—God. We do what we

can and leave the rest to God. The old adage is there to guide us
—that we must act as if all depended upon us but pray and trust
as if all depended on God. That is how God likes it. He wants us
to use the talents he has given us but at the same time to acknowledge how weak and poor we are and in what need of his help.

This consciousness that God is always present with his infinite
knowledge, love, power and goodness grows in intensity with
progress in humility. As King David prayed: "I exult and
rejoice because of thy goodness; for thou dost look upon my
humiliation and bringest rescue to my soul in time of need"
(Ps. 30. 8). And: "The Lord is near to the sad of heart; and to
the lowly in spirit he bringeth safety" (Ps. 33. 19). The reward
of humility is God's help. The person who is always ready to
ascribe to God all that belongs to him can always be confident
that the kind Father will come to help him and lift him in his
mercy and power safely over the perils of life.

There must be many an occasion in the religious life when we
feel like crying out as David did in those psalms—when we feel
that the rule is beyond our strength, that the work assigned is
too hard, that we must before long yield to despair or fail to
persevere—it is at these times that we must present our weakness to God. Once a religious has been admitted to first profession the presumption is strong that perseverance is God's will.
That being so, his grace is always there for our use. It is remarkable what can be achieved by humble surrender to it. That was
St Paul's way of dealing with weakness: "He hath said to me,
'My grace is sufficient for thee, for strength is made perfect in
infirmity'. Most gladly, then, will I rather boast of my infirmities, that so there may rest upon me the strength of Christ.
Wherefore I am well content in infirmities, in insults, in hard-
ships, in persecutions, in straits—for Christ's sake. For when I
am weak, then I am strong" (II Cor. 12. 10-13).

There are many references in the psalms to the spirit in
which humiliations should be accepted. In Psalm 43 the sacred
poet laments the sorry state into which Israel has fallen, having
been beaten in battle and enslaved by her enemies. In the past
God's power had vanquished the heathen; has he now forgotten
those he used to love? Even now they will trust in him. "Thou
humblest us in the place of sorrow; and the shadow of death
overcasts us", the psalmist prays and then cries out, "Arise, O

Lord, help us, and rescue us for thy name's sake" (Ps. 43. 20, 26) We find something similar in the poignant eighty-seventh psalm. The singer puts his unworthiness before God: "Poor am I and wretched since youth; grown up, I have been cast down and dismayed; over me thy anger has swept; thy terrors dismay me. They encompass me like water; they encompass me wholly." Sometimes as we say our Office we may feel just like that. There are days when everything seems to go wrong; times when the lure of the world is particularly strong, occasions when difficulties arising from community life are uncommonly heavy. What is the answer? We find it in the same psalm. It is to turn to God with deepest humility, offering our weakness and temptations to him, the infinitely wise Physician: "O Lord, my rescuing God, I cry to thee . . . . Let my prayer come before thee; bend thy ear to my cry, for my soul is filled with sorrow" (Ps. 87. 2-4). In a short time we will find ourselves able to say sincerely: "Let us rejoice for the days when thou humblest us, for the years when we looked on misfortune!" (Ps. 89. 15). Those are words from the only psalm which is attributed to Moses—if he wrote it, it must have been considerably edited at a later date—a psalm which is a moving meditation on the fleetingness of man compared with the eternity of God, and therefore a help to humility. Who does not know from experience that all the afflictions of life are permitted by God for our good? There is no school as effective as the school of the cross.

I have deliberately concentrated here on the psalms because we priests and religious recite them so frequently and they can and ought to be powerful aids to humility as well as sources of consolation in times of stress. Yet another appropriate thought comes from one of the psalms of thanksgiving: "The pains of death encompassed me, the anguish of Sheol seized upon me; grief and sorrow I found." Once again the inspired singer proclaimed his infallible remedy: "I called on the name of the Lord: 'O Lord, save thou my life!'" He reflects on the reason for his action in the spirit of the little saint of Lisieux: "Gracious is the Lord and kind; And full of pity is our God. The Lord protecteth the little ones [that is the simple souls who rely entirely on his protection]: I was in sorrow, and he gave me help" (Ps. 114. 3-6). There is never a moment when we cannot truthfully confess our littleness before God and our need of help;

the oftener we do it, the more rapid will be our progress in humility. Frequent repetition to God of our conviction that we are nothing before him not only compels his help but increases our own realization that we depend entirely upon him.

On Sundays and greater feasts the small Hours of the Office are largely composed of Psalm 118. When we turn to the translation of it by Mgr Knox we see what a *tour de force* he brought off in retaining the alphabetical arrangement. There are twenty-two stanzas, each of eight verses. All eight verses in each stanza begin with the same letter and the letters follow in the psalm the order of the Hebrew alphabet. It is good to find help for humility in a psalm we say so often. At the beginning of the seventh stanza the psalmist tells God what comforts him when he is wretched and humiliated: "Go not back on the word thou hast pledged to thy servant; there lies all my hope" (Ps. 118. 49-50). If we apply that to our day we might well take it as an instruction of the Holy Spirit never to forget the consoling promises of Christ to all who have left everything to follow him and especially to those who persevere: "He that shall persevere to the end, he shall be saved" (Matt. 24. 13).

How right, too, is the author of the same psalm when he prays: "It was good for me that thou humblest me, that I might learn thy decrees. The law of thy mouth is dearer to me than thousands of gold and silver" (Ps. 118. 71-72). As a master trains his dog by continued repetition of the same command for as long as the dog tends to disobey, so God permits us to be stricken down in order to purify us and reconcile us completely to his will. The humiliation, as the psalmist calls it, may be a yielding to temptation, failure to practise virtue, or some other spiritual shortcoming; it may be a physical disability; it may be removal from an office; it may be an outside circumstance over which we have no control—whatever it is, God permits it for our good. The cross can never be anything but a grace. Or as the psalmist puts it a little later: "I know, O Lord, that thy judgments are just, and that thou humblest me because of thy truth", and "I am greatly humbled . . . teach me thy decrees; look on my misery and rescue me, for I forget not thy law" (Ps. 118. 75, 107, 153). Thoughts like these ought to convince us that the habit of recollection is an indispensable help to the practice of humility. Recollection keeps us aware of

God's never resting protection; humility makes us appeal to it always, but especially when we need it most, in temptation, stress, depression and when the cross presses heavily.

Complete resignation to God's designs is necessarily the result of humility. That is beautifully brought out in the little 130th psalm. It tells how the psalmist, possibly King David, once had an insatiable ambition for great and worldly things; he was clamorous and restless. But now he prays: "O Lord, my heart is not proud; my eyes are not lofty: I strive not after great things, nor after things too far above me. Indeed, I think humbly of myself and exalt not my soul [that is, I have behaved and calmed myself], like a little child on its mother's lap" (Ps. 130. 1, 2). Peace and rest are the fruits of resignation to God's will, which, in turn, comes from childlike confidence in him, and that is the natural result of the humility that recognizes and acts upon the true nature of the relationship between God and man. "O Lord, what is man, that thou shouldst take care of him, the son of man, that thou should take thought for him?" (Ps. 143. 3). Yes, the humble person is always full of wonder that God should, as it were, stoop down to his creatures who are "like unto a breath of air . . . a shadow that passes away" (ibid., 4).

Because humility of its essence acknowledges God's glory and man's nothingness it is particularly pleasing to God. "He is honoured by the humble", the Wise Man reminds us (Ecclus. 3. 21). "To whom shall I have respect, but to him that is poor and little, and of a contrite heart, and that trembleth at my words?" God asks through Isaias (Is. 66. 2). Each of us has a certain capacity for love. Perfection means giving all that capacity to God in himself and in all creatures, including ourselves, for his sake. We love self only in so far as is necessary for our spiritual progress. Proportionate love of self is the way to holiness. True self-love means that we are determined to allow nothing to impede our road to God. So we love self only to lead self to God. If our self-love is excessive we have less capacity for the love of God. In other words, failure in humility necessarily weakens our love of God and makes us less effective in his cause. Pride always falsifies spiritual vision; it nullifies the gifts of the Holy Ghost. Humility enables us to see and judge from God's viewpoint and to make full use of wisdom, understanding and the other gifts of the Spirit. Our Lord himself alluded to this: "I confess to thee, O Father, Lord of heaven and earth, because thou hast hid these things from the wise and prudent, and hast revealed them to little ones. Yea, Father; for so it hath seemed good in thy sight" (Matt. 11. 25-26). Christ is saying that it is humble souls who are really able to penetrate the mysteries of grace and glory he was preaching. The proud are so full of themselves that they are not docile enough to accept a way of life that is so contrary to the principles of the world. It is the humble who can see these things because they are really convinced of their relationship with God, that is of their complete dependence on him. St Paul puts the same thing in another way: "God has chosen what the world calls foolish to shame the wise; he has chosen what the world calls weak to shame the strong. He has chosen what the world calls base and contemptible, yes and even things which have no real existence to explode the pretensions of the things that are—that no man may boast in the presence of God" (I Cor. 1. 27-28; I have paraphrased a little in order to bring out the full meaning). Thus does God unfailingly show his pleasure in humility.

Scripture speaks in glowing terms of the rewards of humility. Job prays to God "who setteth up the humble on high, and comforteth with health those that mourn" and Eliphaz states his conviction that "he that hath been humbled shall be in glory; and he that shall bow down his eyes shall be saved" (Job 5. 11; 22. 29). The Book of Proverbs affirms that "the fruit of humility is the fear of the Lord, riches, and glory and life" and that "glory shall uphold the humble of spirit" (22. 4; 29. 23). The riches are, of course, divine blessings. We have already pointed out how humility leaves the soul free to use to capacity the gifts of the Holy Ghost; it preserves spiritual balance, and that wins God's blessing, as the Book of Proverbs states: "A false balance the Lord hates; nothing but full weight will content him. Pride is neighbour to disesteem; humility to wisdom" (11. 1-2). Pride means, in effect, giving false measure to God. "It is the fear of the Lord teaches the lessons of wisdom; humility goes first, and honour comes in her train" (Prov. 15. 33). The Wise Man is telling us that humble submission to God is the way to honour: "Hearts are proudest where ruin is nearest; humility is the antechamber of renown" (Prov. 18. 12).

12

"HE WAS NOT THE LIGHT, BUT WAS TO GIVE TESTIMONY OF THE LIGHT": II

(John 1. 8)

OUR considerations have so far been prompted mainly by God's word in the Old Testament. Now let us turn to the New. The main feature is the humility of God incarnate, which necessarily is beyond our comprehension. We cannot fathom the greatness of God; therefore we can never fully understand the abasement of Christ. It is a mystery because God is a mystery. "The book of God no man can write; he must lay down his pen. This is the streak of agnosticism in Catholic theology" wrote Father Martin D'Arcy. It follows that the more successful we are in contemplating the nature of God and his attributes, the more we will appreciate his humility as he grew from such littleness in his Mother's womb. The Church contemplates the mystery in the Matins hymn of our Lady's feasts:

> The God whom earth and sea and sky
> Adore and laud and magnify,
> Who o'er their threefold fabric reigns
> The Virgin's spotless womb contains.
>
> The God whose will by moon and sun
> And all things in due course is done,
> Is borne upon a Maiden's breast
> By fullest heavenly grace possesst.
>
> How blest that Mother, in whose shrine
> The great artificer divine,
> Whose hand contains the earth and sky,
> Hath deigned as in his ark to lie.

St Augustine tried to express it: "O manifest infirmity, O wondrous humility, in which all the greatness of God lay hid! The mother to whom his infancy was subject, he ruled with his power; and to her at whose breasts he nursed, he gave the nourishment of truth." My own pen fails when I try to write what is in my mind. I try in prayer to see God as he is in himself, to ponder the mysteries of the Three-in-One and the divine Processions, to realize eternity and immensity as infinite existence concentrated in an unchangeable "now" of time or in a point of space, to adore his glory, his greatness and his majesty, to prostrate before his holiness, to stammer praise of his omnipresence and his immanence, to be enraptured by his goodness, his wisdom, his mercy and his power, to wonder at his changelessness, his justice and his knowledge—and then I have to believe that all this limitless perfection of Being is there as a tiny human body is moulded within a lovely mother. The thought of the humility involved in that is just stupefying; human ideas boggle in the face of it.

One reads sometimes about Christ's humility being remark- able because of the lowly circumstances in which he chose to live. That is only one rather insignificant aspect of his humility. We must apply to Christ the definition of humility; it is the sincere acceptance of our true position in regard to God and our fellow creatures. Now, when God became man he enjoyed human knowledge in all its fullness. There was nothing he did not know about created nature. He knew, for example, that his own human nature was created; it was nothing in itself, apart from God. He owed it to God who created it. All his human thoughts, words and deeds, every tiny detail of his human life he owed to the divine Creator. Christ knew that with absolute perfection; he accepted it; he acted upon it. It was the truth; he was absolute Truth. Humanly Christ lived with perfect humility because he knew that of himself in his humanity he was nothing but owed all to God. That is why he submitted so rigorously to the will of the Father. His humility was beyond compare.

It demanded complete submission to God's will and to his providence. God the Son deliberately chose to join the ranks of his creatures, fallen creatures at that, to take on himself their sins and to submit to all that followed. St Paul says a frightening thing of him: "Him, that knew no sin, for us he hath made sin, that we might be made the justice of God in him" (II Cor. 5. 21). The sinless One became sin, the victim of sin, to reconcile us with God. What that meant is expressed in some of the most famous lines the Apostle ever penned: "For let this mind be in you which was also in Christ Jesus: who being in the form of God thought it not robbery to be equal with God; but emptied himself, taking the form of a servant, being made in the likeness of man, and in habit found as a man. He humbled himself, becoming obedient unto death" (Phil. 2. 5-8).

Oh how can we hope to fathom the humility entailed in this! St Paul tells us that we must cultivate our Lord's dispositions; his mind must be our mind. He was a divine Person. Rightly and justly he could have claimed freedom from the ills our flesh is heir to; he could have demanded to be treated as the God he was; he could have been free from suffering, death and all the other consequences of sin. But he lovingly and freely chose otherwise. He willed to embrace the lot of sinful men. He knew what his choice entailed, all its consequences. That was infinite humility. He volunteered to be sent "in the likeness of sinful flesh and of sin" just as if he were one of Adam's sinful children. He was humble because he accepted all these things; he chose the portion of fallen humanity and he persevered to the very end in accepting all the bitter consequences of his choice. We can only appreciate such humility when we have faithful ideas of the extremities involved—on the one hand the infinite God, who created everything, governs everything, sustains everything, who plans every detail in the affairs of angels and of men, who keeps the stars in their stations and the planets in their paths, and on the other, a member of a race which has rebelled against the ordinances of God and must pay the price of that rebellion.

Long before, God had created men free to obey or disobey him; he wanted them to attain happiness through using rightly their freedom to choose. For reasons known adequately only to his own omniscience God permitted evil to enter his creation; it was part of his providence that disorder should exist there. That was the necessary consequence of his making men free. God willed that evil should enter if man chose that it should. Man did choose. By sin he flung the whole of creation out of harmony. God did not will sin but he permitted it and all its terrible consequences. Once sin had been committed every descendant of the first sinner would have to bear the consequences; he would enter a world torn by strife, afflicted by suffering, buffeted by disorder and largely determined by inordinate passion. The second Person of the Blessed Trinity freely made himself one of our race; he entered this system of fallen men. He submitted, as St Thomas Aquinas says, to the sufferings and disabilities of the present life.

See the consequences of this. When circumstances decreed that he should be born in Bethlehem, he did not use the divine power he possessed to arrange his birth in the most luxurious home; he left his parents to do what anybody else would have done in similar circumstances. Humility caused him to be born in a cattle-shelter. When King Herod sought to kill him, he could certainly have arranged his own protection, but he did not. He did no more than was necessary to fulfil God's plan; he permitted an angel to warn St Joseph that his life was in danger for God did not will him to die then. Apart from that he submitted to his parents, who did what any other parents would have done under the same conditions; they fled. When God permitted injustice, tyranny, cruelty, persecution, ambition and sin, our Lord submitted to the consequences of those things which afflicted him. It was so all through his life, until the moment decreed by God came and the forces of evil were allowed to triumph. Even then we were given a reminder of the reality of the position. It was in Gethsemani. St John tells us about it. When Judas and the Jews came to arrest our Lord he went forward and said to them "Who are you looking for?" They answered "Jesus of Nazareth." "I am the man", he said, and at once they retreated and fell to the ground. There and in the last moment of his life, when he cried out with a loud voice, he publicly revealed that he was submitting with absolute freedom to what God had destined for him as the consequences of human sin. He could have invoked his divine power, he could have summoned twelve legions of angels to defend him, but he did not. With utmost humility he was obedient to the death of the cross.

This picture of Christ's humility is one which could occupy us much in prayer. We can think of him at every moment of his life—as the child amongst other children, the victim often, no doubt, of their unkindness, selfishness, jealousy and all the other things which always cause little ones to suffer, with the exception of shortcomings in his parents. What about the longest span of his earthly visit, the years when he was hidden as the handyman in a tiny village? No doubt he had to suffer then from the sins, imperfections, ignorance or malice of others. He did not exempt himself from these things. Infinite perfection as he was, he meekly submitted to everything. From his public life we have countless examples. The Gospels reveal the failings of those who loved him as well as the malice of those who hated him. But he accepted his position. Never once is there the slightest sign of rebellion against it. Remember that this submission was constant. At every moment he must have been faced with ignorance, incompetence, inefficiency, imperfection and sin; he lived amongst these things because they are inseparable from human life. Yet, can we imagine his being irritated, impatient, morose, fretful, domineering or showing any of the common human reactions to the things about him which were not perfect?

What an example all this is for us! We are by nature what the Son of God became by choice. God deliberately brought into existence a system in which sin is possible; he permitted sin to happen. He willed the human race, including each one of us, to work out its salvation amongst the effects of wrongdoing. He knew that we would be victims of unkindness, injustice, cruelty, inefficiency, ignorance, incompetence and all the other imperfections of men. Each of us knows he is imperfect. Our limitations cause others to suffer as the limitations of others cause us to suffer. That is human life. All men abuse their free wills. The only certain exceptions are Jesus and Mary. All of us are at the mercy of this abuse; we have no option very often about accepting the consequences. Whatever those consequences are we are bound to accept them. We have no right to resent them, to rebel against them. Like those about us, we are members of a race that fell; we fell, too. It is by God's providence, not by a blind chance, that we live amongst sinful men and contribute our share to the common pool of sin. When we rebel against the ordinary circumstances of life, and particularly against the unpleasantnesses which those things entail, we are rebelling against God's providence; we are offending against humility. When we see things like this, we understand more of the humility of Christ. He was not sinful like the rest of us; he did not make his contribution to the common pool of sin. Yet uncomplainingly he submitted to the consequences of sin. It is surely pride for us to complain against God's eternal decree to create men free. Yet that is just what we do when we complain about the ordinary sufferings of life. They come as a result of that decree of God's. We must submit to it; to revolt is pride. The greatest help in the struggle is to "run the race we have to run with patience, our eyes fixed on Jesus, the source and the goal of our faith. For he himself endured a cross and thought nothing of its shame because of the joy he knew would follow his suffering. . . . Think constantly of him enduring all that sinful men could say against him and you will not lose your purpose or your courage" (Heb. 12. 2-3).

When we examine ourselves sincerely we have to admit our many deficiencies. We may not actually have committed each of the seven deadly sins with full deliberation—but we know how prone we are to the inclinations they represent. We can never forget that the war against deviation from God's will is always on. Yet, sinful as we are, we tend to demand exemption from the consequences of sin around us. In our pride we resent having to smart under another's tongue, suffer from his thoughtlessness, be patient with those who are less competent than we are, live with some who are less cultured, help the ungrateful, endure the forward, tolerate the feckless and be cheerful with the sad. We cannot get out of our heads that we are superior at least in some things and that we should therefore be treated with proportionate respect. We tend to indulge and excuse ourselves while we blame and discipline others. Others must make allowances for us, but we are not prepared to make allowances for others. That is pride. Humility means that, while we work to conquer sin and remedy its consequences, we accept our condition as fallen creatures without resentment and do not fret because we cannot live as if the race had never fallen.

Our Lord deliberately came into a world in which all the moral forces were set in battle array against him. His words leave us in no doubt on the point: "I am not of this world; if the world hate you, know ye that it hath hated me before you; because you are not of the world, but I have chosen you out of the world, therefore the world hateth you" (John 8. 23; 15. 18-19). So at every moment of his life the battle was on; he could have escaped it; he could have brought divine armoury into the conflict, but he did not. He conquered but was killed in the process. His Godhead triumphed because of his humanity's annihilation. Because God willed all this, Christ chose it. He kept on keeping on to the bitter end. He welcomed as God's providence the consequences of sin which afflicted him. So he conquered by his humility. And for that cause he was exalted, St Paul says.

During these conferences we have been thinking a lot about the life of grace. We shall return to the subject before we reach the end of St John's prologue. We must understand that sanctifying grace puts a uniquely Christlike element within us. It commits us to battle with all that is unChristlike in ourselves and in the world. What is good in us will be attacked, harassed and tempted by the devil, the world and the flesh. Until Christ finally triumphs in us the battle will go on. So it is with those around us. They and we are all at war; we suffer from what is unChristlike in them; they suffer from what is unChristlike in us. This is the condition of fallen nature; it is wrong to rebel against it. Resentment, bitterness, depression, repining, murmuring, sadness—all these are the fruits of pride and offensive to humility. It is sad to see souls provoking disorder in themselves by rebelling against disorder around them. Those who are genuinely humble see the true situation with the vision of faith; they recognize it as God's providence; they do what they can, always trusting in his grace to remedy evil; but they do not fret or rebel against the situation as such.

What is humiliation? It occurs when we think we have been put in a position inferior to that which we deserve. Yet, honestly, what do we deserve? St Paul asks us in different words: "What have you that you have not received?" (I Cor. 4. 7). Let us face it: as long as we feel humiliated we are not perfectly humble. We resent losing something we think our dignity demands, something which is our right. But that does not exist. All we have of ourselves is sin; the rest is a free gift from God. Why, then, should we feel bitter when it is taken away? If we do we are rebelling against God's providence, against being a member of a fallen race.

"Humility is truth" has become almost a cliché. Yet it is one of the most difficult things to put into practice. Of Satan our Lord said: "He stood not in the truth" (John 8. 44). On the other hand, Christ came to give testimony to the truth. He said that "every one that is of the truth" hears his voice (John 18. 37). So we have opposing trinities: Christ, truth, humility on the one hand, and on the other Satan, falsehood, pride. So long as we have a true estimate of ourselves and our capabilities as God sees them, their origin and their progress, and act upon it, we need have no worries about humility. It is there. God does not ask us to ignore the gifts he has bestowed on us; we must recognize our talents, use them but attribute them, the ability to use them and the good they accomplish to God. St Teresa used to tell her nuns that nothing prevented spiritual progress so much as ignoring or trying to hide from ourselves the graces God gives us.

Is it possible, remembering that we are fallen creatures, to be conscious of our talents without falling into pride by identifying ourselves with them? Yes, it is possible. The way to do it is to try to see our talents in us in the same way as we esteem them if others possess them. Recall St Paul's admonition: "In lowliness of mind let each think the rest better than himself" (Phil. 2. 4). He means that we must subject what is human in us to what is divine in others. But we can go further than that. How do we know all that is divine in others? God's graces are secret. Therefore we can resolve to consider others as superior to ourselves because God may have graced them more than he has graced us. We do not know. But it would be presumptuous on our part to act as if we are superior. In any case, at the end of life our judgment will be based on the extent to which we have succeeded in treating all our fellows as we would treat Christ: "Inasmuch as ye did it to one of the least of these my brethren ye did it to me" (Matt. 25. 40).

The Christian virtue of humility will never be understood by the world; it is completely at variance with all that the world stands for. The pagan philosophers of old knew nothing about it. When God so emptied himself that he took the form of a servant and subjected himself to the consequences of men's sin, humility took on a new dimension. So the duty of those who aspire after Christian perfection is to ponder in prayer over the true nature of humility, to beg to understand its relationship with the truth, to penetrate the details of our position regarding God and, especially, his providence. Until we do that we will never have a right grasp of the fundamentals. If the foundation is weak, the edifice built on it will not·be strong. We do well to repeat until they are indelibly stamped upon our minds St Paul's key questions: "What hast thou that thou hast not received? And if thou hast received it, why dost thou glory, as if thou hadst not received it?" (I Cor. 4. 7). Oh, yes, we have good qualities; we cannot forget them. But we must convince ourselves that they are God's. He has loaned them to us, just as he has loaned time—to be used for him. All we can claim for ourselves is sin. St Francis de Sales explains the position:

> Many people are afraid of thinking about the special graces God has given them in case they become vain and self complacent. In this they are surely in error for, as St Thomas says, the right way to learn to love God is to think about his favours. The more we appreciate them the greater our love will be. Those given us personally move us more deeply than those common to others; therefore they should be considered more attentively. Surely nothing can so humble us before God's mercy as the multitude of his favours, nor before his justness as the multitude of our offences. Let us think about what he has done for us and what we have done against him. In the same way that we think over our sins in detail, let us also consider his graces, having no fear that the knowledge of his gifts will lead to pride, as long as we remember that what is good in us does not come from ourselves. Mules are still clumsy brutes even when laden with a prince's personal possessions.*

To progress in humility demands consummate candour with ourselves. We must face up to our failures and not make excuses. We must be ready to admit faults and that if we had prayed a little more and been less proud we could have avoided them. We must acknowledge that there are, have been and will be countless souls more perfect than we are, not only amongst the Saints but even in our own community. If

---

* *Introduction to the Devout Life*, 3, 5.

we dispute that, we are a very long way from even moderate humility. The thought of the pioneers of our Congregation or of those whose names are remembered for their holiness should humble and inspire us. Coupled with that should always be remembrance of God's perfections and his love and mercy towards us. How unworthily we have repaid him! What a lot more we might have done in the years that have passed if only we had had more love! What graces we have received and how ill we have used them!

We cannot be too insistent on the need and excellence of humility. Could our Lord have emphasized it more than he did? As if his example was not enough he added a vivid illustration. When the disciples wanted to know who is really greatest in the kingdom of heaven, he called a little child to his side and stood him in the middle of them all and said: "Believe me, unless you change your whole outlook and become like little children you will never enter the kingdom of heaven. It is the man who can be as humble as this little child who is greatest in the kingdom of heaven" (Matt. 18. 1-4). There are, too, his words: "Take my yoke upon you and learn of me, because I am meek and humble of heart; and you shall find rest to your souls" (Matt. 11. 29). If we ask why our Lord bade us learn of his humility rather than of all his other virtues we may answer that humility was the unifying, fundamental principle in his human life. He exemplifies every virtue; every incident in his life is for our instruction. Is there any one source of them all? What blends this divine-human life into a compelling unity? Surely it is humility. Everything he did and said was the consequence of his having emptied himself as God and assumed the consequences of sin as man. He was in a permanent state of humility, as we have seen, subject to God's providence. So his words and his works, his virtues and his sufferings, his humiliations and his shame were all fruits of his humility.

Saints are put before us as examples of various virtues— for example, St Francis of Assisi of poverty, St Ignatius of obedience, St Francis de Sales of gentleness, St Paul of the Cross of penance, and so on. Of course, all the saints practised all the virtues and Christ exemplified them all to perfection. Yet there is surely some reason why he should choose humility to name as the one thing we are specially to learn from him. It has been said that the "character" of Christ's personal spirituality is humility. As we have seen his predominant interest was his Father's will, his perfect subjection to his providence. Profound awe and confident familiarity characterize his devotion. He was himself the finished example of spiritual childhood; that was his own way of perfection. From the first moment to the last his life was the fulfilment of the "Behold I come to do thy will, O God" of the Epistle to the Hebrews (Heb. 10. 9).

Little wonder that St Paul and all the masters of spirituality have so insisted on this virtue. "If any man thinketh himself to be something, whereas he is nothing, he deceiveth himself" (Gal. 6. 3). St Cyprian called humility the foundation of holiness; St Jerome said it must be the first virtue of Christians; St Bernard made it the guardian of all the virtues. "To seek to build the edifice of solid virtues on any other base but that of humility is to build on sand," said St Gregory. "No one reaches heaven except by humility," said St Augustine. And St Bonaventure adds: "To try to cultivate virtue without humility is like trying to carry dust in the wind. Pride is the beginning of all sin, humility the foundation of all virtue." This seraphic Doctor tells us that if we wish to be humble we must tread a threefold path. Firstly, we must think of God, the author of all good from whom we have and to whom we owe anything good in us. Secondly, we must remember Christ's example. Thirdly, we must examine ourselves. St Vincent de Paul adds his testimony: "We shall never be fit to do God's work unless we are convinced that of ourselves we are better fitted to spoil everything than to succeed." "Humility and charity are mistresses of all the virtues," St Francis de Sales wrote; "the others follow, as chickens run after the mother hen." All agree that persevering prayer will do more to acquire humility than any other means.

The first step towards humility, after prayer, is to recognize our own insignificance. St Francis de Sales calls it loving our abjection. It means confessing our nothingness with a good grace, admitting that we are bad enough but that without God's grace we would be desperately worse, rejoicing that all the good we have is from God. If we love our position in relation to God we will not be miserable when the cross is offered to us. If we have a true opinion of ourselves and of our nothingness it will not be hard to accept the strictures, censures and criticisms of others. The humble soul rejects at once, as instantly as he would reject an impure thought, every wish to be praised, honoured, admired, reverenced or rewarded. Any seeking after dignities in the Church or the community is quite contrary to humility.

One hardly need say that those who are genuinely humble shun anything which savours of boasting, cultivating the esteem of others, ostentation or display. They have a real horror of praise and admiration and try to hide such qualities or achievements which may win them esteem.

Spiritual writers all insist that to grow in humility we must accept humiliations and contempt. Unless there is an important principle at stake we should not excuse ourselves when we are wrongly accused. If such a principle is at stake, if, for example, evil might be done if such an accusation is not refuted, the explanation should be given with all possible deference, charity and moderation and without bitterness or recrimination. Humble people do not wish to retaliate when they are snubbed, unfairly criticized, made to appear ridiculous or rebuked; they accept these things, saying to themselves, "If it were not for the good God has wrought in me I would be worthy of them all and far more besides. If I am not worthy of them now, it is only by God's grace and through no merit of my own."

In conclusion we might meditate on the words of Thomas à Kempis:

> There is no lesson so profound or so useful as this lesson of self-knowledge and of self-contempt. Claim nothing for yourself, think of others kindly and with admiration; that is the height of wisdom and its masterpiece. Never think yourself better than the next man, however glaring his faults, however grievous his offences. It is humble people God protects and preserves, God loves and comforts; he stoops down and gives his grace lavishly, raising the humble man to heights of glory.*

* *Imitation of Christ,* 1. 2; 2. 2.

13

"THAT WAS THE TRUE LIGHT" : I

(John 1. 9)

THE time has come for us to consider more fully the "light" theme as we find it in the inspired word. Some of the first words of the Bible are concerned with it in the material sense. God created it; the sun, moon and stars radiate it. These heavenly bodies are given a kind of majesty; they rule the day and the night, and the fact that God created them indicates something of his power and glory. In one of the most important prophetic passages he wrote, Jeremias tells of the new dispensation which will be "a message from the Lord, from him, the God of hosts, the same who brightens the day with the sun's rays, night with the ordered service of moon and star" (Jer. 31. 35). The thought is expressed frequently. The psalmist, for example, exclaims: "I look up at those heavens of thine, the work of thy hands, at the moon and the stars, which thou hast set in their places; what is man that thou shouldst remember him?" (Ps. 8. 4). In Psalm 103 light is portrayed as a kind of dictator over the animal world: "He has given us the moon for our calendar; the sun knows well the hour of his setting. Thou dost decree darkness, and the night falls; in the night all the forest is astir with prowling beasts; the young lions go roaring after their prey, God's pensioners, asking for their food. Then the sun rises, and they slink away to lie down in their dens, while man goes abroad to toil and drudge till the evening. What diversity, Lord, in thy creatures! What wisdom has designed them all! There is nothing on earth but gives proof of thy creative power" (Ps. 103. 19–24).

In his 24th chapter, Jesus, the son of Sirach, begins his hymn in praise of wisdom, portraying her speaking "in the court of the most High" and saying: "I am that word that was uttered by the mouth of the most High, the primal birth before ever creation began. Through me light rose in the heavens, inexhaustible; it was I that covered, as with a mist, the earth" (Ecclus. 24. 2–6). Wisdom is described as the spirit of God hovering like a cloud over chaos. Isaias has a similar thought: "It is the Lord that speaks, and there is no other to rival me;" I, the fashioner of darkness, the creator of light" (Is. 45. 6). And Baruch: "What man ever scaled heaven, gained wisdom there, and brought it back from the clouds? . . . Only he who knows all things possesses it, only his mind conceives it. . . . It is on his errand that the light goes forth, his summons that it obeys with awe; joyfully the stars shine out, keeping the watches he has appointed, answer when he calls their muster-roll, and offer their glad radiance to him who fashioned them. Such a God is ours; what rival shall be compared to him?" (Bar. 3. 29–36). Remember, too, how God spoke to Job: "Tell me, if such knowledge is thine, all its secrets; where the light dwells, where darkness finds its home; hast thou followed either of these to the end of its journey, tracked it to its lair? . . . Tell me by what means the light is scattered over earth?" (Job 38. 19, 24).

Do we see the implications of these powerful passages of inspired writing? Light is like a noble ruler, showing itself by day as the king, the sun which seems to dominate all creation, and by night as the moon and stars, the queen with her hand-maids. The creation of these is so far beyond the understanding of the human mind that the God who made them must possess indescribable majesty. Even the sources of light, kings and queens, as it were, in themselves, must praise the Creator: "Praise him, sun and moon; praise him, every star that shines" (Ps. 148. 3). And, in the famous *Benedicite*, which the Church has us recite so often at break of day and after Mass: "Bless him they should, sun and moon, stars of heaven . . . day-time and night-time, light and darkness" (Dan. 3. 62, 72). After all these centuries light still baffles the scientists to such an extent that the thinking ones amongst them acknowledge that it is the work of an incomprehensibly wise Creator and in many ways is like to him.

The transition from the thought of material light's rather special relationship with God to the consideration of God himself is not difficult. How better elevate the mind to God than by the contemplation of light which seems to be so pure and incorporeal? So we are hardly surprised when the inspired writers employ light as a symbol of God. He is eternal Light.

Wisdom is the "pure effluence of his glory who is God all-powerful . . . the glow that radiates from eternal light . . . the untarnished mirror of God's majesty" (Wis. 7. 25, 26). God is clad in light: "O Lord, my God, what magnificence is thine! Glory and beauty are thy clothing. The light is a garment thou dost wrap about thee" (Ps. 103. 2). "See how his glory overspreads heaven, his fame echoes through the earth; the brightness that is his, like light itself, the rays that stream from his hand" (Hab. 3. 4). Ecclesiasticus writes of Samuel's vision of "the God that gives light" (46. 18) and Isaias sings of the glory of the new Jerusalem in terms of light: "No longer wilt thou have the sun to shine by day, or the moon's beam to enlighten thee; the Lord shall be thy everlasting light, thy God shall be all thy splendour" (60. 19). The theme appears again in the Apocalypse of St John. How appropriately the psalmist thought of God's favour as sunshine (Ps. 4. 7); the greatest of all his favours was his coming amongst us, and when he came St John proclaimed that he "was the light". His revelation is the "ray of justice" which enlightens, the "true sun" which shines and the "beacon-light" which shows the track to be followed (Wis. 5. 6 ; Ecclus. 50. 31). "The Lord is my light and my deliverance; whom have I to fear?" the psalmist cried, and declared his conviction that "good men see a light dawn in darkness; his light, who is merciful, kind and faithful" (Ps. 26. 1; 111. 4).

In these extracts from the Old Testament we learn a little of the context of St John's declaration, "That was the true light." They show us that "light" had a special religious significance and associations. It reigned at the summit of the purely material creation; its very existence declared something of the exalted majesty of God; of him it was a fitting symbol, his robe, his wisdom, the favour of his countenance and the source of hope. But more, those ancient inspired writings employed "light" as a symbol of the Messias who was to come. "And now the people that went about in darkness has seen a great light; for men abiding in a land where death overshadowed them, light has dawned. . . . I, the Lord, have summoned thee . . . to shed, through thee, light over the Gentiles. . . . I have appointed thee to be the light of the Gentiles" (Is. 9. 2; 42. 6; 49. 6).

So we turn to the theme of light in St John's writings. Here
in the prologue he states the thesis in the simplest possible
terms. Christ is the true light. We believe that he is essential,
unchangeable, permanent light in a sense proper to himself.
The Precursor could not be light in that sense; he, like all
creatures, received all his enlightening powers from outside
himself. Holy men and women are rightly compared to a light
but their light directs those who follow it to him who is the
essential light, as our Lord said: "You are the light of the
world; a city cannot be hidden if it is built on a mountain-top.
A lamp is not lighted to be put away under a bushel measure;
it is put on a lamp-stand, to give light to all the people of the
house; and your light must shine so brightly before men that
they can see your good works, and glorify your Father who is
in heaven" (Matt. 5. 14–16).

There is another sense in which our Lord is the light. He is
termed the "true food" (John 6. 32), the "true vine" (John
16). In the holy Eucharist he is really, truly and substantially
present to be our food, but he is also our food in the sense that
his truth nourishes the minds of those who accept it in faith.
So we can apply to the light theme the meaning that in our
minds our blessed Lord produces the same effects spiritually as
the sun produces materially when it shines on our bodies. Not
only does the sun enlighten us, and thereby enable us to perform many actions which would otherwise be impossible, and
warm us; it produces also many chemical effects on living and
non-living things the study of which has developed into the
vast science of photochemistry.

Rather than embark alone on the discussion of the implications of this theme let us accept the guidance of the Holy
Spirit and follow it through the inspired lines.

The next important reference to it after the prologue is in
our Lord's words to Nicodemus. I quote them in the more
exact Westminster version: "Now herein is the judgment, that
whereas the light is come into the world, men loved the darkness
rather than the light; for their works were evil. Everyone that
doth evil hateth the light, and cometh not to the light, lest his
works be convicted; but he that doth the truth cometh to the
light, in order that his works may be seen clearly to have been
wrought in God" (John 3. 19–21). I say, "our Lord's words to

Nicodemus" because they have been traditionally regarded as such; but nowadays scholars give much weight to the arguments in favour of taking them to be St John's reflections on his Master's discourse. The general sense is clear enough, but we must not pass on too rapidly lest some of their meaning be overlooked.

St John reflects that what makes men disbelieve is opposition to the light. A guilty man avoids the light because it may expose him. The Apostle wrote elsewhere: "If we say we have fellowship with him (i.e. God), and walk in the darkness, we lie and practise not the truth. But if we walk in the light, even as he is in the light, we have fellowship with one another and the blood of Jesus cleanseth us from all sin" (I John 1. 6). A man with a clear conscience welcomes the light and whatever it reveals. So our Saviour becomes the occasion of a division of men into two groups. In the first are those whose belief in him wins them eternal life; in the second are all whose rejection of him destines them to damnation.

We cannot do better than quote St Augustine's celebrated commentary on this passage. He takes the example of a doctor who comes to cure all the sick. Those who refuse his ministrations die, not on account of the doctor, as if he came to cause their death, but on account of the infirmities they had already contracted and refuse to allow the doctor to cure.

Many loved their sins, and many confessed their sins [he wrote]. He who confesses and accuses his sins is already on God's side. God (that is the light) accuses your sins; and if you also accuse, you are joined to God. There are, as it were, two things: the man and the sinner. God made man, and man made himself a sinner. Destroy what *you* made, that God may save what *he* made. You must hate your own work in you, and love God's work in you. When that which you made begins to displease you, then your good works are beginning, in as much as you are accusing your bad works. The beginning of good works is the confession of bad works. You do truth and you come to the light. What is it—to do truth? You do not fondle yourself, you do not caress yourself, you do not flatter yourself, do not say: I am just, when you are really not—then you are beginning to do truth.

The same holy bishop said: "Sore eyes hate the light; healthy eyes love it."

Thus we are brought face to face with the necessity of knowing ourselves. In so far as our view of ourselves does not coincide with God's view we are wandering in the darkness and always liable to go astray. Faults are bad, but it is worse when one deliberately refuses to face up to them. Then is added the crime of self-delusion. That is one of the easiest of faults, one against which we ought always to pray. We are always prone to see in ourselves only the things we want to see and not the things God wants us to see. A person who is not sincerely interested in the spiritual life nor desirous of loving God more is the prey of many motives and desires; there is no firm direction in his life, no constancy, no singleness of purpose, no dominant resolve. So he wavers this way and that —but, in the end, one force rises to the top and begins to dominate everything else: it is the power of self-deception. "Full wise is he that can himselven know," wrote Chaucer in *The Monke's Tale*. And Thomas à Kempis reminds us at the beginning of *The Imitation*: "The humble knowledge of thyself is a surer way to God than the deepest search after science."

Apart from a reference in the fifth chapter to St John the Baptist as a "burning and a shining light," the theme is not resumed until St John's eighth chapter. It begins with the lovely story of the woman who had been caught in adultery and what somebody has called our Lord's deflation of the rigorists. Immediately after his words of forgiveness, St John goes on: "And now once more Jesus spoke to them, I am the light of the world, he said. He who follows me can never walk in darkness; he will possess the light which is life" (John 8. 12). In the next chapter the same words occur again. As they passed a man who had been born blind and the Apostles asked about him, our Lord took the opportunity of telling them: "As long as I am in the world, I am the world's light" and then follows that very graphic and moving story of the cure of the blind man (John 9. 5).

It is possible that on the first of these occasions the group was standing within sight of the great candelabra which were used to provide light in the Treasury. Maybe there was a remark about them and possibly a reference to the pillar of fire which had guided the Israelites through the wilderness. Christ, as the eternal Word, is indeed the light. He proceeded from all eternity from the Father, being equal in all things to him and in such a way that his eternal generation left the Father unchanged. There is something like it in the lighting of one flame from another. So Christ is in truth the *lumen de lumine*, light of light. But he is the light of all nations also because he is the unique Revealer of heavenly truth. Following his teaching and example means freedom from the darkness of human error, ignorance and malice. His teaching dissipates error, his life and example condemn sin. Those who follow faithfully will have his light within them, the light of faith and grace, and, when this life is over, they will come into the kingdom of everlasting light when his brightness will break on their eyes like the dawn (Ps. 35. 10).

At the end of the ninth chapter, after the story of the blind man's cure, St John reports the Pharisees saying to our Lord: "Are we also blind?" He answered, "If you were blind, you should not have sin, but now you say: We see. Your sin remaineth" (John 9. 40, 41). He told them that if they were humble enough to acknowledge that they were ignorant of many things and sinful, too, they would not be so blameworthy. But because they so arrogantly regard themselves as perfect and beyond correction they are indeed in sin.

From these incidents we can learn to value properly Christ's revelation. Already we have insisted on the absolutely fundamental need of faith on which to build an edifice of sound spirituality. We come back to it here. Our Lord himself insists upon it. His teaching is the way to life. He demands acceptance of it without the slightest reservation. It is true that we can validly distinguish what is of obligation and what is of counsel from the point of view of sin and its gravity; but from the standpoint of love and the ambition of God's true lover there is hardly room for such a distinction. The lover grasps at God's will for him—and that includes the counsels as well as the commandments. In fact, it is the observance of the counsels of perfection that are the true test of love. With the very minimum necessary for salvation one might succeed in keeping the commandments and not gain much extra merit. It is otherwise

with what is not of obligation. One can be a saint without
observing the absolute poverty demanded by the vow of
religious, but no one can be a saint unless he is so detached
from the things of earth that he loves and uses them only in
so far as they lead to God. So with everything: the true lover
ponders Christ's teaching in every detail and, because he is a
lover of the divine will, a little child in spirit, he applies it
within the circumstances of his own life.

Mass mediocrity is something of a mystery. In any Catholic
community the number of those who are sincerely and enthusiastically interested in the pursuit of their spiritual perfection
is desperately small. There is prevalent an attitude of mind
that all is well if we preserve the Faith, if we keep the commandments and avoid mortal sin, if we have good schools for
the children and an organization or two for the youths and
adults who feel like joining them. But, generally speaking, there
is no firm conviction amongst the majority that they, all of
them, are called to be saints. The cry of Christ from the hillside, "You are to be perfect, as your heavenly Father is perfect"
(Matt. 5. 48) does not echo in many hearts and wills. Only an
insignificant minority seems to think of spiritual direction as a
practical matter. That is serious as it affects the laity; it is
vastly more regrettable when priests and religious are concerned. A priest, brother or nun who is not fervently anxious
to love God more and progress in holiness is a living contradiction. Yet we know how easy it is for those who have officially
given themselves to God to become overwhelmed by other
concerns to such an extent that, instead of these being means to
further God's glory, they become obstacles to the perfect love
of him. Weakness of faith is ultimately responsible for mediocrity; the light of Christ is not allowed to burn brightly enough
in the mind; it is not the compelling, compulsive force it ought
to be. Yet we have to face it that to relegate the claims of
Christ to a subordinate place is wholly illogical in one who
believes in him. In fact, when one considers it from all aspects,
it is a species of insanity. Every convinced Christian believes
that this life is merely a preparation for the next, that if heaven
is lost all is lost and that the degree of heavenly happiness
depends only on merit amassed on earth. What a mystery then
is mass mediocrity, the extent to which so many allow them-

selves to be diverted from the primary purpose of life to seek after "the meat which perisheth" (John 6. 27)! The Holy Spirit found something particularly repulsive about tepidity when he bade St John write to the angel of the church at Laodicea: "I know of thy doings, and find thee neither cold nor hot; cold or hot, I would thou wert one or the other. Being what thou art, lukewarm, neither cold nor hot, thou wilt make me vomit thee out of my mouth" (Apoc. 3. 15–16). Set this terrible rebuke in its context and you have a salutary thought for millions of nominal Christians and unenthusiastic religious today.

Laodicea was a rich city, proud and self-sufficient, famous for its banks and traffic in gold. To every part of the world it exported its collyrium, eye-salve. Not far away was Hierapolis, a spa famous for its warm baths. To drink their water when it was only tepid brought on vomiting; hence the allusion in St John's prophecy. Significantly, this self-satisfied city, enriched by the munificence of Hiero and ennobled by the memory of Zeno, is the only one of the seven Asiatic churches to be un-reservedly condemned by St John. He gave the reason: its people were prepared to be too easily tolerant and too readily compromising about eternal values. Read a little more of what the beloved disciple wrote: "If thou didst but know it, it is thou who art wretched, thou who art to be pitied. Thou art a beggar, blind and naked; and my counsel to thee is, to come and buy from me what thou needest; gold, proved in the fire, to make thee rich, and white garments, to clothe thee, and cover up the nakedness which dishonours thee; rub salve, too, upon thy eyes, to restore them sight. It is those I love that I correct and chasten; kindle thy generosity and repent. See where I stand at the door, knocking; if anyone listens to my voice and opens the door, I will come in to visit him, and he shall sup with me" (Apoc. 3. 17–21). What tenderness is mixed with the severity of that appeal! Christ, the outcast, still loves those who insult him by their lukewarmness; he still knocks at the door of the hearts of those who think him hardly worth bothering about; he never despairs of having as companions for all eternity, sharing his throne with him (v. 21), those who have for a time been overpowered by the world's appeal. Notice—spiritual vision is restored by the appeal of love! Those who fear that they are

lukewarm have the remedy in their own hands; it is to contemplate God's infinite love for them. That is the light which
unfailingly guides to eternal life.

St John writes in his eleventh chapter about the raising of
Lazarus from the tomb. When he announced his resolve to
return to Judea the disciples objected. "Master!" they said,
"only a few days ago the Jews were trying to stone you to
death—are you going there again?" "Are there not just twelve
hours of daylight?" he replied, "A man can walk in the day-
time without stumbling, with this world's light to see by; he
only stumbles if he walks by night, because then the light
cannot reach him" (John 11. 8–9). What is the meaning of this
rather enigmatic assurance? It is one that we should find
consoling. Our Lord says: "You must understand that just as
a man walks safely and without stumbling during the period of
daylight, which is a fixed period that cannot be shortened;
so, during the time my Father has decreed my mortal life is to
last, I am safe, and so are you." In other words, so long as we
do God's will we are safe from real harm. The Jews could not
touch our Lord until the Father allowed them to. It is just
another reminder that God's will is the light of life and that
even the most painful things that happen through no volition
of ours must always be regarded as graces permitted by our
loving Father for our good.

Shortly before telling us about the Last Supper, St John
touches on the light-theme again. To the crowds our Lord
said: "The light is among you still, but only for a short time.
Finish your journey while you still have the light, for fear
darkness should overtake you; he who journeys in darkness
cannot tell which way he is going. While you still have the
light, have faith in the light, that so you may become children
of the light. . . . I have come into the world as a light, so that
all those who believe in me may continue no longer in darkness" (John 12. 35, 36, 46). Now he wants them to understand that to believe while he is there to be seen and heard is
easier than it will be after his death. "Do not wait," he says in
effect; "Accept the lights and graces I am offering you now;
believe in me; if you reject me while you can see me, you will
surely be overtaken by the night of infidelity and sin after my
death."

Is it not a very human tendency to shirk from the effort required if we are to grow continually in holiness? Christ is still offering us his light. It comes in many ways—in prayer, in reading, in conferences, from the ordinary happenings of life. It may be that for a long time, even for years, we may know quite well that some flaw remains in our spiritual lives. Usually it is something quite small. We have given ourselves to God; we have been faithful enough to the vows and the rule: we have practised the virtues with fair success—but there is just something that we cling to. Deep down we know it is there and that it is wrong, that we would be better without it; but we just will not face up to the short, sharp sacrifice that is required to rid ourselves of it. We know it is an obstacle to perfection; we want perfection—but we also want this pet weakness of ours. There are so many things it could be—disobedience in some small matter, but regularly practised, attachment to something we have without permission or to some person or habit, a little laziness, a deficiency in regard to the effort we make at Mass, receiving Holy Communion, going to confession, reciting the Office, making our private prayer, saying the Rosary—there are a hundred things it could be; but, so long as it remains, we are unfaithful; we are compelling God to withhold graces he wants to give us. In a word, we are not fully children of the light; we prefer the darkness, at least in that detail. Sometimes these shortcomings are quite obvious to others; every member of the community is conscious of them except their victim. It may be that through long habit one has become so accustomed to a fault that one hardly recognizes it or has even succeeded in convincing oneself that it is not a fault at all. Hence the need of relentlessly following the light of Christ and never refusing even for a time the graces he offers.

In his first epistle St John returns to the theme with even greater vigour. His message concerns the "Word who is life" and it is this: "That God is light, and no darkness can find any place in him; if we claim fellowship with him, when all the while we live and move in darkness, it is a lie; our whole life is an untruth. God dwells in light; if we too live and move in light, there is fellowship between us, and the blood of his Son Jesus Christ washes us clean from all sin" (I John 1. 5–7). Here is repeated a lesson we have learned already—that failure to do God's will is equivalent to rejecting the only true light of life. All the Catholic epistles emphasize how necessary good works are; faith alone will never be enough; evil deeds done for any reason at all destroy the fellowship which should exist between the soul and God. On the other hand, good works make us like God, as far as creatures can be like the Creator, in his uncreated, infinite, unchangeable holiness.

Notice how St John soon relates his light-theme to the subject of brotherly love. It is for him a sign and effect of union with God. He returns to the subject a little later: "It is a new commandment I am sending you, now that it is verified in him and you; the darkness has passed away now, and true light shines instead. He who claims enlightenment, and all the while hates his brother, is in darkness still. It is the man who loves his brother that lives in light; no fear of stumbling haunts him. The man who hates his brother is in the dark, guides his steps in the dark without being able to tell where he is going; darkness has fallen, and blinded his eyes" (I John 2. 8–11).

Let us probe a little further into the Apostle's meaning. Christ has given a new meaning to the commandment of love by dying for his enemies; the light of faith, therefore, proposes now new motives for love, new reasons why Christ's followers must love one another. Our Saviour made this his distinctive commandment, the special badge of all his followers: "The mark by which all men will know you for my disciples will be the love you bear one another" (John 13. 35). There are to be no half-measures in our love: "Your love for one another is to be like the love I have borne you" (ib., v. 34). One who has embraced the faith, St John is saying, but does not love his brethren is equivalently and practically a pagan. Such faith is useless without the leading Christian virtue, charity. So important is this lesson that St John repeats it over and over again. One who does not love is, he says, in the darkness; he walks in darkness; he does not know where he is going; and the darkness has blinded him. The same fact is repeated four times in this one verse. For the beloved Apostle there is no middle way; not to love is to hate; one who refuses to love is still in darkness, that is, without truth and moral goodness. The reason for St John's emphasis is not only that our Lord made charity the principal virtue of his teaching, but because lack of it shows that an individual is not governed by the motives of faith but by the principles of the pagan world.

So the light-theme has led us to the subject of brotherly love. We must be struck by the way in which St John elevates it in his teaching. He is simply following our Lord. When he says that the second commandment is like to the first, he means that it is the same as the first, the same commandment in the sense that we must love one another as we love God, that is, with supernatural motives. The love St John is talking about, the love that brings us to the way of light, is totally independent of likes and dislikes; it applies to everybody—to enemies as well as friends, to the ungrateful, the stupid, the dirty, the ignorant, the proud, the wayward, the sinful. There is not one exception. In each we must see, reverence and love Christ: "When you did it to one of the least of my brethren here, you did it to me" (Matt. 25. 40). We are commanded to love people, not merely qualities. We must love because each is infinitely loved by God who suffered and died for each. God made each, when he could have made a great saint instead; each is destined to live with God for ever. We will never succeed in practising this charity unless we ponder hard, long and prayerfully the sublimity of it, the supernatural truth behind it and the elevated motives which compel it.

14

"THAT WAS THE TRUE LIGHT": II

(John 1. 9)

Now let us seek for the light-theme elsewhere in the New Testament. In the first place we find it used, as in the Old, as a symbol of God. St Paul, for example, tells Timothy that God dwells in inaccessible light (I Tim. 6. 16) and the Colossians that he will shed his light on the saints in heaven. To the Corinthians he says that God, who said, " 'Out of darkness shall shine light,' hath shone forth in our hearts, unto the illuminating knowledge of the glory of God, in the person of Christ " (II Cor. 4. 6). A rather new idea is introduced here. The Apostle is saying that in seeking God's glory and the advantage of his readers, he is simply corresponding with God's designs when he gives the grace of apostleship. Of old God, the same God, said at the beginning of creation, "Let there be light" and there was light; now he shines by his spirit in our hearts, giving us the light of knowledge so that we should be so many lights, illuminating the spiritual darkness of the world. The knowledge we must spread is of the bright glory of God reflected in Christ, his most perfect image. So here is yet another lesson for us: it is that we must always be careful that our zeal is genuinely for God's glory and not for our own advantage or satisfaction; we must preach Christ and never ourselves. We will succeed in this only when the brightness of God's glory and holiness shines forth in our own lives, each of which should be like a brightly burning lamp to bring the light to others.

For the sake of completeness other references may be mentioned. To the people of Ephesus St Paul wrote: "Walk as children of light—for the fruit of the light is in all goodness and justness and truth—and find out what is well-pleasing to the Lord. Have no fellowship with the unfruitful works of darkness, but rather expose them. For the things done by such men in secret it is shameful even to speak of; but all things are exposed and made manifest by the light. For all that is made manifest

is light. Wherefore it is said, Awake thou that sleepest, And
arise from the dead. And Christ shall enlighten thee" (Eph.
5. 7-14). The interest of this passage lies in the words which
introduce it. St Paul is not satisfied with writing "For ye were
heretofore in darkness but are now enlightened in the Lord";
he prefers the abstract as being much more forceful than the
concrete and puts down: "Ye were heretofore darkness but
now light in the Lord." He goes on to explain that one who is
light must be an example of goodness, justness and truth. Some
of the commentators see goodness here opposed to anger
and sharpness, justness opposed to fraud and dishonesty and
truth opposed to hypocrisy and lying. Others note that goodness comes first. They point out that it includes every desirable
quality, is God-like-ness and so reflects the light of him who is
essential light. "God is not a symbol of goodness," wrote
Chesterton, "but goodness is a symbol of God." A good person,
then, is one who tries always to do God's will; that general
attitude of mind shows itself in the qualities which appeal to
others, such as kindness, generosity, helpfulness, deep sympathy
and the like. So it is indeed a quality admirably likened to
light. It embraces justness, which implies that one gives both
God and men their due (and thus includes humility) and truth,
which means that one lives in perfect conformity with eternal
values.

To Timothy St Paul wrote that it was through the Gospel
that life and immortality were brought to light. "Accept all the
hardship that is entailed in preaching the Gospel," he says in
effect; "God gives you the strength. He has rescued us from
everything that is really evil and called us to a life of holiness.
This is not because we deserve it but for his own purpose.
Before time began he planned to give us in Christ the grace to
achieve that purpose of his, but it is only since the coming of
our Saviour that the method has been made clear. For Christ has
destroyed death and has now, through the gospel, opened to
us men the shining possibilities of the life that is eternal"
(II Tim. 1. 9-10). What a telling summary that is of St Paul's
doctrine of divine election: by Christ's blood we have been
delivered, having been freely chosen out by God from all
eternity to be members of his mystical Body, and all that, not
because of any merits of our own but solely on account of God's

goodness. "Is not that motive enough to inspire a zealous service?" the Apostle wrote from Rome, where he was awaiting sentence of death. In this moving passage he likens Christ's coming to an *epiphany*, an apparition which will illuminate the world and point the way to eternal life. The more we ponder these things the more vivid becomes our realization of all we owe to the mercy of God, who has chosen us out to receive the light of faith in Christ. The best way of showing our appreciation is to follow the light without hesitation or deviation, that is, with perfect sincerity, absolute devotion and complete forgetfulness of self.

All these thoughts show how appropriate it is that light should be so prominent in the Church's liturgy. The feast of light *par excellence* is Candlemas. The day's liturgy tries to bring home to us how light symbolizes Christ and the supernatural life of grace. It was instituted to supplant the pagan *Lupercalia*, according to many students of the liturgy. On that occasion, always February 15th, goats and a dog were sacrificed, thongs made of their skins, and the *Luperci*, a kind of priests, ran round the walls of the city striking people with them. A blow from the thong was supposed to cure sterility in women. It is said that these pagan frolics included torchlight processions which the Church "baptized" by incorporating the procession of Candlemas into her worship. Until 1961 the use of purple at this ceremony was a reminder of its penitential institution, to make reparation for the excesses of the *Lupercalia*.

The Church likes to see the faithful lighting their candles at home for family devotions, in times of stress and danger and for special needs. They are to be lighted when Holy Communion is brought to the sick or Extreme Unction administered. They are a continual reminder of the candle we received at baptism, the burning lamp with which we must hasten through life to meet the heavenly Bridegroom. It would be foolish to regard as superstitious or unworthy the use of candles by the Church. Lights, as well as washings, flowers, music, perfumes, bells and vestments, have always been used in worship of all kinds. They are the natural language of mystical expression. They are found in secular ceremonial as well as in the service of God. A firework display and illuminations are always enjoyed and recognized as the expression of joy and celebration.

In pagan times lights were carried before the Emperor in Rome as a mark of respect; it is easy to see how the custom was transferred to processions in church whether of priests, bishops, the missal at Mass or the Blessed Sacrament.

At Candlemas the Church gives each of us a candle to remind us that she never ceases to bring to us the Light of the World. We carry it in procession, signifying the fervour of our imitation of Christ and our desire to carry him to men. The procession enters the church and ends there; so life ends in God's eternal home. If we pass through it always in company with Christ, the Light, we shall be privileged to live there throughout eternity. At the Gospel and during the Canon of the Mass we carry our candles as we remind ourselves that the inspired lives of Christ are the light which ought to rule our lives and that his real presence amongst us, especially as he continues the sacrifice of Calvary in the Mass, should be a special light in our passage through the dark world. The Mass is Calvary, the continuation of the sacrifice which conquered the darkness of the devil and brought to the world the light of salvation.

Fruitful meditation on the light-theme is found in some of the prayers from the blessing of candles. In the first of them we ask God to look down upon us as we signify our yearning to honour him by carrying the candles in our hands. In the second we remember that light is invariably associated with warmth and we pray: "May we be inflamed with the holy fire of thy sweet charity and accounted worthy to be ourselves presented in the holy temple of thy glory." In the third we beg that the candles will be hallowed with the light of the grace of Christ, the light of the world, that "so may our hearts, enlightened by that invisible fire, the radiance of the Holy Spirit, be free from all blindness of sin. May our mind's eye be purified, enabling us to discern those things which are pleasing to thee and of use for our salvation. May we thereby be counted worthy, after the murky hazards of this life, to reach the light that never fails." A similar thought comes in the next prayer in which we ask that the candles "will so provide us with outward light that by God's gift the inward light of his Spirit will not be wanting to our minds."

Another liturgical feast of light is the Easter vigil service. It dates from Apostolic times. Constantine transformed night into day with "pillars of wax," according to the historian Eusebius. Other authors have left vivid descriptions of the brilliance of the churches. Even today there are few moments so solemn as when the new fire is struck outside the church and the celebrant prays that Christ who has enkindled in the faithful the fire of his own brightness will grant that they be so inflamed with desire for heaven that they may attain with pure souls the feast of everlasting brightness. The Easter Candle is solemnly blessed as the symbol of the resplendent risen Saviour. "May his light dispel from heart and mind the evil night!" is the Church's prayer. What a lovely conception it is to carry portions of that new fire to the lamps and candles everywhere in the church in the hope that it will never be extinguished throughout the liturgical year. And how fitting the prayer: "Wherever a portion of this hallowing mystery of fire shall be carried, may the evil of Satan's guile be driven thence and the power of thy majestic glory made manifest." "Behold the light of Christ," thrice the deacon sings. As we gaze upon it and soon the whole church becomes ablaze with light that has been taken from it, we resolve that we will never cease to behold it for the rest of our lives. Fittingly, we hold our candles again as we renew the vows of baptism. Very early in the Church's history baptism was called "illumination". Nor should we overlook the tradition that the *Exsultet,* or a hymn like it, was composed by St Jerome, showing that even in those early times the symbolism of the blessed candle was understood. Using the ancient belief in the virginity of bees, the writer sees in wax a symbol of the flesh of Christ taken from a virgin mother. So the wick may symbolize his soul and the flame his divinity, which dominates his body and soul.

Lest we might believe that candles were originally used in church just because they were necessary to see in the darkness of the catacombs, we recall the protest of the heretic, Vigilantius, at the end of the fourth century that while the sun was still shining they lighted great piles of candles. St Jerome replied that candles were lighted as a sign of joy when the Gospel was read, and not merely to put darkness to flight. The phrase used by Vigilantius reminds us of the massive pile of candles which daily illuminates the grotto at Lourdes. We know that when the Bishop of Carthage, St Cyprian, was buried in the year 258, they carried candles. At a synod held in Gaul early in the sixth century the giving of a candle to acolytes was mentioned. Originally, they were put on the pavement of the sanctuary not on the altar. They were probably put there first about the eleventh century.

So there is little excuse for our forgetting the significance of the light-theme enunciated by St John in his prologue. Every aspect of it is kept before us in the liturgy. Candles are symbols of God, Christ, truth, grace and love; burning out their lives before tabernacles or shrines they symbolize, too, prayer and sacrifice. One called away to daily duty leaves a candle burning to signify his desire to remain there in company with Jesus, his Mother or the citizens of heaven, and to wear himself out in their service.

There are some who rather despise the popular use of candles in church. They would take them from shrines, have just the minimum number at Benediction and permit their use in processions and other ceremonies only when absolutely necessary. This seems to be out of harmony with the mind of the Church. There may be abuses occasionally, but virtue is always found in moderation. There is no doubt that lights in church do elevate the spirit to God. A beautifully decorated Benediction or exposition altar has been the occasion of drawing some converts into the Church. Certainly nobody has the right to scorn a tradition which goes back to the time of the Apostles and beyond. The candlesticks and chandeliers which now grace the greater cathedrals and the museums of the world remind us of the extent to which wax tapers were used. In these days of artificial light it is hard for us to imagine the splendour which magnificent chandeliers ablaze with hundreds of golden flames gave to worship at a time when men were comparatively rude and barbarous. They say Constantine illuminated the first Lateran basilica with no less than 8,730 lights.

Is it possible to sum up all the ideas which have come to us from that simple statement of St John, "That was the true Light"? We have seen how Scripture uses the majesty of the heavenly sources of light to emphasize the majesty of God, how light symbolizes God, how Christ is the true Light, how goodness opposes sin as light opposes darkness, how the light-theme recurs in St John's Gospel with various shades of meaning and application, how puzzling is the mystery of mass mediocrity and how repulsive religious tepidity. We glanced at our Lord's exhortation to accept the grace he offers without procrastination and we saw something of Holy Writ's repeated assurance that acceptance of God's will under all circumstances is to walk in the light. This led us to think of brotherly love as St John emphasized its connection with light and to pursue the light-theme in other places of the New Testament. Then we came to the use of lights in the liturgical worship of the Church and we saw something of its significance. The overwhelming truth emerges that holiness, to which all are called, is simply the following of the Light through love.

Following the light means living in a way worthy of the dignity to which God has called us. St Peter describes it: "You are a chosen generation, a kingly priesthood, a holy nation, a purchased people; that you may declare his virtues, who hath brought you out of darkness into his marvellous light" (I Peter 2. 9). The way to the light is to live as one specially chosen by God to receive the gift of faith, as one who in some way must share in the royal, priestly dignity of Christ and thus make resplendent the spirit of sacrifice, as one of a people all called to holiness and redeemed by the blood of Christ. Faith is the foundation; the life of faith demands sacrifice; when sacrifice is forthcoming it leads to holiness, and that is love, returning generously Christ's love for us. Follow that way and, even in this life, we will rest in God's marvellous light.

Fittingly, then, the New Testament ends on the theme of light. In the Apocalypse, St John describes the dwelling place prepared for the Church triumphant where God will dwell with his saints. It is a sanctuary made holy by the presence of God and the Lamb, whose glory replaces sun, moon and lamp. It will be "clothed in God's glory. The light that shone over it was bright as any precious stone; the glory of God shone there and the Lamb gave it light. There will be no more night, no more need of light from lamp or sun; the Lord God will shed his light on them, and they will reign for ever and ever" (Apoc. 21. 11, 24; 22. 5).

15

"WHICH ENLIGHTENETH EVERY MAN THAT COMETH INTO THIS WORLD"

(John 1. 9)

THERE is some slight controversy about the translation of this verse but all the Latin Fathers and the Greeks, with one exception, would support our Vulgate version. A modern commentator suggests that what St John wants to write is: "There it was—the very Light which enlightens every man coming into the world." "Every man" means Jews, Gentiles, men of all ages, nations, places, generations; there is no exception. Possibly the light referred to is merely that of reason; but more probably it is the light of grace. If any man is spiritually enlightened it is only through Christ; and if one is not enlightened, having come to the use of reason, it is his own fault. Nobody can die in spiritual darkness, in such a state as to lose his soul, without its being his own fault. "It is his will that all men should be saved, and be led to recognize the truth" (I Tim. 2. 4). St John's thought is that Christ's work in general is to make spiritual life and light available to all men. The light is always there but not all accept it. Yet, as St Peter says, God does not will any man to perish (II Peter 3. 9).

There has been so much controversy on this point of salvation in recent years that it seems necessary to set out plainly just what the Church teaches on the matter. To find that teaching we go to certain classical statements and from each of them in turn we draw definite conclusions.

The most important of the Lateran Councils was the fourth, convoked by Pope Innocent III in 1215. In the course of it an official definition of the Eucharist was given, using the word "transubstantiation" for the first time; annual confession was made the law for all Christians. But for our purpose the decrees taught:

(1) For a man to be certain of salvation he must, at the moment of death, be in some way "within" the Catholic

Church either as a member or as one who wishes and prays to enter it;

(2) To this rule there is absolutely no exception. If there were exceptions the statement that "no one at all" is saved outside the one universal Church of the faithful would not be true. But that statement is true. It is an infallible doctrinal statement of a General Council of the Church;

(3) It is completely false and unacceptable to explain the dogma of "no salvation outside the Church" by claiming that the Church is the "ordinary" means, or by imagining that it is necessary only for those who appreciate its dignity and position.

On 18th November, 1302, Pope Boniface VIII, who was quarrelling with Philip IV of France, issued his famous Bull, *Unam Sanctam*. It is an infallible statement of doctrine and stresses especially the following four points:

(1) For both the gaining of salvation and the forgiveness of sins (which is inseparable from the granting of the life of grace) the Church is necessary;

(2) It is necessary because it is the Body and the Spouse of Christ;

(3) Gaining salvation in the Church implies being united with the Bishop of Rome;

(4) The dogma that the Church is necessary for salvation cannot be explained exactly in terms of any "invisible" Church. The Church, outside of which there is no salvation, is the one visible, organized society over which Peter and his successors rule by Christ's own commission.

Here are the exact words with which this powerful document ends: "We declare, state, define and assert that for every human creature submission to the Roman Pontiff is absolutely necessary for salvation."

The *Decree for the Jacobites* is one of the acts of the seventeenth General Council, held at Florence in 1442. The Jacobites were a body of Syrian heretics who had rejected the teaching of the Council of Chalcedon in 451 and took their name from Jacob Baradaeus. The Council of Florence had as its chief objective reunion with the separated Eastern Churches. The Jacobite Decree is a dogmatic statement of high importance concerning what must be believed by members of the Church concerning salvation. Three points call for special mention:

(1) Everyone outside the Church, even one who has never sinned against the faith itself, is so placed that he cannot be saved without in some way entering the Church before he dies;

(2) The alternative to eternal salvation is loss of the direct vision of God. Those who die in a state of mortal sin must pay the penalty of loss and also that of sense in hell;

(3) One who is not "within" the Church, at least by an act of implicit desire, cannot receive the life of sanctifying grace.

This Bull does not teach that in order to be saved all must actually become members of the Catholic Church but it does say that pagans, Jews, heretics and schismatics will not be saved unless at the end of their lives they are joined to the one, true Church. A man is in the Church, though not actually a member of it, if he sincerely, though only implicitly, desires to live within it.

The day after he had defined the Immaculate Conception Pope Pius IX gave an allocution to the cardinals, archbishops and bishops assembled in Rome. It is rich in its dogmatic teaching and has become known by its opening words *Singulari quadam*. Points stated more clearly than in previous documents are these:

(1) It is foolish to hope that those who are dead, but who had not entered the Church in any way during their lives, are saved;

(2) There is no contradiction between the dogmas that there is no salvation outside the Church and that God is infinitely merciful and just;

(3) It is a Catholic dogma, revealed by God through Jesus Christ, that no one is saved outside the Catholic Church; all men must believe it with divine faith;

(4) God does not regard invincible ignorance of the Church or of anything else as a sin. The doctrine that there is no salvation outside the Catholic Church does not in any way mean that invincible ignorance is a sin. (Invincible ignorance is that which is not due to lack of proper diligence on the part of the one who is lacking in certain knowledge);

(5) To believe that the way of salvation can be found in any religion is an impious and deadly error;

(6) We have neither the competence nor the right to search out the manner in which God applies his mercy and his justice in any certain case of a person who is ignorant of the true Church. When we see God ourselves we shall understand how his mercy and justice have worked;

(7) The Church's task is to work and pray that all men will be saved in the Church;

(8) God is infinite generosity. Those who come to him are never rejected. God himself is the source of every movement towards him.

The same Pope, Pius IX, issued an encyclical letter on this same subject. Known as the *Quanto conficiamur mœrore*, it may be summed up under five headings:

(1) Men who die apart from the true faith and Catholic unity cannot attain eternal life;

(2) Through the workings of God's light and grace a person can be saved who is invincibly ignorant of the true religion and carefully obeys the natural law, lives with honesty and uprightness and is prepared to obey God;

(3) A person like that has already chosen God as his last end. That is an act of charity. He is in the state of grace and not in that of original or mortal sin. This act of love includes an implicit desire to enter and stay in God's true supernatural kingdom. Such a person has had his sins forgiven "within" Christ's true Church;

(4) The Church is necessary for salvation with both necessity of means and necessity of precept; necessity of means, that is, no one can be saved unless he dies either as a member of the Church or with a genuine and sincere desire, either explicit or implicit, of entering the Church and remaining in it; necessity of precept, that is, insubordinate refusal to enter the Church or stay within it is gravely sinful;

(5) Catholics have the duty to help all those outside the fold who are in need and a prime duty to bring them to accept God's revealed truth in so far as they are able to do so.

We pass now to one of the greatest letters of Pope Pius XII, that on the mystical Body of Christ. It is very hard to single out points for special mention, but the following five seem most to our point here:

(1) The conditions for being "within" the Church in such

a way as to be able to gain salvation in it and the conditions necessary to be a member of the Church are not objectively and completely identical;

(2) A person can be saved "within" the Church if he has merely an implicit desire to be in it;

(3) To be "within" the Church merely by desire is notably inferior to being actually a member of the Church;

(4) All the Church's members are strictly bound to work and pray for the conversion of all others to the Church;

(5) The visible Roman Catholic Church is identical with the social unit called the mystical Body of Christ.

The most important, complete and explicit statement on the topic we are discussing came from the Supreme Sacred Congregation of the Holy Office in Rome on 8th August, 1949. It was addressed to the Archbishop of Boston but was not published until 12th August, 1950. It is worth our while to go over it in some detail. Known as the *Suprema haec sacra*, it affirms towards the beginning that "we are bound by divine and Catholic faith to believe all those things which are contained in the word of God, whether it be Scripture or Tradition, and are proposed by the Church to be believed as divinely revealed, not only through solemn judgment but also through the ordinary and universal teaching office". Some commentators see here a sign of belief that the topic to be dealt with—no salvation outside the Church—has hitherto been taught more in the day to day teaching of the Church rather than in official definitions.

The next paragraph says that the Church has always taught and will always teach the infallible truth that there is no salvation outside the Church. It is a dogma, part of God's supernatural revelation through Jesus Christ. It must be understood, says the letter, "in the sense in which the Church itself understands it. For our Saviour gave the things contained in the deposit of faith to be explained by the Church's authority and not by private judgment." In other words, changing viewpoints of men and the different circumstances of succeeding generations do not change revealed truth.

The letter goes on: "Not the least important among the commandments of Christ is that one by which we are commanded to be incorporated by baptism into the mystical Body of Christ, which is the Church, and to remain united to Christ and his Vicar, through whom he himself governs the Church on earth in a visible manner." We recall how at the end of his public life our Lord ordered the Apostles to go out, baptize and make converts. The character of baptism makes one a member of Christ's true Church. One may be cast out from the Church by heresy, apostasy, schism or full excommunication. Our Lord imposed the duty of seeking and receiving baptism on all. We see in the Acts how the Apostles acted on this.

Next comes a most important statement: "No one will be saved who, knowing the Church to have been divinely established by Christ, nevertheless refuses to submit to the Church or withholds obedience" from the Pope. The Church was established by Christ "as a means of salvation, without which no one may be able to enter the kingdom of eternal glory". Now comes the distinction between what is necessary for salvation by God's command and what is necessary in itself, intrinsically. For example, there is no reason in itself why washing with water should be necessary for salvation; but God has made it necessary. So this letter says that the effects of the things which are necessary only by God's positive command can be obtained in certain circumstances when those things are "used only in intention and desire". God has willed this in his infinite mercy.

"In its own way, the same thing must be said about the Church", the letter goes on, "in so far as the Church itself is a general help of salvation. Therefore, in order to obtain eternal salvation, it is not always required to be incorporated into the Church *actually* as a member but it is required that at least he be united to it by intention and desire."

Thus, when it is impossible to be baptized, receive the sacraments or even get in touch with the Church—things which are necessary only by God's positive commandment—a man can still have faith, hope and charity. Those who accept God's teaching with divine faith and love God with supernatural charity must belong to God's kingdom on earth; but, if a man belongs to that supernatural kingdom at all, he belongs in some way to the visible Church, Christ's mystical Body.

Suprema haec sacra continues: "This desire [for membership of the Church] need not always be explicit, as it is in catechumens; but, when a person is involved in invincible ignorance, God accepts also an implicit intention which is so called because it is included in that good disposition of the soul whereby a person wishes his will to be conformed to God's will."

Noted commentators on this letter make the point that even the explicit desire of entering the Church does not give anybody a real though incomplete membership of it. So the phrase, "a real, though incomplete membership of the Church", is not in accordance with the teaching of the documents we have quoted, and especially this letter to the Archbishop of Boston. A man who wants to be a Catholic is not already a member of the Church in any way at all; he belongs to it in some way but he is not a member of it. How then does he belong to it? *Suprema haec sacra*, quoting Pope Pius XII on the mystical Body, says he belongs by desire or intention. And that is a thing vastly different from membership, even incomplete membership. "Only those who have received the laver of regeneration, who profess the true faith, who have not miserably separated themselves from the fabric of the Body or been expelled by legitimate authority by reason of very serious offences, are actually to be counted as members of the Church." Thus the Boston letter quoting Pope Pius XII.

The next paragraph is particularly valuable. *Suprema haec sacra* tells how Pius XII invites to unity "those who do not belong to the body of the Catholic Church" and "mentions those who are 'ordered to the Redeemer's mystical Body by a sort of unconscious desire and intention', and these he does not exclude from eternal salvation, but he asserts that they are in a condition in which 'they cannot be secure about their own eternal salvation', since 'they still lack so many and such great heavenly helps to salvation that can be enjoyed only in the Catholic Church'. " So the Pope reproves both those who say that all who are united to the Church by an implicit desire cannot be saved and, on the other hand, those who assert that men can be saved equally in every religion.

The last paragraph that concerns us in the letter to Boston is this: "Nor must we think that any kind of intention of entering the Church is sufficient in order that one may be saved. It is requisite that the intention by which one is ordered to the Church should be informed by perfect charity; and no explicit intention can produce its effect unless the man have supernatural faith." "Perfect charity" in this context means a genuine, supernatural love or friendship for God founded on divine faith.

It is possible to sum up the teaching of this very important document under the following ten points:

(1) "There is no salvation outside the Catholic Church": that is a dogma of the Catholic faith;

(2) It always has been taught, is being taught and always will be taught by the Church's authority, and infallibly;

(3) It must be understood as the Church's *magisterium* understands and explains it;

(4) By necessity of precept and necessity of means the Church is necessary for salvation;

(5) One who knows that Christ, God, founded the Church and yet refuses to join it or to remain within it cannot save his soul;

(6) The Church is a general and necessary means of salvation by God's own institution and not because of any intrinsic necessity; it is necessary because God in his wisdom and mercy made it necessary;

(7) For salvation one need not belong to the Church actually as a member but he must be "within" the Church, that is, it may sometimes be enough to belong to the Church in desire, *in voto*, to be saved;

(8) When a person is invincibly ignorant of the Church his desire for membership may be only implicit but it may be none the less effective;

(9) It is wrong to teach that those who have only an implicit desire of entering the Church cannot be saved; it is also wrong to teach that men may find salvation equally in any religion;

(10) For a desire to enter the Church to be effective, sufficient for salvation, it must be enlightened by supernatural faith and animated or motivated by perfect charity.

One of the most important doctrinal statements issued by the Church in the twentieth century is the encyclical of Pope Pius XII, known as *Humani generis*. In it he listed some false teachings, which he called "deadly fruit". One of them was this: "Some think they are not bound by the doctrine set forth a few years ago in our encyclical letter and based on the sources of revelation, [the doctrine] which teaches that Christ's mystical Body and the Catholic Roman Church are one and the same. Others reduce the need of belonging to the true Church in order to attain eternal salvation to an empty formula."

All the documents quoted show how constant the teaching of the Church on this subject has been. Since the encyclical on the mystical Body, *Humani generis*, and especially the splendid letter of the Holy Office to the Archbishop of Boston, there is no room for talk about the Pope ruling a visible Church while the mystical Body of Christ is a greater thing, an invisible Church, which includes all who have been validly baptized. Nor is there any excuse now to teach that while Catholics belong to the body, non-Catholics belong to the soul of the Church (terminology, incidentally, which arose from the misinterpretation of the teaching of St Robert Bellarmine). Nor can we say that, while the Church is the ordinary means of salvation, some may be saved by some other extraordinary means or that there are exceptions to the general law that all salvation comes through the Church, as, I am afraid, Newman taught in his *Letter to the Duke of Norfolk*. The truth is that God wants all men to be saved; he gives all enough grace to save their souls; nobody goes to hell except through his own deliberate, grave, unrepented sins committed in spite of the superabundant grace of God. Salvation comes only through the Church and it is found only in the Church.

So we see that the two statements: "Outside the Church there is no salvation" and "It is possible to be saved without being a member of the Church at the moment of death" are not contradictory. The answer to the apparent contradiction lies in this, that a man may gain the beatific vision if, without being actually a member of the Church, he sincerely desires, wills or intends to be within it, even though that desire is implicit. But the desire to be in the Church does not give one even partial membership of the Church. The desire to be a member of Parliament does not give one even one foot in the House of Commons. All who are baptized become members of the mystical Body, which is the Catholic Church, by their baptism. But if, when they come to the use of reason, they refuse to be members of the Church, even though their refusal be in good faith and sinless, they are cut off from membership. If they continue in good faith, loving God with supernatural charity and seeking his will, they have surely an implicit desire to join the Church. It is a desire "within the folds", that is, implicit in their desire always to do God's will. This desire, by God's mercy, is sufficient for salvation.

The reason for this is that actual membership of the Church is necessary for salvation not by any intrinsic necessity but by God's command. Supernatural faith, hope and love are necessary by intrinsic necessity, that is, from the very nature of things, but not actual membership of the Church. There can be no substitute for faith, hope and charity as the absolutely necessary requisites for being saved.

How, then, does the possession of the three theological virtues put one "within" the Church, without necessarily being a member of the Church, in the way that is necessary for salvation? Because these three virtues, faith, hope and charity, enter into the very composition of the Church itself; they are the inward, spiritual bond of unity; they join men to God and to each other; they are absolutely, intrinsically necessary components of God's earthly kingdom. There could be no Church without them.

This union through the possession of the theological virtues is an inward one. In addition to it there is an outward bond which comes, not from intrinsic necessity like the inward bond, but from the direct command of God. It is actual membership of his visible Church under his earthly representative, the Pope.

God has been pleased to permit some people to enjoy the benefits of membership of the organized, visible Church when it is genuinely impossible for them to become actual members and remain members. The reason for this, let it be repeated, is because the actual constitution of the Church of the New Testament under a visible hierarchy is a matter of God's positive command only and not of absolute, intrinsic necessity. So those who die in a state of grace, actually possessing supernatural faith, hope and charity, are within the Church by desire and that implicit desire is enough to gain them salvation. It comes from the Church; there is no salvation outside the

Church; they had the essential, constituent, element of the union of God's people; implicitly they desired the additional element made necessary by God's command; by their charity they fought the Church's battle amongst men. "If any one love me, he will keep my word, and my Father will love him, and we will come to him, and will make our abode with him", said our Lord (John 14. 23).

16

"HE WAS IN THE WORLD, AND THE WORLD WAS MADE BY HIM, AND THE WORLD KNEW HIM NOT"

(John 1. 10)

ST JOHN is speaking again of the Word. From the world's foundation, he says, the Word was in the world, upholding it, conserving and ordering it by his providence. His phrases recall the opening of the Epistle to the Hebrews: "God . . . hath spoken to us by his Son . . . by whom also he made the world. Who being the brightness of his glory, and the figure of his substance, and upholding all things by the might of his power. . . . " (Heb. 1. 1-3). But most of all, this verse echoes the terrible words of St Paul in his Epistle to the Romans:

> God's anger is being revealed from heaven;
> his anger against the impiety and wrong-doing of the men whose wrong-doing denies his truth its full scope.
> The knowledge of God is clear to their minds;
> God himself has made it clear to them;
> from the foundations of the world men have caught sight of his invisible nature, his eternal power and his divineness, as they are known through his creatures.
> There is no excuse for them;
> although they had the knowledge of God, they did not honour him or give thanks to him as God;
> they became fantastic in their notions, and their senseless hearts grew benighted;
> they who claimed to be so wise, turned fools and exchanged the glory of the imperishable God for representations of perishable man, of bird and beast and reptile.
> That is why God abandoned their lustful hearts to filthy practices. . . .
> They had exchanged God's truth for a lie, reverencing and worshipping the creature in preference to the Creator (blessed is he for ever, Amen);

and, in return, God abandoned them to passions which brought dishonour to themselves. . . .

And as they scorned to keep God in their view, so God has abandoned them to a frame of mind worthy of all scorn . . .

without prudence, without honour, without love, without loyalty, without pity. . . .

Yet, with the just decree of God before their minds, they never grasped the truth that those who so live are deserving of death (Rom. 1. 18-32).

We will come back to this extract after we have thought a little about the facts of creation and providence. We believe that everything that exists outside God was, as to its whole substance, produced out of nothing by God. The very name, Jahweh, meaning "He who truly is" or "He whose essential property is to be", which was revealed by God to Moses from the burning bush (Exod. 3. 13-16; cf. 6. 3-8), was applied exclusively to God, and no less than 6823 times in the Old Testament. Other things are called nothing in comparison with him. It is not very hard to apply the name to God in the sense of "He who gives being", the Creator. "I am the Lord, whose name tells of power; I will not let the boast that is mine pass to another", cried Isaias (42. 7). "All the nations of the world shrink, in his presence, to nothing, emptiness, a very void, beside him" (Is. 40. 17).

As a substitute for the unutterable Jahweh the Jews called God *Adonai*, the majestic master, the Lord. "Thine are the heavens, thine the earth; author, thou, of the world and all it holds. The north wind and the south are of thy fashioning; thy name wakes the glad echoes of Thabor and Hermon. God of the strong arm, the sure, the uplifted hand. . . . (Ps. 88. 12-14). The same high thought is found in the prayer of Mardochaeus, Esther's guardian: "Heaven and earth and all that heaven's vault contains is thy creation; thy dominion is universal, thy royalty unchallengeable" (Esther 13. 10-11).

Jewish as well as Christian people have always believed that the creation of the world from nothing is expressly taught in the opening words of the Bible: "God, at the beginning of time, created heaven and earth" (Gen. 1. 1). Nothing from which the earth and the heavens, the whole universe, were made is named.

The royal psalmist has the same meaning when he proclaims: "Our help is in the name of the Lord, who made heaven and earth. Blessed is he whose helper is the God . . . who made heaven and earth, the sea and all the things that are in them. He spoke and they were made; he commanded and they came into being" (Ps. 123. 8; 145. 6; 32. 9).

Remember the words of counsel the mother of the Machabees gave to her youngest son: "Nine months in the womb I bore thee, three years at the breast fed thee, reared thee to be what thou art; and now, my son, this boon grant me. Look round at heaven and earth, and all they contain; bethink thee that all this, and mankind too, God made out of nothing" (II Mach. 7. 27-28). In much the same way the Wise Man turns our minds to God's wisdom, might and love: "Death was never of God's fashioning; not for his pleasure does life cease to be; what meant his creation, but that all created things should have being? No breed has he created on earth but for its thriving; none carries in itself the seeds of its own destruction" (Wis. 1. 13-14). Similarly St Paul quoted to the converts in Rome two instances of God's omnipotence, his power to give life to the dead and his power to call non-existent things into being: on them Abraham's faith rested (Rom. 4. 17).

Not only did God create the world, which is the fruit of his infinite wisdom and goodness, he also keeps all created things in existence; he preserves them from relapsing into nothingness. The Wise Man prayed to God: "All things thou lovest, nor holdest any of thy creatures in abhorrence: hate and create thou couldst not, nor does aught abide save at thy will, whose summoning word holds them in being. They are thine, and thou sparest them; all things that live thou lovest, thou, the Master of them all" (Wis. 11. 25-27). Our Lord, too, made a profound revelation, St Augustine tells us, when he said: "My Father has never ceased working, and I too must be at work." He revealed that the Father and Son were united in the creation of the world and its government. In the context he was telling his critics that God continues to work, even on the Sabbath, preserving, holding together, conserving creation, governing the world, moving the heavens, nourishing and feeding every creature. If he were to withdraw his preserving power all creation would crumble. Truly can St Paul write: "In him all

created things took their being, heavenly and earthly, visible
and invisible; they were all created through him and in him;
he (i.e. the Son of God) takes precedency of all, and in him all
subsist" (Col. 1. 16). "All creation depends for its support on his
enabling word" (Heb. 1. 3). To the men of Athens he preached:
"After all, he is not far from any one of us; it is in him that we
live, and move, and have our being" (Acts 17. 28).

What a tremendous thought it is that God co-operates immediately in every act of his creatures! What else can be the
meaning of those last words quoted from St Paul's sermon at the
Areopagus? "What achievement of ours but the doing of it is
thine?" was the prayer of Isaias. It is not for me here to discuss
the manner of this co-operation; for centuries Thomists and
Mollinists have been in controversy about it. The fact is there
that all created being depends on God; activity has a real being
which is distinct from the power from which it flows. Because
it has being it must, of course, depend on the cause of all being,
which is God.

Through his providence God protects and guides all that he
has created. From all eternity infinite Wisdom, Power and Love
had a plan for this world; he knew it and he willed it. In time
he fulfilled it. By providence we mean that eternal world-
plan of God and its fulfilment in time. Scripture is permeated
by belief in it. The Old Testament could hardly emphasize
more God's special provision for his chosen people and even for
individuals, like Joseph, Moses and Tobias. He "made great
and little alike, that cares alike for all" says the Book of Wisdom
(6. 8). And, in majestic words, "Bold is her sweep from world's
end to world's end, and everywhere her gracious ordering mani-
fests itself" (Wis. 8. 1). The reference is to divine Wisdom
which, the Holy Spirit tells us, does all "in exact measure . . .
nicely calculated and weighed" (Wis. 11. 21). "God there is
none save thou, that hast a whole world for thy province. . . .
Nay, here is one that will go a-voyaging, the wild waves for his
pathway, and perishable wood to carry him, yet he makes his
prayer to a piece of wood more perishable yet! As for the ship's
timbers, it was man's covetousness that made need of them, and
man's skill that fashioned them; but it is thy fatherly Providence that brings her safe to port; thou hast made the sea into
a high road men may travel without harm, as if thou wouldst

prove to us how strong is thy protection, though the sailor have little skill" (Wis. 12. 13; 14. 1-4).

Nowhere in literature is there a more moving reminder of God's loving providence, extending to even the most insignificant of creatures, than in our blessed Lord's sermon on the hillside:

I say to you, then, do not fret over your life, how to support it with food and drink;

over your body, how to keep it clothed.

Is not life itself a greater gift than food, the body than clothing?

See how the birds of the air never sow, or reap, or gather grain into barns, and yet your heavenly Father feeds them; have you not an excellence beyond theirs?

Can any one of you, for all his anxiety, add a cubit's growth to his height?

And why should you be anxious over clothing? See how the wild lilies grow; they do not toil or spin; and yet I tell you that even Solomon in all his glory was not arrayed as one of these.

If God, then, so clothes the grasses of the field, which today live and will feed the oven tomorrow, will he not be much more ready to clothe you, men of little faith?

Do not fret, then, asking, What are we to eat? or What are we to drink? or How shall we find clothing? It is for the heathen to busy themselves over such things; you have a Father in heaven who knows that you need them all (Matt. 6. 25-34).

Even greater detail is in the Master's instructions to his disciples: "Are not sparrows sold two for a penny? And yet it is impossible for one of them to fall to the ground without your heavenly Father's will. And as for you, he takes every hair of your head into his reckoning" (Matt. 10. 29-30).

Think of all these things—God, Creation and Providence— and you realize what St John meant when he wrote, "He was in the world, and the world was made by him."

Every passing year, yes, and almost every new day reveals to us some startling scientific discovery. Men are discovering fresh wonders in what God has made. So rapid is their progress that it is impossible for any one man to keep pace with them all. No branch of science is exempt from the progress. The more sensational the progress the greater is its testimony to the wisdom of the Creator. For advance of science depends on knowledge of the laws of science; and the laws of science cannot be without the Maker of law. In the years ahead new and more wonderful discoveries and progress will be made; no doubt if we could see them now we might say, "Such things cannot be." Yet, one and all, they are simply the discovery of the wonders God has hidden in the universe he has created; they are evidence of his wisdom, his power and his providence. They are all the gifts of his love. Only because he wills it are they known by men. Those who think see in each new showing of order in created matter reiterated support for the traditional proofs of God's existence.

"He was in the world"; how marvellously that is described in the psalm: "Where can I go to take refuge from thy spirit, to hide from thy view? If I should climb up to heaven, thou art there; if I sink down to the world beneath, thou art present still. If I could wing my way eastwards, or find a dwelling beyond the western sea, still would I find thee beckoning to me, thy right hand upholding me. Or perhaps I would think to bury myself in darkness; night should surround me, friendlier than day; but no, darkness is no hiding place from thee, with thee night shines clear as day itself; light and dark are one" (Ps. 138. 7-12). He always was in the world; every tiniest motion has depended on God. Not a hair blows in the wind, not a tree falls to the ground, not a thought enters the mind of man but he who is everywhere by his essence, his presence and his power knows it.

Now we return to the passage I quoted from St Paul's letter to the Christians in Rome. It applies directly to the men of his own day; but if we think of it in terms of our day we shall have much food for thought.

St Paul argues vigorously and concisely. He says that God's wrath is revealed in the punishment he inflicts on ungodliness, in appalling blindness, which leads to idolatry and immorality. The cause of that anger is the heathen's sin: they have both known God and disregarded him. St Paul makes it clear that all have sinned, that all are inexcusable because all, the exception proves the rule, have refused God whom they know that honour which is his right. He is not referring only to the "thinkers" of the time; they may be more guilty; he is speaking of everybody.

He says several times very clearly that the heathen knew God. He does not say that it was possible for them to know him or that they could have known him; he says and repeats that they did know him. "They keep truth captive in injustice", he writes; by their wickedness they render it dumb and inoperative. The Knox translation—"denies the truth its full scope"—is rather weak. The Westminster version speaks of those who "in wickedness are repressing the truth". The truth in question is the knowledge of God. They have it, at least to some extent, but they keep it captive.

The next verse is admirably rendered by Knox: "The knowledge of God is clear to their minds; God himself made it clear to them." But their sin is that "they did not honour him or give thanks to him as God". There is the sin: they knew God but did not honour him. He is referring to the great mass of the non-Jewish people. They had real light about God but they did not worship him. The original text makes it quite clear that they knew him unreservedly but acted in a way contrary to their knowledge. They did evil things or approved of others doing evil things.

How did the pagans receive this light? How can they be so guilty? A modern author translates the Apostle's words by writing that they are "without a rag of an excuse". St Paul gives the answer: "The invisible things of God, his eternal power and divinity, intellectually perceived in his works, are clearly seen in the creation of the world" (v. 20). Note how he specifies the divine attributes reflected in the world: his power, his eternity, his divinity. For him God's creatures prove God; they are also a kind of mirror which reflects the divine attributes. "Look at the universe", he says in effect; "there you find evidence that an all-powerful Creator exists. It must always have existed. It could not produce itself; it is eternal."

In the next chapter St Paul will show how the natural law is engraved in men's hearts in indelible characters (Rom. 2. 11-16). The knowledge of the law and its sanction implies belief that there is a Lawgiver. He is God. So the heathen knew God as first Cause and supreme Lawgiver. Relying on this text the Vatican Council has defined that God *can* be known by man with certainty, by the light of reason alone, by means of his creation, as Creator and Lord, as the only and true God. St Paul goes further than that. He does not say only that the Gentiles could have known God in this way, but that they did know him.

Read again through what follows in the quotation from the letter to the Roman Christians and you see the terrible things which followed the disregard of God whom the Gentiles knew through reason. What is meant by the statement, thrice repeated, that God "abandoned them"? Does God really abandon the souls he loves? Perhaps we can think in terms of three stages of abandonment by God. In the first place, God must permit every evil which befalls; in the second, he may withdraw some of the chosen graces he has previously offered in vain, but still leaving the individual free, with sufficient grace to avoid grave evil; and in the third place, God withdraws his graces as a punishment for man's malevolence, ingratitude and obstinacy. Thus does godlessness grow in the world. Men reject the super-generous graces God gives them; he leaves them then with the ordinary graces necessary to remain in his favour; but these, too, they reject and soon find themselves completely turned against God. Left to themselves they fall into all the wickedness which St Paul so graphically describes. Lest we should think that those who have become so degenerate are excusable, he comes back with yet another affirmation that "those who so live are deserving of death".

What we have to ask ourselves is whether the men of our day are better placed than those of whom St Paul writes? It is a grim picture. Here we are thinking of the non-Christians. In the next verse we shall think about those who are "his own". According to reliable estimates the non-Christian population of the world is approaching two thousand million, more than twice the number of Christians, and nearly four times the number of Catholics. In view of what St Paul wrote we cannot be very hopeful about their eternal salvation. How many of them have accepted the light God gives them "through his creatures"? How many honour the Lawgiver, having discovered the law written in their hearts? How many of them have "exchanged God's truth for a lie" and worship the creature in preference to the Creator? Is it any wonder that the saints of every century have burned with zeal to convert the pagan? Is it surprising that almost every Pope in modern times has appealed to generous young people to devote their lives to missionary work?

We must not presume too much on the often quoted words of St Paul to Timothy: "It is his will that all men should be saved, and be led to recognize the truth" (II Tim. 1. 4). The last thing God could desire would be that these inspired words should be used as an excuse for minimizing efforts for the salvation of the souls of pagans. Certainly God wills that all men should be saved; surely he gives each enough grace to save his soul; but how many today accept that grace? The missionary strivings of the Church for twenty centuries are sufficient proof that Popes and saints have been convinced that unbelievers are in serious danger of losing their souls. Recall the burning words of the prayer of St Francis Xavier: "Permit not, I beseech thee, O Lord, that thy Son should be any longer despised by unbelievers, but do thou graciously except the prayers of holy men and of the Church, the Spouse of thy most holy Son, and be mindful of thy mercy. Forget their idolatry and unbelief. . . . "

Similarly in the exhortations of Popes. There is never any presumption there that large numbers of pagans are going to save their souls purely by God's mercy and their own good faith. For example, in one of the most celebrated missionary encyclicals of all time, Pope Benedict XV used these words:

. . . the duty of . . . delivering them [i.e. the natives] from the cruel slavery of demons. . . . There are still vast numbers of the human race who are yet sitting in darkness and in the shadow of death. We have compassion on the miserable lot of this immense multitude of souls. . . . The head of a mission . . . is bound to seek the eternal salvation of all who live in that region. . . . What class of men is in graver need of brotherly aid than the heathen, who, since they know not God, are bound by blind and unbridled lusts and enslaved in the worst kind of slavery, that of the devil? . . . How much more strictly is the the law of charity to be observed in this case, where it is a matter not only of giving assistance in hunger and want and a multitude of other miseries, but also, and primarily, of rescuing so vast a number of souls from the arrogant dominion of Satan.*

* Encyclical, *The Missions*, C.T.S. edition, pp. 5-22.

Those words could not be applied to men in good faith or invincible ignorance. It could not be said that those who were not guilty are under the cruel slavery of demons, in the shadow of death, enslaved in the worst kind of slavery, that of the devil, and under the arrogant dominion of Satan. We cannot allow presumption of God's mercy to amount to a denial of St Paul's clear teaching concerning the pagans, that "the knowledge of God *is clear to their minds; God himself has made it clear to them;* from the foundations of the world men have caught sight of his invisible nature, his eternal power and his divineness, as they are known through his creatures. *There is no excuse for them*" (Rom. 1. 19 ff.).

If this is true of the heathen in far off missionary lands, how much more does it apply to many of our contemporaries in these advanced nations who call themselves humanists, thinkers, philosophers or progressives and somehow or other manage to get enormous publicity for themselves and their always "leftish" ideals? They may now be in good faith but is it possible, in view of St Paul's strong, inspired words to maintain that they are without guilt? If the heathen of 2,000 years ago was without excuse, is it conceivable that intelligent men educated in modern universities can be more favourably placed in regard to the prospects of salvation? Calamitous, indeed, it would be to fail to pray and work for them on the grounds that their sincerity will save them. These men and women, who in some strange manner seem to have formed an unholy alliance amongst themselves so that they support the same minority causes, attack the same traditional beliefs and are particularly vehement in their hatred of the Church and everything associated with it, are a most powerful and particularly dangerous element in modern society. They should be the object of our very special prayers.

"He was in the world . . . and the world knew him not"; how pathetic those words are and, when we probe their implications, how frightening. Meditation on them will cause us to attach ourselves ever more faithfully to God's will, manifested in his loving providence. Devotion to divine providence, because it is centred in the will of infinite Goodness and Love, is a high-road to holiness. It involves humility, self-surrender, obedience, patience and, above all, charity—humility, because it recognizes that all one is and has comes from God, self-surrender, because it sees him as the absolute Lord and Master, obedience, because his will is infinite majesty, wisdom and goodness, patience, because all that befalls is by the permission of an infinitely kind Father, and charity, because every moment of life is spent under the care of infinite Love.

"The world knew him not", yes, and still knows him not. "There is no excuse for them"—those words of St Paul vibrate within us; "the knowledge of God is clear to their minds; God himself has made it clear; they had knowledge of God, they did not honour him. . . . God abandoned their lustful hearts. . . . They exchanged God's truth for a lie. . . . God abandoned them . . . they scorned to keep God in their view. . . . God abandoned them to a frame of mind worthy of all scorn, without prudence, without honour, without love, without loyalty, without pity . . . deserving of death." Were more terrible words ever written? Were they ever more applicable than in this atomic age in which, according to Pope Pius XI, men are more neglectful of God than at any time since the deluge? Such sombre thoughts drive us to passionate prayer, sincere penance, inspiring example and untiring apostolate.

"Almighty and everlasting God, whose will is that all men should be saved and that none should perish, look upon the souls that are deceived by the guile of Satan, in order that the hearts of them that are gone astray may put aside all perverseness and turn to the knowledge and love of thee.

"O Mary, most merciful, the refuge of sinners, hear our supplications and pray to thy Son, that Almighty God may take away all iniquity from the hearts of the heathen; that, having forsaken their idols, they may turn to the living and true God, and his only Son, Christ our Lord and God. Amen."

17

"HE CAME UNTO HIS OWN, AND HIS OWN RECEIVED HIM NOT"

(John 1. 11)

WHAT a pathetic lament this is! The natural reaction nowadays is to think of it purely in connection with the visible coming of Christ, the Incarnate Word. But St John seems to have a much wider vision. "His own" means his own domain and his own people, Israel and the Jews, and the coming to which St John refers embraces all the dealings of the Word with them, culminating in the Incarnation.

God freely chose Abraham's descendants to be his own in a special way. They alone of all the nations of the earth knew and worshipped the true God; revealed religion was deposited with them; they had a special mission. "My covenant shall pledge them prosperity, a covenant that shall never be revoked; I will make them . . . and give them increase, and set up my sanctuary in their midst forever. My tabernacle over them; they are my people and I their God; proof to all the world that I, the Lord, have set Israel apart, I that dwell apart in their midst forever" (Ezech. 37. 26–28). Thus did God speak of them.

In the ninth chapter of his letter to the Christians in Rome St Paul gives a list without parallel in the Bible of the privileges of Israel. It is worth our while to study it, because it brings home to us another aspect of God's love and mercy. Is it not indescribable generosity to live amongst men and die for them when the people he chose as his own and so specially graced had, throughout the centuries, been so unfaithful to him? Here are St Paul's words: "They are Israelites, adopted as God's sons; the visible presence, and the covenant, and the giving of the law, and the Temple worship, and the promises, are their inheritance; the patriarchs belong to them, and theirs is the human stock from which Christ came; Christ, who rules as God over all things, blessed for ever, Amen" (Rom. 9. 4–5).

Note how the Apostle lists no less than nine special privileges
which God's favour had given to Israel. The first was the very
name "Israel". Remember how Jacob wrestled with an angel
who said to him: "Jacob is no name for thee, thou shalt be
called Israel, one that prevails with God" (Gen. 32. 28). And
how the psalmist sings: "The Lord took Juda for his sanctuary
and Israel for his own dominion" (Ps. 113. 2). The writer of
Ecclesiasticus strikes the same chord: "To every Gentile people
he [God] has given a ruler of its own; Israel alone is exempt,
marked down as God's patrimony" (17. 15), the Saviour's
portion. The name is applied by St Paul to the Church "God's
true Israel" (Gal. 6.16).

Secondly, the Israelites had been adopted as God's sons, not
in the sense in which St Paul could say that "the spirit of
adoption makes us cry out, Abba, Father" (Rom. 8. 15), but
in the sense explained by God to Moses: "Israel is my first-born
son" (Exod. 4. 22), and he explained to his people: "Learn to
carry yourselves as the children of the Lord your God. . . .
What, reckless still, inconsiderate still! Is this the return thou
wouldst make to that father who calls thee his own?" (Deut.
14. 1; 32. 6). When Jeremias prophesied Israel's return from
banishment he put into God's mouth these moving words:
"Weeping they shall come, and I, moved to pity, will bring
them to their journey's end; from mountain stream to mountain
stream I will lead them, by a straight road where there is no
stumbling; I, Israel, thy father again, and thou, Ephraim, my
first-born son" (Jer. 31. 9).

The next privilege mentioned by St Paul is that of seeing
something of God's glory in his special presence at Sinai as the
inspired word tells us: "Even as Aaron was speaking to the
assembled Israelites, they looked round towards the desert, and
saw the glory of the Lord revealed there in a cloud. . . . The
mountain was veiled in cloud; for six days the glory of the Lord
abode there on Sinai, wrapping it in cloud, and on the seventh
day, from the heart of that darkness, the Lord called to him.
To the Israelites, as they looked upon it, this glory of the Lord
wore the semblance of a fire, burning there on the summit of
the mountain" (Exod. 16. 10; 24. 16–18). Later the sign of
God's visible presence overspread the tabernacle "and it was
filled with the brightness of the Lord's presence", so radiant

that Moses could not enter the tabernacle, radiant, says the inspired writer, with the majesty of God. Magnificently the sacred scribe describes how the cloud of the divine presence enveloped the first Temple in Jerusalem: "The whole of the Lord's house was wreathed in cloud; lost in that cloud the priests could not wait upon the Lord with his accustomed service; his own glory was there, filling his own house" (Exod. 8. 11). God has, indeed, taken possession of his Temple.

The fourth mark of God's favour was the divine covenants or agreements made by God first with Noe, Abraham and Isaac and then with Israel as a nation. Moses was the mediator. The book of Exodus tells how, in a spirit of reverential fear and holiness, the people were to prepare themselves for this covenant. Let us read the inspired description of its inauguration: "Morning broke, and all at once thunder was heard, lightning shone out, and the mountain was covered with thick mist; loud rang the trumpet blast, and the people in the camp were dismayed. But Moses brought them out from the camp itself to meet the Lord, and they stood there close by the spurs of the mountain. The whole of mount Sinai was by now wreathed in smoke, where the Lord had come down with fire about him, so that smoke went up as if from a furnace; it was a mountain full of terrors. Louder yet grew the noise of the trumpet, longer its blast; and then Moses spoke to the Lord, and the Lord's voice was heard in answer" (Exod. 19. 16–19). It was concluded by sacrifices, one half of the blood of them being sprinkled on the altar and the other half on the people, with the words: "Here is the blood of the covenant which the Lord makes with you, in accordance with all these words of his" (Exod. 24. 8).

God made the covenant with Israel to separate it from the pagan and idolatrous nations, to nominate it freely as the true bearer and guardian of revelation and the prophecies concerning the Messias and thus to make it God's special possession, "a royal priesthood, a consecrated nation" (Exod. 19. 5). There was nothing one-sided about it. In return for this special love, Israel was to observe God's Ten Commandments, practise the virtues and try to attain national holiness. Covenants were made again with Phinees when he stopped the licentious idolatry of Beelphegor (Num. 25. 1–18), by Josue at Sichem (Jos. 24. 25), with David as related in Psalm 88, by Joiada, the High Priest, when he had Joas recognized as king (IV Kings 11. 17), by King Ezechias when he opened the Temple which Achaz had closed (II Par. 29. 10), by King Josias after his successful efforts to eradicate the idolatry which had been allowed in Juda for too long (IV Kings 23. 3) and by the priest and scribe, Esdras, who led the second group of exiles from Babylon to Jerusalem in 458 B.C.

The Old Testament often has as its theme the teaching of the prophets that Israel was breaking the covenant and their foretelling of its dissolution. It would be punished, but there would be a future restoration, a New Covenant, which was to be primarily spiritual, as well as universal and perpetual. Isaias, Jeremias and Ezechiel are all emphatic about it. The fulfilment of the promises God made in the covenants is salvation through the Messias: "Blindness has fallen upon a part of Israel, but only until the tale of the Gentile nations is complete; then the whole of Israel will find salvation, as we read in Scripture, a deliverer shall come from Sion, to rid Jacob of his unfaithfulness; and this shall be the fulfilment of my covenant with them" (Rom. 11. 27). St Paul there formally predicts that when the Gentiles have been converted Israel will be saved and he quotes from Isaias (59. 20; 27. 9) to prove it. The author of the letter to the Jewish Christians says explicitly that the New Covenant promised to the Jews was inaugurated by God through the Mediator, Jesus Christ (Heb. 8. 10; 10. 16).

Returning to St Paul, we find that the next of the privileges of the Jews he mentions is the Law of Moses; then comes the worship of God, the liturgy carried out first according to the law of Moses in the tabernacle and then in the Temple. After that are mentioned the Messianic promises, which are surely one of the greatest of the treasures given by God to his chosen people. To this day they are an admirable means of elevating the heart and mind to God in prayer.

There will always be some lack of agreement as to how many texts of the Old Testament are prophetic of our Lord. The Jewish rabbis say there are nearly 460; a well-known Catholic scholar recently gave his opinion that the number should be restricted to 50. Nor should we forget that, in addition to the directly prophetical texts, which most scholars would estimate

as being about 120, there are those which are called typical.
They have two meanings, the literal and obvious one, which
applies to the words in their original setting, and a typical sense,
which is a further meaning to be realized later in Christ. Most
modern writers name about thirty such passages.

To survey all the prophecies of the Old Testament here
would be far beyond my purpose, but, as we are thinking about
how the Word of God came to his own people and how they
rejected him, it seems necessary to indicate just a little of the
more important aspects of prophecy. There are certain important passages which contain the key truths. The first is in the
third chapter of the Bible, the celebrated *protoevangelium*: "I will
establish a feud between thee and the woman, between thy
offspring and hers; she [better, he] is to crush thy head, whilst
thou dost lie in ambush at her [or his] heels" (Gen. 3. 15).
Here is the first good news of Christ's conquest of Satan and,
incidentally, a prophecy of his Mother's Immaculate Conception, since the enmity between her and Satan is said to be as
complete as that between Christ and Satan. The next key
passage is the twelfth chapter of the Book of Exodus, the story
of the origin of the Paschal Lamb and the feast. After that we
pass to Moses' promise that God would raise up a line of
prophets, culminating in the Great Prophet, by which he would
communicate with his people, a passage to which there are
several references in the New Testament (Deut. 18. 18; cf.
Jn. 6. 14; 1. 45; Acts 3. 22; 7. 37; Heb. 1. 1–2).

Now comes the promise of the prophet Nathan of an
"eternal" kingdom to the house of David, which has always
been understood to mean that the Messias would be descended
from King David and would exercise spiritual dominion for all
time (II Kings 7. 13, 16). After that we turn to the prophecies
in the Psalms, the most important being the second, which
foretells Christ's universal and divine kingship; the fifteenth,
with its statement of belief in the resurrection of the body
(which St Peter quotes to prove our Lord's resurrection, Acts
2. 25–31); the twenty-first, which so vividly describes the details
of our Lord's passion, death and resurrection; the thirtieth, with
its prayer of confidence quoted by our Lord on the cross; the
thirty-ninth, on Christ's obedience (quoted in the Epistle to
the Hebrews, 10. 5–12); the forty-fourth, foretelling Christ as

the bridegroom of the Church (also quoted in the letter to the Jewish Christians, Hebrews 1. 8–9); the seventy-first, which depicts Christ as the universal, eternal, just and peaceful King; the eighty-eighth, known for its emphasis of our Lord's Davidic kingship to which the announcing angel alluded (Luke 1. 32–33); and, perhaps the best known of all because of its place in Sunday Vespers, the hundred and ninth, in which Christ's kingship, priesthood and divine sonship are foretold, as he himself argued (Matt. 2. 42–46).

The Book of Proverbs speaks of Christ as eternal Wisdom, the Master-workman at the Creation (Prov. 8. 22–36). The seventh chapter of the Book of Wisdom is important in connection with the divinity of Christ, to prove which it is quoted in the letter to the Hebrews and equivalently in that to the Colossians (Heb. 1. 3; Col. 1. 15). Its second chapter anticipates the Son of God's passion and death, while the twenty-fourth chapter of Ecclesiasticus pre-figures the coming of Christ, the Wisdom of the Father, to dwell on earth.

The most important chapters of Isaias are the seventh, with its well-known prophecy of our blessed Lady as the virgin Mother of God; the ninth, speaking of Christ, prince of peace; the eleventh, telling of the seven gifts of the Holy Ghost; the forty-second, with its insistence on the gentleness, humility and obedience of the Saviour; the forty-ninth, also referring to Christ's obedience; the fiftieth and fifty-second, which foretell our Lord's confidence and constancy as he suffered death for our sins; and the sixty-first and sixty-third where the divine, universal and all-embracing vocation of the Messias is stressed as God's Champion bringing deliverance to men.

Eight more key prophecies should be mentioned. One is the unique reference in Jeremias to the new and eternal covenant (Jer. 31. 31–34); the second and third are passages from Ezechiel concerning Christ as the true, Davidic shepherd of Israel with his own special flock (Ezech. 34. 16, 23; 37. 24–25); the fourth is the famous words of Daniel foretelling the Son of Man's eternal reign (Dan. 7. 13–14); the fifth is that of Micheas to the effect that the Messias would be born in Bethlehem (Mich. 5. 2–14; cf. Matt. 2. 6); the sixth and seventh are from Zacharias foretelling the entry of the Prince of Peace into Jerusalem and the repentance of the Jews when they witnessed the events of the first Good Friday on Calvary (Zach. 9. 9; 12. 10; cf. Matt. 21. 5; John 19. 37; Apoc. 1. 7); and the last key prophecy is that of the last of the prophets about the Mass (Mal. 1. 11).

To go over the above passages carefully and prayerfully will reveal something more of the poignancy of St John's lament, that "He came unto his own and his own received him not". Only when we study the amazing detail of Old Testament prophecy can we have anything like an adequate conception of the appalling blindness and malice of the Jewish leaders in rejecting their Saviour.

The eighth of the chosen people's special privileges was that God raised up amongst them "the fathers", Abraham, Isaac and Jacob. St Peter proclaimed this after curing the lame man at the Beautiful Gate of the Temple: "Men of Israel, he said, why does this astonish you? . . . It is the God of Abraham and Isaac and Jacob, the God of our forefathers, who has thus brought honour to his Son Jesus. You gave him up and disowned him. . . . You disowned the holy, the just, and asked for the pardon of a murderer, while you killed the author of life" (Acts 3. 12–15).

The last and crowning privilege of the Israelites was that the Messias was one of their race. But in spite of all their privileges the Jews rejected Christ. The more we ponder it the more astonishing and mysterious it becomes. How our Lord himself lamented their blindness: "The heart of this people has become dull, their ears are slow to listen, and they keep their eyes shut, so that they may never see with those eyes, or hear with those ears, or understand with that heart, and turn back to me, and win healing from me" (Matt. 13. 15). He was referring here to the prophecy of Isaias (6. 9) but he toned its language down. He did not wish them to think that their failure to receive his teaching was due to some arbitrary decree of God's and not their own fault. Nor did he speak to them in parables principally to punish them but rather because, having already rejected the sufficient light all Jews received from God, they would be unable to grasp the full meaning of his teaching. Those who were well disposed, like the Apostles, did understand his message. He tried to appeal to them again when he said: "It is only in his own country, in his own home, that a prophet

goes unhonoured" and St Matthew adds, "Nor did he do many
miracles there, because of their unbelief" (Matt. 13. 57–58).

Our Lord's words about the Jews denote a general attitude,
not just resentment at certain incidents by individuals. For
example: "The Jews took occasion to rouse ill-will against
Jesus for doing such things on the sabbath. And Jesus answered
them. . . . The Father who sent me has himself borne witness
to me. You have always been deaf to his voice, blind to the
vision of him, and his word is not continually present in your
hearts; that is why you will not trust one whom he has sent.
You pore over the scriptures, thinking to find eternal life in
them (and indeed, it is of these I speak as bearing witness to
me): but you will not come to me to find life. . . . I can see
you have no love of God in your hearts" (John 5. 16, 38–42).

Writing to the Thessalonians St Paul has an unparalleled
outburst against the Jews. He writes of them as "the men who
killed the Lord Jesus and the prophets, and persecuted us;
the men who displease God and show themselves the enemies
of mankind. . . . They must always be filling up the measure
of their sins, and now it is God's final vengeance that has fallen
upon them" (I Thess. 2. 14 16). The Apostle is so sure of the
terrible penalties awaiting the Jews that he writes as if they had
already happened. What are they? Traditionally three are
named in this connection: eternal damnation, for the unre-
pentant who deserve it; the destruction of Jerusalem, which
occurred about twenty years after St Paul's letter, and the
exclusion of the Jews from the Church.

This very sad fact, the rejection of infinite Love consistently
through the centuries by his own people, ought to make us think
hard and long about the situation amongst Christians in the
world today. Perhaps it is true that Christ still comes to his
own and his own receive him not. Compare the privileges we
have been considering of the Jews with those God has given
to us, and see how the majority of Christians in the world
repay God for them.

The first privilege was the name "Israel"; we are twice
called Christians in the New Testament, first by Herod Agrippa
(Acts 26. 28) and then by St Peter (I Peter 4. 16); we are known,
too, as disciples, i.e. of Christ (Acts 9. 25; 11. 29; 14. 21),
brethren (Acts 9. 30; 10. 24; 11. 12; 15. 1), saints (Acts 9. 13,

32, 41; 26. 10), faithful and believers. St Ignatius of Antioch was the first to name us "Catholic". All these names have a meaning of which we ought to be proud and for which we should thank God.

Secondly our adoption far surpasses that of the Israelites, making us children of God, brethren of Jesus and sharers in the divine nature, as we have seen elsewhere in these conferences. Thirdly, instead of the presence of God in a cloud we have his real, true and substantial presence under the appearances of bread and wine; we have, too, his mystical presence in the Church, his Body; and we believe that he lives in the soul of every person in the state of grace. Fourthly, the covenants between God and the Jews have been succeeded by the many promises of Christ to those who love and serve him and the guarantee of infallibility he gave to his Church. Fifthly, the Mosaic Law has found its complete fulfilment in the doctrinal and moral teaching of the Gospels, preserved by the living voice of the Church. Sixthly, the worship of the Temple has been supplanted by the holy Mass, the sacrifice of Calvary preserved for us by the love and power of God, and the marvellous liturgy which embellishes it. Seventhly, prophecy has given way to reality, the Gospels have fulfilled the teaching of old. Eighthly, the Fathers are represented in the new dispensation by our blessed Lady, St Joseph, St John the Baptist and all the saints whose example the Church places before us in the liturgy day by day. And lastly, the Messias, Christ himself, remains with us all days, even to the consummation of the world (Matt. 28. 20). Here are nine precious gifts of God's merciful love. Cold words fall far short of bringing home their meaning; only by prayer and loving familiarity with them can we appreciate how wonderful they are.

Indeed Christ still comes to his own. He offers us indescribable privileges—but how have his own people received him? The picture of the Christian world today is a frightening one. In the first place Christians are divided amongst themselves. We Catholics proudly count our 525 million souls; but there are probably well over 400 million other Christians wandering outside the fold of Christ and Peter, divided amongst hundreds of denominations which contradict one another in the essentials of doctrine, worship and authority. In many cases loyalty to a denomination or a country is, consciously or unconsciously, put before loyalty to Christ. And of the non-Catholic Christians how many really live up even to the tenets of their particular denomination? Figures recently published by the Church of England estimate that there are more than 27 million baptized Anglicans in this country today; but only just over two million receive Holy Communion on Easter day. We Catholics are little better in South America and some other parts of the world. The men of France and Italy seem to think that God's revelation through Christ is not meant for them. The size of the communist parties in those countries which are regarded as Catholic should not be brushed aside as of no concern.

Consider the Christian people of England from the norm of their observance of the Ten Commandments alone and what do we find? Certainly the first three are honoured in the breach. Only about one in twenty of the residents of our island, apart from Catholics, goes to church on Sunday. There is precious little reverence for God. His holy name is used more often as an expletive on the sports field than in reverence elsewhere. Nor is there any evidence that the people as a whole have any idea of prayer as a necessary exercise of the day. In fact, the worship of God is being challenged by the new generation of self-styled humanists, those whom a popular journal appropriately named the "lilac gang", in a concerted way. They dominate the so-called serious programmes on radio and television; their views are heard in parliament and every other public forum; they lose no opportunity of attacking traditional Christian beliefs and practices. On the other hand religious advertising is forbidden on television and religious programmes so diluted as to become almost entirely ineffective.

The fourth commandment concerns the sanctity of family life. It is attacked on all sides today. Government interference makes it impossible for parents to fully perform the duties for which God has destined them; they can educate them at Catholic schools only at the cost of sacrifice. The traditional teaching that children must obey and that parents have the right to punish is continually under attack by modern psychology. Social conditions often make it necessary for the mother to take a job as well as manage her home. When we pass to the fifth commandment there is no need to go abroad and think of

the millions who have been liquidated behind the iron curtain
or in Nazi concentration camps nor to anticipate what will
happen if nuclear war breaks out; we need only glance at the
wards in so many hospitals in which human life is taken away
regularly as pregnancies are terminated and the aged and
suffering "given a happy release". There is little need to dwell
on the violations of the sixth commandment which are going
on all around us. Birth prevention is the accepted order of
things; divorce is far too prevalent; young people commonly
experiment with the use of sex before marriage; sexual sin is
the common theme of novels, plays and films. The prevailing
view is that our traditional Christian teaching is outmoded and
in need of revision. As for the seventh commandment—justice!
Is justice the principal concern of governments, political parties,
trade unions, employers' federations, landlords and business
men? There is precious little evidence that it is. The eighth
commandment forbids lying—yet it is probably indulged in
today more viciously than at any time in history. Never has
propaganda been so important nor its means more potent. So
the great machines pour out the lies through all the media of
mass communication. Advertising has become one of the biggest
forces in the life of man, and such evidence as there is indicates
that it is not exactly scrupulous in regard to the truth. Put the
ninth commandment with the sixth and the tenth with the
seventh, and you have a picture of the way men in a Christian
country are returning the love and generosity of God towards
them. Indeed he comes unto his own and his own receive him
not.

Glance at the Catholic community almost anywhere. See
the empty churches at daily Mass—when the most ardent
desire of Christ is that all should receive him frequently in
Holy Communion. How few of our people pay a daily visit to
their eucharistic Lord; how few spend any considerable time
in mental prayer; how few offer themselves for the organized
work of the apostolate; how few are enthusiastic for holiness.
Only very exceptionally does one find layfolk who are interested
in serious Catholic reading. In most parish churches the
attendance at Benediction of the Blessed Sacrament on Sundays
and weekdays is pathetically small. Perhaps worse than all these
depressing manifestations is the attitude of mind that they must

be accepted as beyond our control. In other words, it is inevitable that Christ must still come to many of his own and be not received, must still stand at the door, knock and remain unheard (Apoc. 3. 20).

Disregard of the Ten Commandments by the majority of the so-called Christian people of our day and the low standards which apparently satisfy many Catholics are only two indications of the return which is being made to God for so many signs of his infinite, merciful love for men. Our duty is clear. In the first place it is to make sure that whenever Christ comes to us, in whatever way—in his Church, by his grace, in the holy Eucharist, through the commands of superiors, in the ordinary happenings of life which make his will known to us, in our neighbours, with whom he has identified himself—we respond with the utmost generosity. Making that response lies at the heart of holiness; it is the essence of devotion to Christ's Sacred Heart, which Pope Pius XII has spoken of as embracing in its practice the essentials of the religion Christ revealed. Oh, how different the situation would be if all Christians realized that their religion does not demand merely the performance of a series of exercises and duties but a heart overflowing with love and the desire to return to Christ love for his infinite love. We must emphasize generosity, our duty to try by his grace to be as generous in our return of love for him as he was in his proofs of love for us, especially when he poured out his blood to the very last drop. Lack of fervour betokens weakness of faith, failure to appreciate our duty to Christ and the extent of his love for us. We should take to heart St Paul's words to the Christians at Ephesus: "May he (God the Father of our Lord Jesus Christ) strengthen you through his Spirit with a power that reaches your innermost being. May Christ find a dwelling place, through faith, in your hearts; may your lives be rooted in love, founded on love. May you and all the saints be enabled to measure, in all its breadth and length and height and depth, the love of Christ, to know what passes knowledge" (Eph. 3. 14–20).

We should remember, too, our duty of making reparation for all the shortcomings within Christ's Body. Like St Paul we should "help to pay off the debt which the afflictions of Christ still leave to be paid, for the sake of his body, the Church"

(Col. 1. 24). Christ suffered for the sins of all; but some are
indifferent to all he has done for them; they make no contribution of their own. Of course, our Lord's sufferings were more
than enough; but it is surely fitting that all of us who believe
should try to trust for those who do not trust, love for those
who do not love, pray for those who do not pray, strive after
holiness for all who are not enthusiastic for it, practise the
virtues for those who indulge in the opposite vices and suffer
in union with Christ for those who unite no sufferings of theirs
to his. Reparation through love can become a rapid road to
progress in holiness. Our Lord appealed for it when he appeared
to St Margaret Mary; it is an essential element in devotion to
his Sacred Heart. Is it not significant that Mary, the lovely
Mother God created for himself, whom he graced and loved
more than any other creature, should have been called upon to
suffer most, to become the Queen of Martyrs? That is what
union with Christ means. Nowadays there is usually very little
need to look for extra suffering, although voluntary mortification is an absolute necessity for progress in holiness. Each day's
round has much to offer us to unite with Christ's passion. The
constant battle with the devil, the world and the flesh, unceas-
ing efforts to do all things well and the sum of the afflictions,
frustrations, disappointments and trials of life can all be
accepted, consecrated and offered to Jesus through his Mother,
so that the spirit of our morning Sacrifice of the altar unites
every moment of the day.

18

"BUT AS MANY AS RECEIVED HIM, HE GAVE THEM POWER TO BE MADE THE SONS OF GOD, TO THEM THAT BELIEVE IN HIS NAME"

(John 1. 12)

AFTER lamenting that the Jews as a nation had consistently rejected the Word in spite of the many ways he had come to them, St John writes that there were, however, some who believed in him. Whether they were Jews or Gentiles, once they had co-operated with his grace and believed, he mercifully gave them the grace by which they would be justified and thus be God's adopted children. The last words of the verse, "to them that believe in his name", explain the meaning of "as many as received him". "In his name" is a Hebrew way of writing, meaning simply in him or his authority.

Earlier in these conferences we have touched on the nature of the adopted sonship God bestows on believers. Now let us search the Scriptures in order to learn more about it.

In the Old Testament the terms "sons" or "children of God" were used of the entire Jewish nation, especially before the exile. For example, God bade Moses say to Pharao: "Israel, says the Lord, is my first-born son, and when I bade thee give this son of mine leave to go and worship me, that leave was refused; I come to claim the life of thy first-born in return" (Exod. 4. 22-23). The prophecy of Isaias opens like this: "Listen, you heavens, and let earth attend to this, a divine remonstrance; my own sons, that I reared and brought to manhood, hold me in defiance!" (Isaias 1. 2). And through Jeremias God asked his people: "Must I ever be offering thee sonship, and a land so fair that all the peoples of the world might envy thee its possession? Must I ever be pleading with thee to acknowledge me as thy father, and forsake my guidance no more?" (Jer. 3. 19). When the prophets prayed to God they called him "Father", not primarily as individuals but in the name of the entire nation. Thus, "Who is our father, Lord, if not thou? Let Abraham disown us, Israel disclaim his own blood, we are thy sons still; is it not thy boast of old, thou hast paid a price for us?" (Is. 63. 16). And again: "Yet, Lord, thou art our father; we are but clay, and thou the craftsman who has fashioned us" (Is. 64. 8).

Later, after the exile, we find individual Jews addressing God as Father, but it was in much the same sense in which our Lord was to say of the peacemakers, "they shall be counted the children of God" (Matt. 5. 9), or that if we love our enemies, do good to those who hate us and pray for those who persecute and insult us, we will be "true sons of our Father in heaven" (Matt. 5. 44). An ethical relationship is indicated here, not the divine adoption of which St John is writing in his prologue. People who live in a virtuous way are God's sons because they resemble him in a special way.

The privilege of sonship of God which can be enjoyed under the new dispensation is something far and away more wonderful than anything known to the children of Israel. When he spoke to Nicodemus our Lord said that an entirely new life, a spiritual regeneration, a complete change in a man was required to become a member of the messianic kingdom. "A man cannot see the kingdom of God without being born anew. . . . No man can enter the kingdom of God unless birth comes to him from water, and from the Holy Spirit. What is born by natural birth is a thing of nature, what is born by supernatural birth is a thing of the spirit" (John 3. 3-5). The Council of Trent has defined that our Lord was speaking here of natural water and that natural water is necessary for baptism. We read later on in this same chapter that our Lord was himself baptizing: "Jesus and his disciples came into the land of Judea, and there he remained with them, baptizing. . . . John's disciples . . . told him . . . he is baptizing now and all are flocking to him" (John 3. 22-26).

This discourse with Nicodemus reveals to us something of the splendour of baptism. Our Lord says we are to be born again; St Paul wrote about it to Titus: "Then the kindness of God, our Saviour, dawned on us, his great love for man. He saved us; and it was not thanks to anything we had done for our own justification. In accordance with his own merciful design he saved us, with the cleansing power which gives us new birth, and restores our nature through the Holy Spirit, shed on us in abundant measure through our Saviour, Jesus Christ. So, justified by his grace, we were to become heirs, with the hope of eternal life set before us" (Titus 3. 5-7). Here the Apostle emphasizes that all this comes to us through the absolute goodness and mercy of God through no merits of ours. Baptism, he teaches, gives us a new spiritual essence. It makes us God's children. It renews us perfectly. It invests us with faith, hope and charity. The entire blessed Trinity works in us; each divine Person contributes something to our new spiritual existence. The eternal Father is the principle of the divinity itself; from him the Son is begotten and from him and the Son the Holy Ghost proceeds. So he is the Father of the baptized, the principle of the pouring out of the Holy Ghost into souls. With him the Son, too, is the principle of that outpouring just as he is the instrument of the Holy Ghost's eternal procession within the Trinity. And the Holy Ghost, who is the Spirit of the Father and the Son, becomes also the Spirit of the baptized.

This action of the holy Trinity within us, this second birth, is absolutely necessary if we are to enter God's kingdom. Our Lord said so to Nicodemus; he repeated it at the end of his life: "He who believes and is baptized will be saved; he who refuses belief will be condemned" (Mark 16. 16). St Peter told his first converts: "Be baptized, every one of you, in the name of Jesus Christ, to have your sins forgiven" (Acts 2. 38). St Paul makes it clear that this new birth in baptism implies two things, firstly death to sin, "in our baptism, we have been buried with him, died like him" (Rom. 6. 4), and secondly, birth through the gift of divine grace to the new life which makes us God's adopted children: "You, too, must think of yourselves as dead to sin, and alive with a life that looks towards God, through Christ Jesus our Lord" (Rom. 6. 11).

A little later he is even more emphatic: "The spirit you have now received is not, as of old, a spirit of slavery, to govern you by fear; it is the spirit of adoption, which makes us cry out, Abba, Father. The Spirit himself thus assures our spirit, that we are children of God; and if we are his children, then we are his heirs too; heirs of God, sharing the inheritance of Christ" (Rom. 8. 15-17). When we recall all that we have said earlier in these conferences about the infinite perfection of God, we are filled with wonder and gratitude as we come to understand the meaning of these words of St Paul. Sons of God, adopted children, heirs of God, sharing Christ's inheritance—these are breathtaking phrases to men of faith. God's love for each of us is so great that he comes to dwell within us, bringing with him the gift of a new life, which really makes us members of his family. Then he works upon us, enlightening our understanding and directing our wills to call upon God as our Father, implying that we are what we profess to be, his loving, humble and obedient little children. So full was St Paul of his theme that he could not omit it from his writings. He had used almost the same words a little earlier when he wrote to the Christians of Galatia and he returned to the theme four or five years later when he wrote from his Roman prison to the converts at Ephesus: "He [God the Father] has chosen us out in Christ, before the foundation of the world, to be saints, to be blameless in his sight, for love of him; marking us out beforehand (so his will decreed) to be his adopted children through Jesus Christ. Thus he would manifest the splendour of that grace by which he has taken us into his favour in the person of his beloved Son" (Eph. 1. 4-7; cf. Gal. 4. 6 ff.).

"In Christ" is an expression which comes constantly from St Paul's pen, just as he often writes of our being "in the Spirit". He wants us to realize that God has been so good to us that he has put us spiritually in Christ as we are naturally in the atmosphere around us which sustains us. We cannot live in a vacuum; so we cannot live spiritually apart from Christ; we are members of his Body, his living cells. He acts upon us like the human soul acts upon the body in which it dwells: "I am alive; or rather, not I; it is Christ that lives in me. True, I am living here and now, this mortal life; but my real life is the faith I have in the Son of God, who loved me, and gave himself for me" (Gal. 2. 20-21). Christ is the source of all grace, holiness and justness; he died for men; he is now the source of spiritual life. We must live in the atmosphere of faith; as reason dominates the men of the world, so God's light in faith should dominate the life of those who are his sons.

Notice how St Paul's mind is fixed in eternity. He tells the Ephesians that when God so enriches us in time with his grace, making us his adopted children, he is simply carrying out his eternal decree regarding us; we have never been out of the sight of his eternal, timeless gaze. Our spiritual blessings began in eternity and in eternity they will be completed as we share in the glory of Christ (Rom. 8. 17). God chose us to be holy; apart altogether from any merits of ours he has made us holy beings, endowed with the life which makes us his children, sharers in his divine nature (II Peter 1. 4). He could have made us holy without making us his children; but he has willed in his infinite mercy to make holiness and adopted sonship identical. If grace is in our souls we are holy, and if we are holy we are God's children. St Paul uses the word translated by Mgr Knox as "splendour". Is there anything in the material, artistic, cultural or scientific worlds as splendid as the mystery of our divine adoption in Christ? It came about "in him and through his blood". Oh, how very easily we take it all for granted—that the Creator poured out his blood for the creature he had made from nothing, that quite gratuitously a God should die to make it possible for one infinitely beneath him to see him face to face for ever, that infinite Goodness should be tortured for the evil he could never merit to save us from the eternal damnation we actually did merit. It is God whom sin offends; we who are responsible for that sin; yet it is the offended God who atones for us the offenders. Oh, how can we ever understand such love! We should at least try to bring it home to ourselves in prayer. If we do, we shall never be less than enthusiastic to grow in the spirit of sons, to respond to the efforts of the Holy Spirit to form our spirit to the likeness of God's only-begotten Son become man for love of us.

"When a man is in Christ Jesus, there has been a new creation", St Paul wrote (Gal. 6. 15). What did he mean? Surely that the state of grace by which we become God's children transforms our minds, hearts and actions. He has been writing in the epistle about Christ's passion. Now he says that the fruit of the cross and passion of the Saviour is the renovation of the interior man by sanctifying grace. Therefore, "God forbid that I should make a display of anything, except the cross of our Lord Jesus Christ through whom the world stands crucified to me and I to the world" (Gal. 6. 14). In other words, only the thought of what God-made-Man has done for me should be dominant in my life; it is through that that I have been reborn, through that that the evil things around me no longer matter to me, through that that I have become a new creature, God's own child, with a new life far surpassing the life of nature. Much the same phrasing is found in the second letter to the Christians in Corinth, which was probably written at the end of the year 57, immediately after that to the Galatians: "Even if we used to think of Christ in a human fashion, we do so no longer; it follows, in fact, that when a man becomes a new creature in Christ, his old life has disappeared, everything has become new about him" (II Cor. 5. 16-17). We might paraphrase like this: "When we become Christians we must die to ourselves and live to Christ; we must not pay attention to the merely earthly or carnal qualities of people; if, at any time, we have loved Christ from only human motives we must do so no longer but we must adore and serve him from high, spiritual motives. One who has been reborn in Christ has received a new existence; old things have passed away; he must live according to what he has become" by God's favour, that is, God's adopted child.

The same practical conclusion is drawn by the Apostle writing to Ephesus: "If true knowledge is to be found in Jesus . . . there must be a renewal in the inner life of your minds; you must be clothed in the new self, which is created in God's image, justified and sanctified through the truth" (Eph. 4. 21-24). And to the Colossians: "You must be clothed in the new self, that is being refitted all the time for closer knowledge, so that the image of the God who created it is its pattern . . . there is nothing but Christ in any of us" (Col. 3. 10, 11). The Holy Ghost is exhorting all of us through the Apostle to live according to our inner spiritual greatness as children of God, to let the new life within us shine forth in our lives. The Spirit of Christ within us must be evident in the spirit in which we live. God has re-created us; he has justified us; he has made us holy. He has given us closer knowledge of spiritual things; we must model ourselves, our lives and our outlook anew. We are made naturally according to God's likeness, having intellect and will; but now, by grace we receive a new likeness to God, having essential holiness and truth in the new life which gives us real sonship of God. Only

Christ, therefore, matters. We must study him in order to love him.

As we search the Scriptures for information about the marvellous sonship with which God has graced us we soon come to the places where it is described in terms of generation, of being born. We have already touched on our Lord's revelation to Nicodemus; now we turn to St John's first epistle: "If a man is born of God he does not live sinfully, he is true to his parentage; he cannot be a sinner if he is born of God. . . . Love springs from God; no one can love without being born of God, and knowing God. How can the man who has no love have any knowledge of God, since God is love? . . . Everyone who believes that Jesus is the Christ is a child of God, and to love the parent is to love his child. . . . Whatever takes its origin from God must needs triumph over the world; our faith, that is the triumphant principle which triumphs over the world" (I John 3. 9; 4. 7; 5. 1, 4). St Peter writes in much the same sense when he says that we must love "unaffectedly as brethren should, since" we "have all been born anew with an immortal, imperishable birth, through the word of God who lives and abides for ever" (I Peter 1. 23).

We have earlier explained the metaphor of the seed. St John, writing about sixty-five years after our Lord's death and twenty-eight after St Paul's, stresses the nature of our supernatural birth. The life it brings to us is incompatible with mortal sin; one who commits that kind of sin is false to his parentage, that is, he runs away from home, ceases to be a real child of God, loses supernatural life. This life is the seed of future glory as well as the principle of our spiritual activity on earth; it remains permanently in the soul. It is inseparable from love, and love of God must overflow upon all whom God loves. Brotherly love, then, is God's gift; it emanates from his grace. We cannot practise it unless God gives it to us. All the members of the Church are given this charity by God. It matters not whether they be triumphant in heaven, struggling on earth or suffering in purgatory—all are endowed with this new life of love and grace. Practical brotherly love is the hallmark of Christ's brethren, God's children. Faith, hope and love are gifts which come with adoption into God's family. One who does not love the members of his own family, which is

God's family, is a living contradiction; he cannot remain in the family; he cannot persevere as God's child. Note again how the beloved disciple stresses the importance of faith. He means, of course, effective faith—believing in Christ to the point of accepting him and living up to his teaching through love. That makes one God's child; it brings about the rebirth St John refers to in his prologue. And we must remember that every word of Christ is the word of God; every deed is the deed of God. We cannot pick and choose in him. He demands our whole allegiance. If we give it we will surely conquer the world and all other spiritual enemies. Faith alone is the foundation of all this; we cannot love Christ unless we know him; the more we know him by faith, the more we will love him, and the more we love him, the more will we triumph over all that stands against him.

What sublime truths these are—and how little they are appreciated today, even by many who would call themselves the faithful followers of Christ. There is too much apathy concerning the spiritual life, too little enthusiasm for the love of God, too little interest in searching the Scriptures for knowledge of him, too little appreciation of the sublime things that are found there. For example, glance at the words of St Peter quoted above. There he tells us that the brotherly love we must have for one another is based on the spiritual new birth we have all received in common; for it is a fact that all of us have been born again, have received a new spiritual existence, an existence which comes not from a corruptible source but from the word of God, that is the Gospel. These are the main grounds for brotherly love; it is something which flows inexorably from justification in Christ. So necessary is it that one who does not love has, in fact, reverted to paganism; he has cancelled out the effect of God's life within him.

When we analyse further this surpassing gift of sonship of God we find Holy Writ telling us that it is the gift of God's infinite love. He is perfectly free to adopt us or not, but his love causes him to take us to himself: "See how the Father has shown his love towards us; that we should be counted as God's sons, should be his sons. . . . We are sons of God even now . . . when he comes we shall be like him; we shall see him, then, as he is. Now, a man who rests these hopes in him lives a life of holiness; he, too, is holy" (I John 3. 1-3). It is as if the beloved disciple is saying to us: "Think again about the tremendous proof of his unbounded love God the Father has given us. He not only gives us the exalted title of sons of God; he makes us his children in reality; he gives us a new spiritual birth; he adopts us; he makes us co-heirs with his only-begotten Son, Jesus. Yes, living in an unbelieving world we should console ourselves with the thought that we are really children of God. The degree of glory that will be ours after death is hidden from us. But we do know that, provided we do not forfeit our sonship by grave sin, Christ when he comes to judge the world will find us clad with all the properties of glorification. We shall be like him in a special way; we shall see him, too, not as we see him now like 'a confused reflection in a mirror' but face to face (I Cor. 13. 12). Hope like this of the direct vision of God must cause us to try to be like Christ, pure and holy in this life. After death we shall be like Christ in a unique way; we must begin that likeness here by the life of grace, by living faithfully as God's children, by returning to God generous love for the infinite, unbelievable love he has shown to us."

Nor must we forget that all these wonders are only possible because God became man, suffered and died in agony for us. St Paul says it: "God sent out his Son on a mission to us. He took birth from a woman as a subject of the law, so as to ransom those who were subject to the law, and make us sons by adoption. To prove that you are sons, God sent out the Spirit of his Son into your hearts, crying out in us, Abba, Father. No longer, then, art thou a slave, thou art a son; and because thou art a son, thou hast, by divine appointment, the son's right of inheritance" (Gal. 4. 4-7). In that magnificent passage some of the ideas we have already discussed are recapitulated. It is, in fact, a splendid summary of the revelation of the nature of our divine sonship. But the point to be underlined is that it all comes to us through Christ's bitter passion and death. Therefore we have a grave duty of trying to thank him as far as we can for everything he has done for us. The best thanks is, of course, a fervent life, the return of love for love, centred especially in the sacrifice of thanksgiving, which is the meaning of the word Eucharist, the Mass.

In this teaching is the whole basis of ascetical theology. As St Paul says again: "Through faith in Christ Jesus you are all now God's sons. All you who have been baptized in Christ's name have put on the person of Christ . . . you are all one person in Jesus Christ" (Gal. 3. 26-28). Because grace makes us God's children and Christ's brethren, we should try to live as Christ would live. His Spirit should appear in all we do. We have been made members of his Body, transformed into him. But Christ's principal preoccupation during his rather brief passage through our vale of tears was to do his Father's will; so holiness consists in seeing in God's will the desires of him who is infinite love and longing to fulfil it to the smallest detail, knowing that all it demands and requires is for our good.

The life of God's children is outlined in Holy Writ. "The man who belongs to God listens to God's words" our Lord says (John 8. 47). We cannot be worthy as his children unless we do that. St Gregory comments on this passage that it is a sign of predestination to hear God's word and obey his holy inspirations. Did not our Lord promise that he would regard as his mother and his brethren those "who hear the word of God, and keep it" (Luke 8. 21)? Too many of those who wish to follow Christ pick and choose in God's word; they will go so far but no further; they will not surrender that last strong-point of self-will which prevents progress towards the higher reaches of sanctity. In this way they are only partially loyal members of Christ's flock. He is the good shepherd; freely he has given his life for his sheep, those who are loyal to him always listen to his voice; he knows them and they know him (John 10. 14 ff.). This is a practical result of faith.

God's true child also does battle ceaselessly with the world and its spirit. There are few things so emphasized in the New Testament as this. "Do not bestow your love on the world, and what the world has to offer; the lover of this world has no love of the Father in him . . . the world and its gratifications pass away; the man who does God's will outlives them, for ever" (I John 2. 15-17). Read through our Lord's discourse after his last supper and you will see how seriously he taught his disciples about the menace of the world. St James sums it up as briefly as possible: "The world's friendship means enmity with God, and the man who would have the world for his friend makes himself God's enemy" (James 4. 4). In spite of these repeated warnings of the Holy Spirit the vast majority of Catholics today succumb to the allurements of the world and give Christ only a very small place in their lives. The other texts we have already considered have taught us that divine sonship and grave sin are incompatible, and also that God's sincere child strives not only to avoid grave sin but to do the divine will in the smallest detail.

St Paul touches on another requirement in the life of a worthy child of God; it is zeal. Here are his words: "Do all that lies in you, never complaining, never hesitating to show yourselves innocent and single-minded, God's children, bringing no reproach on his name. You live in an age that is twisted out of its true pattern, and among such people you shine out, beacons to the world, upholding the message of life" (Phil. 2. 14-15). Is not this an echo of our Lord's own words: "Your light must shine so bright before men that they can see your good works, and glorify your Father who is in heaven" (Matt. 5. 16)? Divine sonship means identity of outlook within the divine family; we must have the mind of Christ: "Yours is to be the same mind which Christ Jesus showed" (Phil. 2. 6). What is that mind of Christ? To save men, to bring light and life to men, to call sinners to repentance, to give his life as a ransom for all, to make God's name hallowed, his kingdom come, his will be done on earth, to preach the gospel to every creature. So every Catholic, in virtue of the divine life that is in him, must not only use opportunities of apostleship, but make them.

God adds his grace to every effort which is made to work for souls purely for his honour and glory. So far in these conferences I have refrained from personal reminiscences. I have done my best to follow the lead of the Holy Spirit through the inspired word of God. But there is a remarkable story I must tell to show what might happen if every effort were to be made to bring wandering sheep back within the fold of Christ.

At the end of 1959 I preached at every Mass in the church of a large parish, appealing to the people to volunteer to go round taking a census from door to door and at the same time offering all an invitation to attend a week of talks on the Faith. A good number of people responded to the appeal, and so did a community of nuns in the parish. About 9,000 homes were visited. At very few was the reception anything but friendly. But one of the nuns went with a girl companion to a certain house where she was greeted with many insults. The lady was only a visitor to the district; her husband was a Baptist minister. The rain was pouring down very hard and the nun was kept standing out in it. Insult followed insult, but the nun returned them with a sweet smile. In the end she said that although the lady would not then accept an invitation she might well change her mind and come to the church some evening.

During the week I received a letter in the question box. It was an apology. The writer said that she had insulted the nun who had called on her, but had been so moved when her insults were repaid by a sweet smile that she had come to the talks after all, and she had been most impressed. She added a question she wished to hear answered on behalf of her husband, the Baptist minister. The following week a letter was sent on to me from the same lady saying that during the week she had come to Mass, and when the people bowed their head and the bell rang, she knew that the little white disc the priest raised in his hands was indeed God himself and this was his one, only true Church. She said that all her objections had been swept away and that she intended to take instructions.

I was so moved by this that I wrote a simple account of it in *The Catholic Times*. No more news came until the following November. It was a letter from the lady telling me that on the feast of Corpus Christi she had been received into the Church and confirmed on the feast of St Francis. She had told her husband of her wish to become a Catholic. He then told her that before she knew him as a Baptist minister he had been a Catholic and a student for the priesthood. He, too, had seen that nun's smile from inside the house behind the curtains and, unknown to his wife, he had attended the last of the talks. His one desire was to return to the Church, which he had left and against which he had worked for thirty years. Of course, his marriage was invalid also. So on the feast of Corpus Christi they parted, never to see each other again. He went to live with a religious community.

There was no further sequel until I was actually at the same place giving another series of talks the following year, 1961.

In the question box I received an astonishing letter. The writer said she had sent it by a friend who was passing through the place. She had been a nun for fourteen years; had then left her order and the Church and had gone around lecturing against the Church and had even joined a secret society in Paris. There somebody unknown to her had sent her a copy of *The Catholic Times* containing the account of the effects of that nun's smile. From it she recognized the nun and realized that she had known her before either of them entered religion. The effect was so immense that she obtained a copy of *This is the Faith*, studied it, returned to the Church and passed it on to her brother, who had also apostatized. I learned later that he had probably been a cleric and possibly more. Brother and sister by God's grace both came back to the Church.

Those are just the broad outlines of the story. More details could not be given without violating confidence. Does it not show that God is always waiting with his graces to help on our poor efforts? Who is to say what wonders would follow similar "crusades for souls" in other parishes? Because they do not take place thousands of those outside the Church who could be approached are not approached and God is denied a powerful means of bringing grace to them.

19

"WHO ARE BORN, NOT OF BLOOD, NOR OF THE WILL OF THE FLESH, NOR OF THE WILL OF MAN, BUT OF GOD"

(John 1. 3)

O UR first problem in discussing this verse is its meaning. The issue at stake is illustrated by quoting some modern translations. The Douai is given above. Mgr Knox has: "*Their* birth came, not from human stock, nor from nature's will or man's, but from God." Father Boismard, O.P., in his book called *St John's Prologue*, has "*His* birth came, not from human stock, not from nature's will or man's but from God's." The Westminster version translates: "that were begotten not of blood, nor of the will of the flesh, nor of the will of man, but of God." The French Bible translated under the direction of the Bible School of Jerusalem has: "*Lui* que ni sang, ni vouloir de chair, ni vouloir d'homme, mais Dieu a engendré." J. B. Phillips, an Anglican, puts: "*Their* birth depended not on the course of nature nor on any impulse or plan of man, but on God."* So out of six translations we have found that two make the subject of the verse "the Word" while four make it "the sons of God", from the previous verse. In the second century the subject was commonly taken to be the Word but such a reading has only negligible authority from the Latin and Syriac manuscripts. In addition to the Jerusalem Bible some non-Catholic critics defend it. Every known Greek manuscript makes the subject the children of God and not the Word. Supporters of both views argue that their opinion is more perfectly in line with St John's thought. The fact is that we shall never know what St John really meant until we can ask him in the next world; but for our purpose here we will keep to the traditional Douai, Knox and Westminster translations. The verse refers to those St John was writing of already, those

* The New English Bible has: " To all who did receive him . . . he gave the right to become children of God, not born of any human stock, or by the fleshly desire of a human father, but the offspring of God himself."

187

who received the Word, believed in him and thus became God's sons. He says now simply that they were born not in a carnal but a spiritual manner—not of *bloods*, according to St Thomas Aquinas. "Nor of the will of the flesh" seems to refer to sinful generation as against "of the will of man", lawful generation. The spiritual generation to the life of grace is contrasted with carnal generation of any description.

In our last conference we pursued this idea of divine adoption through the New Testament. It is something so tremendous that we would never have dared to think that God would bring it about. At Mass, when we are about to recite the prayer our Lord taught us, the Church bids us say: "Taught by our Saviour's command and following his divine instruction we make bold to say: our Father. . . ." One of the main contrasts between the Old Testament and the New lies precisely in this, that in the New Christ revealed the loving fatherhood of God. He wanted the practice of the spiritual life to be based on this relation of love; he wanted the title of Father given to God to be the keynote of the devotional life of his followers. What else are we to gather from the gentle words our Lord spoke on the hillside: "You are to be perfect, as your heavenly Father is perfect" (that is complete, all-embracing in our charity as God is all-embracing in his charity), "then thy Father, who sees what is done in secret, will repay thee. . . . Your heavenly Father will forgive you your transgressions, if you forgive your fellow men theirs. . . . I say to you, then, do not fret over your life. . . . You have a Father in heaven who knows. . . ." (Matt. 5. 48; 6. 4, 14, 25-32).

St Paul speaks expressly of adoption. We are not, of course, sons of God in the same sense that Jesus Christ is; the substance of God is not communicated to us, nor even a part of it, because there are no parts in God. Our spiritual sonship is not "natural" sonship. It is adopted, and therefore free. Even when a father disinherits his son in the way of the world, the lad still remains physically his son; natural sonship can never be terminated; as long as the boy lives he is his father's son. How different is our sonship of God! It does not begin with life, as natural sonship does; it may not take place at all; it is not obligatory; it comes as the free gift of God with sanctifying grace and it ends when grace leaves our souls. "Adoption" may be misunderstood. Our supernatural adoption by God far, far surpasses the legal fiction we call human adoption. We have already quoted St John (I John 3. 1) as saying that we really are God's sons; we are born of God; we are God's "seed"; we are like to him.

What, then, is this sonship? It stands between the natural sonship of Christ, to whom the divine essence is wholly communicated, and earthly adopted sonship, which is not real sonship at all but only a legal substitute for it. It is something unique; it is God's creation; we would know nothing about it unless he had revealed it to us.

Another point is worth mentioning. When husband and wife adopt a child they cannot give him their own blood stream nor can they give him the dispositions he ought to have towards them. Very often an adopted child will have those dispositions but they are not directly produced by the parents. On the other hand, when God adopts us, we not only share in his nature in the way we have explained in an earlier chapter, but God infuses into us the dispositions a child should have towards him. St Paul twice tells us (Rom. 8. 14; Gal. 4. 6) that God's Spirit makes us cry out "Father". We receive grace and with it the theological virtues and the gifts. Faith makes us accept God's word as children; hope makes us trust him, especially his love and his promises, as children; charity gives us the loving tenderness children must have for their Father. The gifts make us docile to the action of the Spirit of God in us; in particular, the gift of piety enables us to behave like God's true children.

Why do husbands and wives adopt children? Very often it is for their own sakes; they feel that a child will bind them together, bring completion to their lives. It may exceptionally be purely for the child's sake. When we apply this thought to our spiritual adoption as God's children we realize at once that we can give to God nothing that he has not already. He is already infinitely self-sufficient. He adopts us in order to give; he pours out, as St Thomas says, something of his own perfection. "As by the work of creation the divine goodness is communicated to all creatures in a certain likeness, so by the work of adoption the likeness of natural sonship is communicated to men." Absolutely freely God takes us into his family, with not the slightest merit on our part nor the slightest need on his. He does it because he loves us and wishes to give himself to us. He had an only Son; he did not wish him to remain alone; he sent him into the world to gain for himself many brethren. He becomes "the eldest-born among many brethren" (Rom. 8. 29).

We have noted how the Holy Ghost reveals to us that the inheritance of Christ is ours. What is that inheritance? God himself; nothing less. We are to possess him throughout eternity. The earthly son, be he natural or adopted, has to wait until his father dies before he acquires his inheritance; he has to become an orphan to attain it. Moreover, the more children there are, the less, normally, is his share. The inheritance is divided between them. God's love has made things otherwise when supernatural sonship is in question. We begin to receive our reward as soon as grace is given to us; we then become sharers in the divine nature; we begin on earth the possession of God which will be perfected after death. Moreover, the inheritance is the same for all God's children; the degree of their participation depends on God's grace and their co-operation with it.

We should think, too, of the glory of the God who adopts us. We are born of God. The fact is too wonderful to describe. On earth any child is fortunate to be adopted by kind people, but how much more fortunate would one be if he were adopted into a royal family, with every happiness that could be possessed on earth and the prospect of the royal succession as well! Our adoption by God infinitely surpasses even that. He has taken us into his family; we are really his children, really sharing his inheritance with his only-begotten Son—and the inheritance is not something created, it is himself.

On earth men and women are proud of their lineage and their noble titles. Royalty is honoured by all right-minded men. A nation is proud of an illustrious ruler. But how many Christians ever think about the royal dignity of the family to which grace makes them belong? We are God's direct descendants; he himself has called us to be his children; we share in his nature; we are princes of royal blood, the precious royal blood of Jesus Christ. To the eternal Father we can truly say "our Father", to his only-begotten Son, Jesus Christ, we can truly say "our Brother", to the Holy Spirit we can truly say "our Soul". Child of the Father, brother of the Son, temple of the

Holy Spirit—such is the dignity of a Christian. Nothing can exceed it, but nothing is less recognized. Nothing is more priceless, but nothing is less appreciated. On all sides men betray their divine sonship by making terms with the devil, the world and the flesh, the bitterest enemies of their Father and their King.

Children of God we are, and God wants us to behave as such. In our own time he has raised one up amongst us to teach us to live in the spirit of childhood. The Church has canonized her and proposed her as a model to all the faithful "of every nation, no matter what may be their age, sex, or state of life". She is St Teresa of Lisieux, popularly known as the Little Flower of Jesus. It is a pity that there has been so much misunderstanding concerning her mission. At first some were genuinely repelled by the sentimentality associated with the devotions held in her honour and the propaganda on behalf of her *cultus*; now others try to tell us that that early picture of her was so essentially distorted that it did not convey her spirit at all, that hers is not really the mission to teach the way of spiritual childhood, trust and absolute self-surrender and that devotion to her has so far been misdirected. But the fact is that the closest study of the full, authentic version of her writings demands no essential change in what we have always believed concerning her. On the contrary, first impressions are deepened by it.

Love lies at the heart of the relationship between father and son. When the Father is infinite Love and the spiritual life is devotion to him, everything is resolved by devotion to his love. Our Father is limitless love in himself; he has shown boundless love to us; we must return it with all the generosity his grace permits. God's will is the will of a Lover; God's presence is the presence of a Lover; God's providence is the guidance of a Lover—and so it is throughout every aspect of our relationship. Love is the magnet, the centre, the pivot of the spiritual life. The Saint of Lisieux thought of Love especially from the aspect of mercy. She loved to contemplate God as the infinitely kind Father, who was always showering his favours on his creatures in spite of their sins, weaknesses, infidelities and failures. He never ceases to search for the wandering sheep. Nothing happens without his permission; even sin is permitted by him.

If we have to suffer sin's consequences, it is because our infinite Lover permits it. Our Father wants us to use that trial as an instrument of sanctification; he will offer us the grace to do so. The spirit of childhood implies love, humility, trust, self-surrender, immolation, victimhood. It means loving slavery to God's will, not because it is the will of the Lord of the universe, but because it is the will of an infinitely loving, gentle, kind and merciful Father. So one who lives according to what God has done for him in making him his child is dominated by the desire to return love for infinite love. When he prays, it is the prayer of love; if he must suffer it is with the surrender and acceptance of love; he practises the virtues because that is the way of love. Every exercise, every hour, every sacrifice, every effort after perfection is the gift of love. In this way the spiritual life is reduced to its simplest terms.

To understand more fully some of the consequences of our being adopted into God's family we ought to think about what it means to be the brethren of Christ. He is God's Son; we are God's children—but there are vital differences. He is the only begotten Son of God the Father; we are children of the one God, that is of all three divine Persons. We share in the divine nature, which they possess in common. Because of this distinction our Lord never spoke of God as "our Father", meaning the Father of himself and the Apostles. Intentionally he said: "My Father and your Father" (John 20. 17). When he told us to pray, saying "Our Father", he was not included in the "our". He is himself our Father as the Word of God; and so is the Holy Spirit our Father.

We have already seen how the eternal Word was begotten by the Father within the most holy Trinity. He is God's Son by nature. His personality is constituted by his being the Son of God. From the Father he receives the one divine nature in all its infinite fullness. The Holy Spirit receives the same nature from the Father and the Son not by generation but by being breathed forth, spiration or procession. So the Word is God's only-begotten Son. By nature there is only that one Son, the Word, the second Person. By love there are many sons, all who partake in the divine nature by grace.

In what way, then, are baptized souls God's sons? If he cannot communicate his nature to them, how can he make them his children? We have answered the question when we were discussing our sharing in the divine nature. God creates outside of himself reproductions of his nature. Only through the hypostatic union can he communicate his nature. So our sharing, our sonship, is created and accidental; that of God the Son is uncreated and substantial. Our sonship comes about by the free act of God; Christ's sonship is of the very essence of the Trinity. Our sonship began in time, when we were baptized; Christ's sonship is eternal.

Is it not a marvellous demonstration of God's love for us that he should create in us reflections of the unique sonship which exists within the blessed Trinity? What joy we derive from listening to a record of a masterpiece finely played; what pleasure comes from studying perfect copies of great works of art! In such we see faintly something of what God has done when he makes us his children. He has reflected the eternal sonship of the Word in the souls of men by placing in each one in grace a created image of the unique reality. Thus will that unique sonship receive more glory. St Thomas sums up the doctrine and shows our relationship to the three divine Persons like this: "Adoptive sonship (that is the sonship we receive through grace) is a certain likeness of the eternal sonship. . . . Therefore adoption, though common to the whole Trinity, is appropriated to the Father as its author; to the Son as its exemplar and to the Holy Spirit, as imprinting on us the likeness of this exemplar."

God became man to teach us the way to heaven, that is to show us how God's true children live. Grace impels us to live like that. So long as we do, that is so long as we avoid mortal sin, we remain God's children. And the more perfectly we imitate Christ the more intense is the grace of sonship within us.

We owe our sonship to God the Son. In theological terms, he is its efficient cause. Because all the acts of Christ were the acts of God the Son and infinite in value, he was able to merit the grace of adoption for us. He is the instrument by which it comes about. He became incarnate to merit the grace of sonship once again for fallen humanity. "He took birth . . . so as to ransom" (Gal. 4. 4).

When a person gives an alms to a beggar that alms is himself under another form. Most probably he has worked in order to have that money to pass on. His work is the result of his capacity, his toil, his sweat and everything he puts into it. Similarly, by dying for us Christ merited grace; it is the price of his blood; it is the abundance out of which we have all received something (John 1. 16). It is the equivalent of the life he laid down in sacrifice for us. That life given for us won grace for him; from him it comes to us, still belonging to him; and it makes us God's children.

Living amongst us God the Son made known to us his Father's secrets. "My Father has entrusted everything into my hands; none knows the Son truly except the Father, and none knows the Father truly except the Son, and those to whom it is the Son's good pleasure to reveal him" (Matt. 11. 27). His revelation is God's way of belief, worship and authority. He did not merely teach it to us and exemplify it in his own life; he merited and brought about such an internal transformation in us that we are really God's children, with special grace to believe, worship and obey as he wills. He made his Father our Father.

He made his mother our mother, too. We are his brothers in the spirit. The grace that makes us his brothers comes, with all other graces, through his mother. She was the channel by which he came to us. By her prayers she still brings him to us. Her vocation in heaven is to mould us to be the perfect images of her Son, just as she moulded his body for nine months within herself.

Our Brother remains with us in the Eucharist. The life of sonship must be fed according to its nature; the food is God the Son himself. The more frequently and fervently we receive him, the more will the spirit of sonship intensify in us. "He who eats my flesh and drinks my blood lives continually in me, and I in him. As I live because of the Father, the living Father who has sent me, so he who eats me will live, in his turn, because of me" (John 6. 57-58). Our Lord means that just as he lives through the eternal life communicated to him in his eternal generation by the Father, so the communicant lives in virtue of the spiritual life communicated to him or sustained in him because of union with Christ in the blessed Eucharist. Devotion to Mary and to Holy Communion are essential marks of the spirit of sonship.

Is it not terribly sad that so few of our Catholic people are aware of their intrinsic dignity as children of God? Our Lord does not look upon his relationship with us as being a mere symbol. He loves us as a Father and a Brother; he showers his graces upon us; he sends his Spirit to form us to his likeness; he never ceases to sacrifice himself for us eternally in heaven; he is always our Redeemer and our Saviour. The more we resemble him through holiness of life, the more powerful will be our prayers and the more intense our sharing in the divine nature. Those bonds make us one with him, branches of him the true vine, members of him, still living in his fullness, the Church (John 15. 1-2; Eph. 1. 23).

Need it be added that because we are God's children and brethren of Christ, with his mother for our mother, we are also brethren of all the just? To what an immense multitude we are joined; to the vast crowd of all the saints, "a great multitude past all counting, taken from all nations and tribes and peoples and languages" (Apoc. 2. 9) in heaven, on earth and in purgatory—apostles and martyrs, doctors and confessors, virgins and widows—with all we have kinship in Christ. What an honour this is—and what an advantage, for we share in all the prayers, merits, good works, indeed in all that our brethren in Christ have to offer to God. The mysteries and privileges of membership of the communion of saints are inexhaustible. We are never alone, isolated, abandoned, helpless. We have millions of spiritual brethren all the world over; we do not know them, they do not know us; yet, because we are all born of God we love, sustain, protect and help each other. We are all one body in Christ and just as the ailing members of any organism are helped to strength by those who are strong, so is it in the Communion of Saints.

Is there not something particularly applicable to the tensions of the present day in the lessons we are gathering from this verse of St John? When the world is split into east and west; when the black races are demanding their rights; when the once "dark continent" might soon prove to be the cross-roads of civilization, the Holy Spirit, speaking forcibly through the beloved Apostle, reminds us that God wills to embrace us all in a universal spiritual brotherhood. As St Paul wrote to Galatia: "You are all now God's sons. All you who have been

baptized in Christ's name have put on the person of Christ;
no more Jew or Gentile, no more slave and freeman, no more
male and female; you are all one person in Jesus Christ"
(Gal. 3. 26-28).

What mighty social and political revolutions would come
about if this lesson were seriously accepted throughout the
world! Immediately would be solved the bitter conflicts between capital and labour; men of every colour would love and
help one another as brethren in Christ; peoples would not be
amassing nuclear weapons of destruction through fear of other
nations; statesmanship would be freed from the poisons of
ambition, greed and expediency; workers everywhere would
receive not only a just, living family wage but, as brethren in
Christ of their employers, they would reap the benefits of
prosperity; the sick, the poor, the backward, the unfortunate of
every description and from whatever cause would be loved
and cared for by those more fortunate than themselves. Charity,
said Pope Pius XI in his *Quadragesimo anno*, is the "soul of the
social order". With justice it must be the foundation of all
worldly peace, "the compendium and most general expression
of the Christian ideal",* "the essence of Christian life",† the
remedy for envy, hatred and war.

"If thou knewest what it is God gives!" said our Lord to the
woman of Sichar (John 4. 10). In order to give us grace God
gave us his own Son. From that alone we gather something of
the immense worth of grace. And also from what it is in itself—
a communication of God's own nature, his beauty, his life, his
activity, his possessions, his happiness, his indwelling. Giving
is a proof of love; an immense gift means immense love. Could
God have given us more than he has given us through the
marvellous, indescribable sharing in his own nature? What a
proof it is of his affection for us! Nor is it merely something we
possess to remind us of God; it is something which actually
unites us with God by sharing in his own life and bringing
him to live, Three in One, within us. The nature of the gift
implies very special affection; it shows that because God loves
us so intensely that he does not wish to leave us, that he wants
to be united with us always, he makes us resemble him in a

* Pope Pius XII, *In Questo Giorno di Santa*
† Pope Benedict XV, *Pacem Dei*

most extraordinary way. The more we are God-like the more
God loves us; so our loving Father has done this unbelievable
thing for us—he has created within us the sharing in his own
nature which we call sanctifying grace. As St Thomas Aquinas
wrote: "The grace that unites man to God is the grace that
makes him pleasing to God." The more we ponder it the more
we understand of God's love for us. True, he loves everything
he has made, even the inanimate creation, but how much
more does he love the immortal beings in whom he has placed
something of himself and who shall when he comes be like him
(I John 3. 2), whom he has stamped with his effigy, made reflect
his own personal traits, knowing as he knows and loving as he
loves, sharing in the very love he has for himself!

Any father naturally loves his child. God is the supreme,
infinitely perfect Father, "that Father from whom all fatherhood in heaven and on earth takes its title" (Eph. 3.15). Between
him and earthly fathers is this enormous difference, that
whereas the latter do not even produce the most important
being, the soul, God gives us everything lovable we have. Freely
he made us to his own likeness, united himself to us, reproduced
himself within us, begot us to the life of grace and made us his
children. He caused everything in us there is to love. As St
Thomas says: "When a man is said to be in another's good
graces, it is understood that there is something in him pleasing
to the other; even as anyone is said to have God's grace—with
this difference, that what is pleasing to a man in another is pre-
supposed to his love, but whatever is pleasing to God in a man
is caused by the divine love." God does not love us in the first
place because we are perfect; we only have any perfection
because God loves us. St John tells us: "What has revealed the
love of God, where we are concerned, is that he has sent his
only-begotten Son into the world, so that we might find life
through him. That love resides, not in our showing any love
for God, but in his showing love for us first, when he sent out
his Son to be an atonement for our sins" (I John 4. 9-10).

God's love for us now is the same as that with which he will
embrace us throughout eternity. During our time of trial he
cannot manifest himself to us intuitively in all his glory because
we must be free to accept him or reject him. But, short of that,
the effects of his love within us far surpass anything we could

have desired of ourselves. Our Lord, indeed, calls human love evil in comparison with God's fatherly love: "Why, then, if you, evil as you are, know well enough how to give your children what is good for them, is not your Father in heaven much more ready to give wholesome gifts to those who ask him?" (Matt. 7. 11).

What consolation there is in all this! God loves me. Do we not forget it too often? How many spiritual books one reads which are full of information about the spiritual life and self-perfection but have scarcely a word about God's love for us on which everything depends. It is far more important for us to believe that God loves us and to try to understand something of that personal, fatherly love than to concentrate on the mechanics of asceticism and external practices of spirituality. If we want to love God passionately we should try to realize that he first of all loves us passionately and that our desire to love him is the gift of his infinite love. Why do we allow ourselves to be upset by the disturbing trifles of life? Compared with God's love of us these little things are negligible. Human comings and goings are like matches lighted and extinguished in comparison with the noonday sun. The thought of God's love should dominate us as the sun dominates the firmament. It will console us, inspire us, perfect us and burst forth in all the virtues, which are like handmaids assisting the queen, which is charity. And charity in action is zeal. "My little way is all love," wrote St Teresa of Lisieux. And that is true of any direct way to God. It must be all love. There is no other.

20

"AND THE WORD WAS MADE FLESH
AND DWELT AMONG US"

(John 1. 14)

A T once we feel confronted with the impossible when we are required to comment on these, probably the most significant words of all Holy Writ. Almost as if what had gone before was a parenthesis, the Apostle takes us back a decade of verses: "In him [the Word] was life, and the life was the light of men; and the Word was made flesh." Yes, the article is used to indicate that it is the same Word—the Word that was in the beginning with God, the Word that was God, the Word by whom all things were made, the Word in whom was life, the Word whose life was the light of men.

This same infinite Word was made flesh. The divine nature could not change. The Second Person of the Blessed Trinity assumed a full, entire human nature, a created body and soul. That human nature had no distinct human personality of its own. So the Word incarnate had two distinct natures, divine and human, but only one person, the Person of God the Son. Into the unity and dominion of the divine Person the human nature was assumed. Henceforth the divine Person, God the Son, would operate in the human nature and through it.

The Council of Chalcedon, confirming the famous dogmatic letter of Pope St Leo the Great in 451, defined: "We teach that one and the same Christ, the Son, the Lord, the only-Begotten is to be recognized in two natures unmixed, untransformed, unseparated, undivided whereby the difference of the natures in consequence of the unification was never abrogated, but the peculiarity of each of the two natures remained preserved." Each of those two natures in Christ possesses its own natural will and its own natural manner of operation. The union of the two natures in the one Personality took place at the moment of conception; it has never been interrupted; it will never cease.

St John chose to use the Greek word which means "flesh". He

could have written simply "man" but he wanted to stress particularly the infinite contrast between the Word, whom he had
just described, and the greatest weakness, for the flesh is the
weaker part of human nature.

When Mary bowed her lovely head with consenting words on
her lips there took place incomparably the greatest event in the
history of creation. Greatest seems such an inadequate word.
Call the Incarnation amazing, astounding, astonishing, startling
and you are far from the mark; describe it as inenarrable, inex-
pressible, ineffable, unspeakable, unutterable and you are still
falling short; say it is sublime, splendid, superb, glorious and
you touch but one of its facets; tell of its importance, significance,
consequences and momentousness and yet all you say must be
inadequate. It is absolutely unique, utterly and completely
indescribable in its infinite fullness. It dwarfs into nothingness
all the otherwise most momentous happenings to matter, man
or spirit. It infinitely transcends all comparison, outstrips all
analogy and excels all parallels. To compare it with anything
is to belittle it.

Is it not strange that familiarity has so dimmed man's per-
ception that he no longer estimates the importance of other
human happenings by their relationship to this one pivotal
thing, the union of God and man in Mary's womb? Indeed
most of the men who call themselves Christians hardly ever
pause to think of the meaning of that happening in history which
made Christianity possible. Stop twenty men in the Strand,
London, tomorrow and ask each of them which, in his opinion,
is the greatest event of all time—how many would reply without
a moment's hesitation the coming of God into a virgin's womb?
Yet that is the true answer.

The universe is so replete with wonders that we have ceased
to show surprise when even the most electrifying advance is
made in the world of science; we have come to expect these
things. We take for granted the reflection in material things of
the infinite attributes of the Creator. We are so accustomed to
the harmony which prevails about us and to the laws according
to which everything operates that the knowledge of them does
not turn us to the infinite Designer or the omniscient Lawgiver.
The creation of the universe from nothing is a thrilling manifestation of the goodness and the power and the wisdom of God—

but his coming amongst us in human form displays those attributes even more magnificently. Could he reveal his goodness more than by espousing the very human nature which had rebelled against him? Could he disclose his power more effectively than by making one and the same Person God and man? Could he manifest his wisdom more significantly than by restoring fallen humanity to grace, displaying his infinite mercy yet leaving intact his infinite justice?

Why did God wait all those thousands of years before taking our human flesh from Mary? St Paul says it happened "when the fullness of the time was come" (Gal. 4. 4). St Thomas Aquinas, commenting on it, tells us: "God decreed everything by his wisdom. He became incarnate at the most fitting time." He goes on to say that since the purpose of the Incarnation is principally "the restoration of the human race by blotting out sin" it was not fitting for the Incarnation to take place until sin had been committed. Nor yet immediately after sin because man had to be made to see how much he needed a redeemer. Moreover, the dignity of the God-man demanded a worthy preparation: "The greater the judge who was coming, the more numerous was the band of heralds who ought to have preceded him."

There is another reason. Had not man, in his first parent, set himself against God, proclaimed his determination to carve out his own destiny and attain independent happiness? He looked forward to the triumph of unaided human reason, to evolution after evolution leading ultimately to perfect prosperity and complete contentment. God left him to himself and his materialistic ambitions; he let him develop successive civilizations at Sumer, 3500 years before Christ, then in Egypt, then in China, then in Babylon, then in Egypt again, then in Greece and finally in Rome. Many of these civilizations attained astonishing heights of achievement in science, art and culture. But to what did they all lead? To the frightful state of moral degradation we have already studied in the first chapter of St Paul's letter to the Romans. There was what man could do by himself; that appalling picture represents the summit of refinement, culture and civilization. So, with good reason St Thomas wrote:

Man was to be liberated in such a way that he might be humbled and see how he stood in need of a deliverer. . . .

With great wisdom was it so ordered that the Son of Man should not be sent immediately after man's fall. For first of all God left man under the natural law, with the freedom of his will, in order that he might know his natural strength; and when he failed in it, he received the law; whereupon, by the fault, not of the law, but of his nature, the disease gained strength; so that having recognized his infirmity he might cry out for a physician, and beseech the aid of grace.

See the infinite mercy of God! Not only does he become man to redeem man, which he could have done by a single act of his will, but he lived amongst us so that we could learn how God would live a human life. In such a life is the whole secret of happiness. The more our lives reflect his life the less disorder afflicts us. Christ's life focuses the Godhead into a human life; it shows us God worshipping, God praying, God teaching, God working, God suffering, God obeying, God humbling himself, God practising every virtue. It shows us God as a baby, God as a child, God as a teenager, God as a man, God in the home, God in the village, God in the community, God in the countryside, God with his friends, God and the state, God on trial. It has been well said that God chose to come like this just when the world had become a vast temple of Satan. Man's life had to be changed in every department; it had to be re-focused; its whole direction had to be altered. God had to be brought into work and play, art and science, state and politics, civic and social life, domestic economy and international relations, family life and education. The whole order of paganism had to be uprooted; long-established vested interests had to be challenged and over-thrown; evil customs had to be exposed for what they were; selfishness, greed and injustice had to be conquered; idolatry and lust had to be supplanted. Almost everything in human life at the time of God's birth of Mary had to be transformed into its opposite: pride into humility, lust into purity, hate into love, greed into generosity, slavery into freedom, cruelty into gentle-ness and so on.

Suppose it had never happened? Suppose the Word had never been made flesh? Can we imagine the state of mankind today? Not only would there be no Church, no sure guidance, no sacraments, no supernatural life, no Mother of God, no

saints, no Real Presence, no Mass, no knowledge of the Holy
Trinity, no certainty as to what happens after death, but men
would have sunk into unbelievable depths of immorality and the
consequences of that would be only too evident. Disease and
despair would ravage our race. Suffering and every kind of
evil would be infinitely more rife than they are now and
—this is even worse—men would have no explanation for
them. When we are afflicted we can turn to our crucifix and
learn from it that God does indeed care for us; in fact we have a
thousand proofs of his infinite love for each of us. If Christ had
not come that would have been impossible. If, in spite of the
coming of God amongst us, the human race has reached such a
dangerous state today that it is threatened with annihilation in a
nuclear war, what would have been the extent of the bloodshed
in twenty centuries if the Incarnation had never happened?
Suppose the state of affairs described by St Paul had progressed
in the direction in which it was moving then, from evil to evil—
is it not likely that the soil of Europe would have been stained
with the blood of millions of young bodies mutilated in warfare?
If after twenty centuries of Christianity man could destroy his
brethren to the number of eleven million in the First World
War, what would have happened if there had been no Christianity? Dare we think of it—the battlefields, the graveyards, the
asylums, the orphanages (would there have been any?), the hospitals (without Christian charity), the devastated cities, the
scorched countryside. Yes, and the cry of the multitude to the
faithful few—"See all these things and how can you still believe
in a merciful God!" But how different it all is. "The Word *was*
made flesh." In that fact we have our answer and our consolation.

If God had not lived amongst us we would have had no
answer to the problem of sin. It would have abounded in the
world; the natural law would have been disregarded; the sinners
would prosper; the rich would grind down the poor; evil would
seem to triumph—and God would seem to be unmindful. It was
stated in an earlier conference that men today hardly care about
the Ten Commandments. George Bernard Shaw said they have
become mere lumber. If the situation has developed like this
with Christianity in the world, what would it be like if Christian
influence had never been known?

In the mystery of the Incarnation also we have the solution of yet another problem which puzzles the materialistic world of our day, the problem of the human body. To some it is vile and disgusting; to the majority it is little more than a plaything from which they are to extract the maximum amount of sensual pleasure. The purpose of marriage is pleasure, pleasure and yet more pleasure. Yet, "the Word was made flesh". God was not ashamed of what he had made. He loved it so much that he had to be united with it, raise it up and glorify it. How utterly anti-Christian it is to regard the body as a dirty thing, a source of sensuous amusement, a bait on stage or screen or advertisement! The figure of God in the flesh should be a sign and a warning to a wicked world that degrades the body, with which he was united, to the level of the beasts. It should be a reminder to all Christ's followers that they should not be ashamed of maintaining his standards of purity and modesty under all circumstances. There is nothing to be ashamed of in being pure as Christ was pure, nothing to apologize to the world about because we cannot follow it into the slough of lust.

God might have made Christ's human nature in ways utterly unknown to man's finite mind. It was by no means necessary that he should have been born of a woman. Yet the fact is that he was so born, that he thereby became a member of our human family, our Brother in the flesh. From Adam's day until ours one blood stream has coursed through the veins of men; God himself deigned to fill his veins with blood from that same stream. It still flows in the veins of every human being, but realize how it has been ennobled beyond measuring because God willed to draw from it his own Precious Blood, the blessed price of the ransom of the human race.

In every nation there are families which rightly glory in the nobility of their blood; they are the privileged ones; in them much of the national heritage is enshrined. By the Incarnation we have been all ennobled, become privileged and been made the shrines of the same blood stream upon which the Creator deigned to draw. The Son of God is in our family; he is one of us. We look forward to the day when he will welcome us to our true home, realizing that one of us is already reigning there, with another, his Mother, by his side. At every moment God is still a man; he will never cease to be a man; so, for all eternity our Brother in the flesh is seated at God's right hand. There is the glory of our manhood; God is really and truly our brother. We have already seen with St John how this natural brotherhood with God incarnate is infinitely surpassed by the supernatural brotherhood with which he has endowed us, making us partakers in the divine nature. "The Word of God, Jesus Christ, on account of his great love for mankind, became what we are in order to make us what he is himself", wrote St Irenaeus at the end of the second century.

For our further meditation we will glance quickly at some of the thoughts of the Doctors and Fathers of the Church about this sublime mystery. "By becoming man the Saviour was to accomplish two works of love", wrote the Doctor of orthodoxy against Arius, St Athanasius; "First, in putting away death from us and renewing us again; secondly, being unseen and invisible, in manifesting and making himself known by his works to be the Word of the Father and the Ruler and King of the Universe." Already we have quoted those other tremendous words of the same saint: "He was made man that we might be made God." Insisting on the reality of the human nature which God's eternal Word assumed St Cyril of Jerusalem wrote: "If the Incarnation was a phantom, salvation is a phantom also." St Gregory Nazianzen pledged his belief that the "Son of God, the eternal Word, who was begotten of the Father before all ages and without body" after being born of Mary is "in his own person at once entire man and perfect God". And St Ambrose asks: "What was the purpose of the Incarnation but this—that the flesh which had sinned should be redeemed by itself?" His famous convert, St Augustine, tells us: "God died, that a kind of celestial exchange might be made, that men might not see death. Forasmuch as he is both God and man, wishing that we should live by that which was his, he died by that which was ours. For he had nothing himself whereby he could die, nor had we anything whereby we could live. What an exchange!" In another work of his we find words which are echoed daily in the offertory prayers of the Mass: "By being made partaker of our mortality, he made us partakers of his divinity."

On a more devotional theme St Bernard stated that the chief reason "why the unseen God willed to appear in flesh and mix with men was that he might draw to himself in flesh the love of those who were not yet able to love save in a carnal manner, and so to lead them gradually on to spiritual love". Repeating the thought of the Fathers, the Angel of the Schools declared: "From Christ's fullness grace is poured out on us. The Son of God was made man that men might be made gods and become the children of God. Not from necessity was Christ a debtor to death but from love of God and man."

Is it not a pity that so many millions of Catholics are unaware of the gems of consolation concerning the mystery of the Incarnation which are to be found in the prayers, antiphons, responsories, readings and hymns of the sacred liturgy? Throughout the year the Church, through her official worship, lives again the earthly life of the eternal Word. Each succeeding season and feast is a renewal in his mystical Body of the mysteries and events of the thirty-three years he spent amongst us. Moreover, throughout the centuries, through the legitimate development of the life of the Church new insights have been given into devotion to Christ, God and man. It would be a tragic mistake to undervalue them. For example, the popular devotions promulgated by St Francis of Assisi and his followers to the Sacred Infancy, the Crib, the Way of the Cross, the Holy Name and Mary's Immaculate Conception as well as devotion to the Sacred Heart are the legitimate expressions of orthodox spirituality and should never be reprehended on the grounds that they conflict in some way with the true stream of liturgical development. Countless souls have found in them highroads to holiness. The wealth of the devotional life of the Church through the centuries, with its appeal to men and women of every condition and walk of life, is just one of the many proofs of her infinite vitality.

To all go out the touching words of the martyr-poet, Blessed Robert Southwell:

O dying souls; behold your living spring!
O dazzled eyes! behold your Sun of grace!
Dull ears attend what word this Word doth bring!
Up, heavy hearts, with joy your Joy embrace!
From death, from dark, from deafness, from despairs,
This Life, this Light, this Word, this joy repairs.

Christ's life, portrayed in the Gospels by the Holy Ghost, and in many excellent works by saints and scholars, should be the subject of ceaseless study, thought and, above all, prayer. It is the model of every life, the source of all true spirituality, the inspiration for all holiness, the example of all virtues. The more we know Christ the more we will love him. Prayerful reading and devotional study will surely merit for us the increase of faith for which we ought to pray with the Apostles: "Give us more faith" (Luke 17. 5).

He dwells amongst us still. We have studied already under the guidance of St John how he is present in the life of grace in every soul. We know, too, how our judgment is going to depend on our seeing him in each of our fellow men and serving him there: "Believe me, when you did it to one of the least of my brethren here, you did it to me" (Matt. 25. 40). But he lives on also in his mystical Body, the Catholic Church, and he is really, truly and substantially present under the appearances of bread and wine in the Holy Eucharist.

Let us recall again the moment of the conversion of Saul on the road to Damascus. "Saul, Saul, why dost thou persecute me?" the voice of Christ said to him and at once grace illuminated his mind and will to understand that in persecuting a Christian he was really persecuting Christ. He knew in that startling moment that each individual is a member of Christ and that Christ who died on Calvary still lives on in his Church. As St Augustine was to write: "If we consider ourselves, if we think of his Body, we shall see that he is ourselves. If we were not he, those words would not be true: 'Saul, Saul, why dost thou persecute me?' Therefore, we, too, are he, because we are his members, because we are his Body, because he is our Head, because the whole Christ is Head and Body."

Is it not, humanly speaking, astounding that after thirty-three years on earth, years spent in prayer, toil, preaching, miracles and works of charity, God himself should leave behind only a few fearful, hesitant disciples? He could hardly have been further from his stated goal of preaching the "gospel to the whole of creation" (Mark 16. 16). But "who has ever understood the Lord's thoughts, or been his counsellor?" (Rom. 11. 34). What man could have conceived that that Person pierced by a lance on the cross was not really leaving the world at all, that at that very moment new life was springing forth with the

stream of blood and water that followed the weapon's with-
drawal? We know that Christ lived on in his other self, his
Church, his fullness, his Body. What the Church would do in
the years that remained of human history after man attempted
to murder his God, he, that same God, would do for men. He
would do it in her.

The same truth emerges from all that our Lord said about his
"kingdom". It is to be intimately united with his own Person; it
is to have its own life, its "mystery". He will remain with it until
the end of time. Those who hear it will hear him; those who
receive it will receive him; what it will forbid he will forbid;
what it will allow he will allow; what is done to the least of its
members he will regard as done to himself (cf. Mark 4. 11;
Luke 10. 16; Luke 9. 48; Matt. 18. 18; 28. 20; 25. 40). "The
Kingdom of God", someone has well said, "is Jesus, known,
tasted and possessed."

There is little need here to dwell in detail on the comparison
used by our Lord as the end of his life was near: "I am the vine,
you are its branches" (John 15. 5), nor yet on St Paul's undying
phrases: "So it is with Christ and his Church; we are limbs of
his body; flesh and bone, we belong to him" (Eph. 5. 30). We
know the truth only too well, the Church is Christ himself still
dwelling amongst us, alive in every age, teaching, encouraging
and comforting all peoples, always bestowing mercy and blessing, giving infinite glory to God and offering redemption and
grace to men. The implications of it all are inexhaustible; the
whole edifice of sacred theology might well be erected around
the scaffolding of the doctrine that the Church is Christ.

Here is how Father Emile Mersch, S.J., sums up in the last
chapter of his monumental book, *The Whole Christ*:

In the Church, which is the continuation of Christ, there
exists between the Incarnate Word and each Christian more
than any bond of love, however ardent, more than a relation
of resemblance, however close, more than the bond of total
dependence that binds to their one Saviour all men who have
received the grace of pardon and sanctification. There is
something more than the union of subjects to any king, more
than the insecure incorporation of members in an organism,
more than the closest possible moral union. There is a

"physical" union, we should say, if the very term itself did not
appear to place this bond in the category of mere natural
unions. At all events it is a real, ontological union, or, since
the traditional names are still the best, it is a mystical, trans-
cendent, supernatural union whose unity and reality exceed
our powers of expression; it is a union that God alone can
make us understand, as he alone was able to bring it into
being.

Let it be solemnly noted that our devotion to the Church must
correspond to our belief.

Christ dwells amongst us still in the Eucharist. He is, as the
prophet proclaimed, still the hidden God (Is. 45. 15). He who
was thought by the pagans when the human race was young to
speak in the thunder, he who possessed in a mysterious way the
Holy of Holies of the chosen people, he who lay as a little baby
in the straw of Bethlehem's manger, he who was taught by his
mother, worked and preached, he who was transfigured, he who
hung naked, nailed in infamy to Calvary's tree—it is of him
that we sing "O Godhead hid, devoutly I adore thee". He is our
King, living incognito amongst his subjects; only we, with faith,
have been let into the secret. There is his tent, the appearances
of bread and wine. Daily the priest raises him that his people
might see him, but still he remains hidden as always before.
No earthly power can penetrate that veil, no human force
pierce that tent. There he dwells still, the Word who was in the
beginning, who was with God, who is God.

In his eucharistic presence he relives amongst us still his
earthly life. Faith sees in every Mass not only the Last Supper
and Calvary but Bethlehem, too, in the ceaseless presence of the
tabernacle the hidden life of the Worker of Nazareth, the
healing mission of him from whom power went out during his
public life, the inspiring example of every virtue and the infinite
devotedness which made him far more than the Apostle, who
applied the words to himself "all things to all men" (I Cor. 9.
22). Devotion to his eucharistic presence is surely a test of the
measure of our love of the incarnate Word.

For the man of deep faith there is nothing on earth so sublime,
so enthralling, so stupendous, so compelling as the Holy
Eucharist. It is the greatest work of God, the mirror of the

divine perfections, the type of all the divine operations. It is the continuation and parallel of the Incarnation, the sum of its wonders, the reflection of the earthly life of Christ. It is the triumph of the Church, its food and its life and the explanation of its phenomena. It is a compendium of miracles, an example of virtues, a fountain of grace and a magnet of souls.

Faith makes us yearn to proclaim the glory of the Eucharist with the voice of its martyrs who for it gave their all, with the fervour of the confessors who spent themselves to enlarge the kingdom of their tabernacled Creator, with the learning of the Doctors, who strove to explain the manner of his presence, with the zeal of the Apostles who knew that under the created veils he lives whom they hailed as Master in Galilee, with the love of the choirs of angels who adore the Host on the altar as they cease-lessly adore the majesty of God in heaven. Is it too much to imagine Mary herself pleading with the men of every age to recognize and love in the Eucharist the baby she bore at Bethlehem and carried to Egypt, the child she cared for at Nazareth, the man by whose toil she lived, the preacher on whose words she hung, the priest and the victim nailed to the tree beneath which she stood? If she lived on earth today would not her loving service be concentrated on his eucharistic life amongst us? Would she not adore him there, thank him there, intercede with him there and propitiate him there? Does she not long now as she reigns in heaven for an immense revival of devotion to his presence here in this mystery of faith and love?

21

"WE SAW HIS GLORY, THE GLORY AS IT WERE OF THE ONLY BEGOTTEN OF THE FATHER, FULL OF GRACE AND TRUTH"

(John 1. 14)

IN the previous phrase St John has said that the eternal Word dwelt amongst them. They could see that he was really man. He was a member of the human family, eating, walking, talking, weeping, bleeding, suffering and dying like other men. As St Luke had put it years before, "The Lord Jesus came and went among us" (Acts 1. 21), and Baruch, centuries before him, "Not till then would he reveal himself on earth, and hold converse with mortal man" (Baruch 3. 38).

Now the evangelist turns to the Godhead of the Word. They saw his glory. When? Surely at his Transfiguration, as St Peter also testified: "When we preached to you about the power of our Lord Jesus Christ, and about his coming; we had eye-witnesses of his exaltation" (II Peter 1. 16). And also after his Resurrection, at his Ascension and in the miracles he worked. The glory they saw was such as was becoming the only-begotten Son of God. St John Chrysostom comments: "As if he said: we have seen his glory such as it was right and becoming that the only begotten and true Son of God should have." The glimpses of glory to which St John alludes were not of the Word in himself but they were enough to convince them that Christ was indeed that Word, the eternal, consubstantial Son of the Father, who is equal to him in all things.

The words "full of grace and truth" go with the preceding, "the Word was made flesh and dwelt amongst us". He it is who is full of grace and truth. A couple of verses later on St John writes: "Through Jesus Christ grace came to us, and truth" (John 1. 17): therefore it seems better to think that in the verse we are considering grace and truth represent two realities.

We may think of grace in this context in its widest sense. Not only had Christ the grace of union, as it is called, by which his humanity was hypostatically united to the Godhead, but, in addition, Christ's human soul was full to capacity with created grace. Not only did it sanctify him; it was through him a source of our sanctification also.

Our Lord's human nature is substantially holy. It was anointed by the Godhead, as the name "Christ" signifies, and by that anointing sanctified. As St Gregory of Nazianzus puts it: "He is called Christ on account of the Godhead; for this is the anointing of humanity; it sanctifies not through an alienation of power, as in the case of other anointed, but through the presence of the totality of him who anoints." St Augustine says it this way: "In the Word the Son of man was himself sanctified from the beginning of his creation when the Word was made Flesh, for the Word and the man became one person. Then accordingly he sanctified himself in himself, that is, himself the man in himself the Word, for the Word and the man is one Christ, who sanctifies the manhood in the Word." St John of Damascus emphasizes that the very flesh of Christ was anointed not by the mere operation of God but also by the full presence of the one anointing. It is infinite grace for it is the gift of an infinite divine Person granted to human nature. Christ's humanity is holy, independently of his sanctifying grace, through uncreated, infinite divine holiness. Of course, we must not think of this substantial holiness as a form inhering in our Lord's humanity, for God's attributes cannot belong to a created nature. It is rooted exclusively in the personal union of Christ's human nature with the Word of God.

In his encyclical letter on the mystical Body of Christ, Pope Pius XII wrote: "He (Christ) is adorned with all those supernatural gifts which accompany the hypostatic union; for in him the Holy Spirit dwells with a fullness of grace than which no greater can be conceived." To him has been given "power over every flesh", and "all the treasures of the wisdom and knowledge of God" abound in him (Col. 2. 3). He also enjoys the beatific vision in a degree, both as regards extent and clarity, surpassing that of all the saints in heaven. Indeed, so "full of grace and truth" is he that of his inexhaustible "fullness we all receive" (John 1. 14-16).

The grace of union is the greatest of all graces; by it Christ's humanity was sanctified formally, and that sanctification we attribute to the Holy Ghost. To him also we attribute the endowment of his soul with sanctifying grace. "God anointed him with the Holy Spirit and with power, so that he went about doing good" (Acts 10. 38). Once, preaching in the synagogue of his village, he applied the words of Isaias to himself: "The Spirit of the Lord is upon me; he has anointed me" (Luke 4. 18). Not only in the infinite grace of union was this anointing bestowed but also in all the other graces and gifts which adorned Christ's soul. In the most perfect way possible divine grace dwelt in him with absolute fullness. Isaias had foretold: "One shall be born, on whom the spirit of the Lord will rest; a spirit wise and discerning, a spirit prudent and strong, a spirit of knowledge and of piety, and ever fear of the Lord shall fill his heart" (Is. 11. 2). In his encyclical letter *Divinum illud* Pope Leo XIII wrote: "By the conspicuous apparition of the Holy Ghost and by his invisible power in his soul, the twofold mission of the Spirit is foreshadowed, namely, the mission which is evidently manifested in his Church and that which is effected by his secret descent into the souls of the just."

But we are anticipating. We must consider more fully the grace and truth of Christ. A comparison may make clear the distinction between substantial holiness and what we might call holiness of operation. Anything which is consecrated for use in divine worship, like churches and chalices, or blessed, like vestments, is substantially holy. We see the distinction especially in the Pope, bishops and priests. In virtue of their office and their Orders they are essentially holy; they are men apart; but, unfortunately, they have not always been actively holy, holy in their conduct. Now nothing could be more closely associated with God than our Lord's humanity. It is therefore holy in itself, substantially holy, infinitely holy, in the sense in which a consecrated chalice is holy. That is why we honour the humanity of Christ, and that means, for example, his Sacred Heart and his Precious Blood, with the worship which is due to God alone.

This substantial holiness is the root of his operative, active, living, dynamic holiness, of the absolute perfection of his life. God made our Lord's soul his own in a unique way. It is unthinkable that it should be stained by sin or the slightest imperfection. He could neither inherit sin nor commit it. Every thought, word, deed and omission of Christ was the thought, word, deed or omission of the infinitely perfect Word of God, and he is not only sinless but incapable of sinning.

Not only that. We have already seen in some detail how, during our earthly trial, God permits us to become his children, to share in his divine nature, to anticipate in limited measure the direct vision of himself. To be holy in God's sight means to have this divine life in one's soul. That is why it is called sanctifying grace, that is, the grace which makes holy. Our Lord is the source of all that grace; he possesses it in all its fullness. St Thomas Aquinas tells us that this grace in Christ's soul emanates from the hypostatic union "as light proceeds from the sun". As the eternal Word, equal in all things with the Father, our Lord possesses the infinite, indivisible life of the Godhead. It surely follows that as man he is made in the fullest possible sense a partaker of the divine nature. The grace of union which makes Christ's human nature substantially holy does not of itself necessarily make that nature also a partaker of the divine nature. For that to happen sanctifying grace, which is a finite entity, and the supernatural virtues, which are the principles of supernatural action, must be infused into Christ's soul. That infusion undoubtedly took place; on every count it is due to the human nature which is so closely united with the Godhead.

Christ as man does share in the divine nature, is the living temple of the Holy Ghost and is full of habitual, sanctifying grace. This does not result physically from the union of the human nature with the divine in one person; it is God's only-begotten Son's hereditary right. Therefore he possessed it from the first moment of his conception in the womb of his immaculate Mother, and he possessed it in all its fullness. How then does St Luke write: "And so Jesus advanced . . . in favour both with God and with men" (Luke 2. 52)? St Thomas Aquinas has the answer: "Anyone may increase in wisdom and grace in two ways. First inasmuch as the very habits of wisdom and grace are increased; and in this way Christ did not increase. Secondly, as regards the effects, that is, inasmuch as they do wiser and greater works; and in this way Christ increased in wisdom and grace even as in age, since in the course of time he

did more perfect things, to prove himself true man, both in the
things of God, and in the things of man."

Not only is the Word made flesh full of grace; he is full of
truth also. His human intelligence is the mind of God made
man. From the first moment of his human life he is humanly
conscious that he is God and with his human mind he contemplates God face to face. Even when, with the psalmist, he cried
out on Calvary "My God, my God, why hast thou foresaken
me?" (Matt. 27. 46; Ps. 21. 2), he still saw the glorious light
of God's countenance with nothing intervening. In the vision
all his pain and sorrow appeared not as evil things but as
appeasements of God's justice, manifestations of his love and
instruments of the salvation of souls and so of his Father's glory.
Even when he was sorrowful unto death his inmost soul rejoiced
to do his Father's will.

He is full of truth because he is infinite Truth become flesh
to bring truth to mankind. Recall his lesson to Nicodemus:
"Believe me, we speak of what is known to us, and testify of
what our eyes have seen, and still you will not accept our testimony. You cannot trust me when I tell you of what passes on
earth; how will you be able to trust me when I tell you of what
passes in heaven? No man has ever gone up into heaven; but
there is one who has come down from heaven, the Son of Man,
who dwells in heaven" (John 3. 11-13). Commenting on this
verse St John Chrysostom remarks that of all the senses sight is
the most certain. When we say we saw such a thing with our
eyes we compel men to believe us. So our Lord, speaking in
human fashion, does not mean that he has seen the mysteries he
is revealing with his human eyes but he does mean that he has
the most certain, absolute and immediate knowledge of them.
He teaches with authority; he must be believed. As St John puts
it, "No man has ever seen God; but now his only-begotten Son,
who abides in the bosom of the Father, has himself become our
interpreter" (John 1. 18). He is the truth of God. So also in other
words: "The Father, instead of passing judgment on any man
himself, has left all judgment to the Son" (John 5. 22). Yet
again St John says concerning those who believed in our Lord
through his miracles: "Jesus would not give them his confidence;
he had knowledge of them all, and did not need assurances
about any man, because he could read men's hearts" (John 2.

25). By the Jews who believed that God alone could read men's hearts, as the Old Testament says so often (Jer. 17. 10; 3 Kings 8. 39; 1 Par. 27. 9; Job 42. 2; Ps. 7. 10), such a manifestation should have been seen as proof that Christ was God.

It will not be inappropriate for us to conclude our meditations on the last gospel by thinking about the most startling manifestation of his glory our Lord made to his three chosen Apostles on Mount Thabor. The sequence of events adds significance to the story. After curing the blind man at Bethsaida (Mark 8. 22-26), our Lord went to the Caesarea Philippi district. It was there that St Peter made his profession of faith, "Thou art the Christ, the Son of the living God" (Matt. 16. 16) and was promised in return the primacy over the Church, inerrancy, the continual presence of Christ and the power of the keys. Then came our Lord's first prediction of his Passion and his startling rebuke of the very man to whom he had just promised such honour and power: "Go behind me, Satan, thou art a scandal unto me, because thou savourest not of the things that are of God, but the things that are of men" (Matt. 16. 23). What merited such a reprimand? Simply Peter's attempt to take his Master to task when he proposed to go to Jerusalem to suffer and die. "Heaven forbid!" Peter said in effect, "Nothing like this must happen to you." Our Lord's reply told him that he was standing right in his way because he was looking at things from a man's point of view rather than God's.

Next come our Saviour's words about self-denial. Harmonizing the text of the three evangelists we might translate with Knox:

He called his disciples to him, and the crowd with them, and said to them all alike, "If any man has a mind to come my way, let him renounce self, and take up his cross daily, and follow me. The man who tries to save his life will lose it; it is the man who loses his life for my sake and for the gospel's sake, that will save it. How is a man the better for it, if he gains the whole world at the expense of losing his own soul? For a man's soul, what price can be high enough? If anyone is ashamed of acknowledging me and my words before this unfaithful and wicked generation, the Son of Man will be ashamed to acknowledge him, when he comes in his glory, with his Father and the holy angels to glorify him; he will recompense everyone, then, according to his works." And he said to them, "Believe me, there are those standing here who will not taste of death before they have seen the kingdom of God present in all its power" (Matt. 16. 24-28; Mark 8. 34-39; Luke 9. 23-27).

Notice the sequence of poor Peter's ups and downs! At first he was bubbling over with enthusiasm and faith, but it was not so very solid. As soon as "the Son of the living God" talked about his Passion, renunciation, suffering and self-denial he wavered to the extent of opposing him and meriting a stern admonition. We are like that, too, when we fail to recognize God's will in the many happenings of life, in our daily crosses, frustrations, disappointments, sicknesses, behests of superiors, human limitations of companions and the rest. When the Prince of the Apostles jibbed at the programme offered him his Master thought it opportune to remind him of the value of the soul, the reality of eternity and the reward God gives to those who are faithful. We need that consolation, too. We should often think of these comforting verities.

Six days later Peter's act of faith received its divine confirmation. According to early tradition it happened on Mount Thabor. Hermon, 9,000 feet high, is preferred by some modern critics, or even some other spot on the chain of heights. Thabor, only five miles east of our Lord's childhood home and twelve west of the southern end of the Sea of Galilee, is a modest hill, half as high as Snowdon. On its flat summit there may have been some fortifications but its steep slopes were thick with trees, especially oak, carob and terebinth.

Up the steep path with their beloved Master walked the three men who were to be the first Pope, the first to die for Christ and the last of the twelve Apostles, Peter, James and John. This is not the James who wrote an epistle, was Bishop of Jerusalem and was called the "brother of the Lord" (Gal. 1. 19), but James the Great, St John's elder brother, the son of Zebedee, one of the "Boanerges", the sons of thunder (Mark 3. 17), who is traditionally regarded as the Apostle of Spain. We might think of these three privileged men as representing repectively authority, martyrdom and love. It is as if our Lord had decided that to faithfully exercise divine authority, to be courageous even to death and to love to perfection required more than ordinary faith in his Godhead.

We note that St Luke writes that Jesus took the three "to pray" and that it was as he prayed that he was transfigured. How very human is the sentence: "Meanwhile, Peter and his companions were sunk in sleep; and they awoke to see him in his glory, and the two men standing with him" (Luke 9. 32). Perhaps it is not wrong for us to take a little consolation from that when we find it so hard to keep alert during our daily prayer.

What does "transfigured" mean? It indicates a change of nature, not just the glorification of our Lord's human nature but his divine nature shining through his mortal body. He displayed for precious moments the glory with which he will appear in his heavenly kingdom and when he comes to judge our race. His face shone like the sun; his clothes became bright, dazzling, "white as light, white as no fuller here on earth could have made them". The Apostles were seeing something of the gift of clarity which arose from the glory of our Lord's Godhead and the beatitude of his soul. So far this gift had been concealed. In virtue of the grace of union it belonged to Christ, as did all the gifts of a glorified body, but by God's dispensation, which involved a continual miracle, it was repressed in his body, prevented from taking effect.

Now Moses and Elias are seen in glory talking with our Lord about his death in Jerusalem. Why Moses and Elias? We can only suggest that they represented the Law (Moses was the supreme lawgiver amongst the chosen people) and the Prophets (Elias was one of the most important of them). The three Apostles thus learned in a way they could never forget that these leaders, whom the Jews professed to follow, acknowledged their Master as the Messias. Thus were the Jewish leaders, who charged him with opposing the Law and the Prophets, refuted. Moreover, it was now evident that he was the Lord of Moses and so of the Law, and of Elias, and so of the Prophets; nor could he be himself Moses or Elias as the crowds falsely imagined. How did the Apostles recognize them? By a special revelation, by the talk they heard or by their appearance as the Jews usually recognized them. St Luke tells us that they spoke of his death in Jerusalem; thus they corroborated the prophecy with which he had so upset St Peter a few days earlier.

"Just as these were parting from him, Peter said to Jesus, 'Master, it is well that we should be here; if it pleases you, let us make three arbours in this place, one for you, one for Moses and one for Elias.' But he spoke at random; he did not know what to say, for they were overcome with fear." He was taken out of himself, lost in his delight mingled with reverential fear. Could not such happiness last for ever? Why should it be altered? Why could not Moses and Elias remain with his Master here, away from the crowds on the hilltop? He would soon put up three tents; there were plenty of tree branches about. He was used to erecting them on the feast of Tabernacles. But, says St Mark, who wrote down details supplied by Peter himself in Rome, he did not know what he was saying. Only a few days before he had been sharply corrected for trying to prevent the accomplishment of the Redeemer's mission. Now he tried to detain him on a mountain top, which would leave his redemptive work unfinished. It was thoughtless. And it was rather inconsiderate, too, to imagine that the glorified lawgiver and prophet needed tents to protect them. There was an element of selfishness about it also; he must keep all his glory here on the mountain, confined to the six who were present there. Little did he realize how foolish it was to prefer this passing glimpse of glory to the overwhelming, lambent, resplendent glory with which the saints would see God face to face for all eternity. Yes, indeed, "he spoke at random; he did not know what to say".

While he was speaking a bright cloud overwhelmed the party. Frequently in the Old Testament God displayed his majesty in a cloud. "They saw the glory of the Lord revealed there in a cloud" (Exod. 16. 10; cf. also 19. 9; 24. 15; Ps. 103 etc.). Later St Peter would describe it as "the splendour which dazzles human eyes" (II Peter 1. 17). The cloud certainly made it clear that our Redeemer was in need of no tent made by men. An interesting little point is that the cloud of the book of Exodus is said to be a "thick" one; this is a "bright" one. Thus, say the commentators, is shown the difference between the Old Law, the covenant of terror, and the New, the covenant of love.

Not only did the three Apostles see the most convincing evidence that their Master was indeed God; they heard it, too. From the cloud came the same words which had been uttered at his baptism: "This is my beloved Son, in whom I am well pleased". Literally the translation would be: "This is the Son of mine, *the* beloved", and the word translated by "beloved" is also used for "only-begotten" because an only-begotten son is singularly beloved. The Father's words clearly indicate that Jesus is his eternal Son, Son in a way far excelling all who are sons by other titles, such as creation, redemption or adoption. The form of words used by the inspired writer indicates that God's pleasure in his Son is continuous; it embraces past, present and future; it is unique; he alone singularly pleases the Father; in him there is nothing to cause displeasure.

"Hear ye him", said the voice of God. St John Chrysostom observes that it was only when Moses and Elias had disappeared that the voice was heard so that it would be absolutely clear that the words referred to Christ and to him alone. "Hear ye him" implies believe in him, keep his commandments, do his will, embrace his law now—not that of Moses and the Prophets. They have witnessed to the divine mission of Christ; their office has now ceased. Christ alone is enough. If we listen to him, obey him, love him and follow him in all things we shall obtain a share in the heavenly glory he displayed in those precious minutes on Thabor.

Now as we come to the end of our meditations on the few inspired sentences the Church bids us read every day as Mass ends, we must make our act of faith with St Peter. As long as we live we shall be engaged in battle with the enemies of our spiritual lives; never for a single second will that battle be called off. Our surest guarantee of victory is the outlook which follows logically from all we have learned from St John. Christ is God; he is full of divine life; he gives that life to us; he makes us share in his own life. At baptism we are transfigured, born again, made new creatures, take up a new life, become the dwelling places of the Trinity, children of God, brethren of Christ.

The details of the Transfiguration offer us a programme. We must be faithful to Peter, loyal always to the Holy See, loving God's will as it is made known to us by Christ's earthly representatives, shunning all craving for novelty, embracing the solid traditional ways of spirituality. Like James we must be courageous, always ready to die for Christ, to die, not only physically if he wills that of us, but especially in our intentions, dying to anything and everything which prevents our perfect love of him. Like John we must concentrate on the perfection of love which is not only the way to holiness but the essence of it, love of God and of all creatures for God's sake.

"We saw his glory", St John wrote. Yes, they saw him as the consummation and fulfilment of the Old Law; he must be to us all that matters in life. Daily we must pray for greater faith in him, that we will realize more and more what we mean when we hail him as the Son of the living God, the Splendour of the Father, the Brightness of eternal Light, the King of Glory, the Sun of Justice, the Author of Life, the Model of Virtues, true Light, eternal Wisdom, infinite Goodness, infinite in majesty, glowing Furnace of Charity, in which are all the treasures of wisdom and knowledge and where dwells all the fullness of the Godhead. Or in the words of the Creed at Mass: "the only-begotten Son of God, born of the Father before all ages; God from God, light from light, true God from true God; begotten, not made, of one essence with the Father; through whom all things were made. He for us men, and for our salvation, came down from heaven and was incarnate by the Holy Ghost from the virgin Mary; and was made man."

Peter, James and John saw his glory when they were on a mountain away from the world. So it will be with us. Growth in spiritual insight demands a conscious effort to detach ourselves from all that is not of God. They saw Christ's glory when they went to pray; so with us, prayer is absolutely indispensable; there is no substitute for it. "Tell the vision to no man", our Lord said; expediency made silence necessary at the time. But how different it was after that other evidence of glory, his Resurrection and his final triumphant ascent to his Father. Then they were to go out "making disciples of all nations", preaching the Gospel "to the whole of creation" (Matt. 28. 19; Mark 16. 15), knowing that he was with them to whom "all authority in heaven and on earth has been given". That is our vocation now; that is why the Church exists; that is the object of all our prayers and works. Only by absolute fidelity to Christ can we accomplish it. To his and our Mother we turn for the message in its briefest form: "Whatsoever he shall say to you, do ye" (John 2. 5).

INDEX

Abandonment, 26, 83
Abandonment by God, 157
Abia, Course of, 47
A-c-t-s, 78
Adonai, 151
Adoption, divine, **Chapter 18**, 188
Adoration, 13, 78
Advent, 23
Advertising, religious, 170
Affective prayer, 77 ff
Ambition, 98
Angels, 11, 94
Apostolate, 26, **Chapter 10,** 132, 171, 184
Ascetical theology, 183
Atonement, 178
Awe, 56

Balance, 106
Baptism, 42 ff, 136, 143 ff, 175 ff, 226
Beatific Vision, 31, 35, 182
Beatitudes, 62
Beauty, 36
Beginners in prayer, 82
Benediction, 171
Benedictus, **Chapter 7**
Birth, supernatural, 180
Body and soul of the Church, 147
Body, human, 204
Books, use at prayer, 83
"Born of God", 30
Boston, Letter to Archbishop of, 143
Brethren of Christ, 192
Brotherly love, 130 ff, 180 ff

Candlemas, 134
Candles, 134 ff
Candour, 115
Capital and labour, 196
Catholic, 169
Cenacle. the, 46
Ceremonies, 70, 81
Charity, 67, 71, 92, 130 ff, 146, 159, 196 (*see also* Love)
Childhood, spiritual 117, 192 (*see also* Teresa of Lisieux, Saint)
Christ, divinity of, 9 ff, 17, 199 ff, 220
Church, the, 54, 85, 94, 207 ff (*see also* Mystical Body)
Colour prejudice, 195-6
Commandments, Ten, 170
Communion, Holy, 39, 40, 45, 61, 171, 194 (see also Eucharist)
Communion of Saints, 195
Communism, 170

Considerations in prayer, 77-82
Contemplation, 79, 96-7
Contrition, 78
Conversion story, 184 ff
Co-operation, God's, in our actions, 152
Covenants, divine, 60, 163
Creation, **Chapter 3,** 151 ff
Cross, the, 103-4, 118
Crusades for souls, 186

Depression, remedy for, 101, 105
Desire for membership of the Church, **Chapter 15**
Detachment, 85, 221
Devotions, popular, 206
Discursive prayer, 76
Distractions, 16, 82, 86-7
Disunity, Christian, 169
Divine Office, 62

Easter vigil, 135
Efficiency, 68
Effort, 63
Election, divine, 133
Elias, 52, 218
Elizabeth, Saint, 48 ff, 57 ff, 62
England, 90
Eternity, 1 ff, 45-6, 69, 71, 177
Eucharist, Holy, 81, 92, 122, 139, 194, 201, 209-10 (*see also* Communion, Holy)
Evil, 109, 203
Exsultet, 136

Faith, 26, 35, 45, 55, 64-5, **Chapter 8,** 77, 79, 83, 92-3, 97, 113, 125-6, 138, 146, 172, 176-7, 181, 207, 217, 220
Family life, 170
Father, God our, 64, 188 ff
Feasts, 81
Feelings in prayer, 80, 86
Fervour, 172

Gazing on God, 61, 84-5, 117
Generosity, 172
Goodness, 54, 133
Grace, 31 ff, 39, 61, 92, 101, 113, 178 ff, 190 ff, 212
Graces of Christ, 212 ff

Heathens, salvation of, 156 ff
Holiness, 56, 75, 126, 129, 138, 159, 172, 178-9, 183, 213
Holy Ghost, 51, 88, 106, 176, 178, 192, 213

"Horn of salvation", 58
Humanists, 159, 170
Humility, 70, **Chapters 11 and 12,**
    159; of Christ, **Chapter 12**

Ignorance and salvation, 141 ff
Illuminative Way, 80
Immaculate Conception, 165
Inaction, Catholic, 89
Incarnation, the, 33, **Chapter 20**
"In Christ", 177
Incomplete membership of the Church,
    145
Indwelling, divine, 34 ff, 40, 177
Inheritance of Christ, 190
Intellectual interests and prayer, 87
Intelligence and holiness, 65
Intention, purity of, 71
Invisible Church, 147

Jahweh, 151
Jesus, holy name, 58–9
Jews, **Chapter 17**
John the Baptist, Saint, 47 ff, **Chapter
    6,** 67 ff, 76 ff, 86, 98, 169
Judgment, last, 25
Justice in our time, 171

King, Christ the, 22 ff
Knowledge, divine, 157

Law of Moses, 164 ff
Laws of science, 155
Life, Christ the, 28 ff, 40 ff
Life-light theme, **Chapter 5,** 66
Life of Christ, 91, 206–7
Life of grace, 38–46
Light, 34, 38 ff, **Chapters 13 and 14,**
    132 ff
Lights in worship, 134
Liturgy, 54, 63, 81, 169, 206
Lord's prayer, the, 15, 90
Lourdes, 81
Love, Christ's, 8, 12
Love of God, 26, 64, 69–74, 83, 95,
    105, 178, 182, 188, 191–2, 196 ff,
    221
Loyalty, 169–70
Lukewarmness, remedy for, 128

Marriage, 204
Mary, Blessed Virgin, 19, 37, 46, 54–59,
    61, 65–6, 75, 81–83, 85, 91, 93–96,
    107–8, 111, 160, 166, 169, 172, 194,
    200, 204, 210, 222
Mass, holy, 53, 63, 135, 167, 169, 171,
    173, 182
Mediocrity, mass, 127
Meditation, 76 ff

Membership of the mystical Body,
    Chapter 15
Members of Christ, 91
Mental prayer, 76 ff, 171
Merciful love, God's, 50, 55, 64
Mercy, 55, 64, 83, 100, 191, 202
Messianic Prophecies, 164 ff
Missionary work, 158 ff
Mortification, 56, 86, 173
Mystical Body of Christ, 42–3, 54–5,
    88, 97, **Chapter 15,** 183, 206 ff

Natural law, 156–7
Nazarites, 51
Necessity of means and precept, 142 ff
Non-Catholics and the mystical Body,
    Chapter 15
"No salvation outside the Church",
    Chapter 15

"O" antiphons, 24
Obedience, 26, 69, 70, 159
Oriens ex alto, 65–6

Pagans, salvation of, 157 ff
Partakers of the divine nature, **Chap-
    ter 4,** 101, 178, 190 ff
Passion of Christ, 182
Patience, 159–60
Perfection, 65, 105, 126, 129
Perseverance in religious life, 102
Petition, prayer of, 55, 83–4
Prayer, 13 ff, 50, **Chapter 9,** 102, 218,
    221
Precious Blood, 213
Presence of God, 61, 84, 102, 169
Preservation of creatures by God, 152
Pride, 105–6, 112
Privileges of the Jews, nine, **Chapter
    17**
Progress in prayer, 80
Promises, God's, 50, 62, 104
Proofs of God's existence, 155
Prophecy, 165 ff
Providence, divine, 69, 74–5, 151 ff
Psalms on humility, 100 ff
Purgative Way, 76
Purity, 204

Recollection, 61, 104–5
Recollection, prayer of, 79
Reparation, 81, 83, 172–3
Resignation, 105
Resolutions in prayer, 84

Sacred Heart of Jesus, 12, 25, 55, 63,
    83, 90–1, 97, 172, 206, 213
Sacrifice, 138
Salvation outside the Church, **Chap-
    ter 15**

Scientific discoveries, 154–5
Seed, metaphor of the, 30, 159
Seeing God, 73 ff
Self, 105, 118, 124
Self-denial, 56
Self surrender, 27, 55, 65–6, 82, 85, 91, 93–4
Service, 68–9
Sex, 171, 204
Shepherd, the Good, 41, 92, 183
Silence, 62
Simplicity, 65
Sin, 93, 109 ff, 112, 115, 180, 203
Social order, 196
Solitude, 61
Sonship, divine, **Chapters 18 and 19**
Soul of the Church, 147
Spiritual life, 34, 41 ff, 88
Spiritual reading, 80, 171, 207
Subjects of prayer, 83

Talents, 114
Television, 170
Tepidity, 127–8
Teresa of Lisieux, Saint, 50, 64, 92, 97, 103, 191, 198
Theological virtues, 17, 148, 176
Time and eternity, 1 ff
Transfiguration, the 25, 211, 216 ff

Transubstantiation, 139
Treasures of the Church, 92
Trials in prayer, 82
Trinity, Blessed, 6, 22, 35, 61, 82, 176, 193
Trust, 100, 102 ff, 105
Truth, 114, 215

Union with God, 43, 45, 63, 65, 70, 92
Union with Mary, 66

Victims of merciful Love, 55
Vine, Christ the, 43
Visible Church and the mystical Body, 143 ff
Visitation, the, 52, 65
Visiting the Blessed Sacrament, 171

Weaknesses, 102 ff, 129
Will of God, 69, 73–4, 100, 125–6, 128, 183, 192, 217, 220
Word of God, Christ our Lord, the, 5 ff, 21 ff and passim throughout
Work, 63, 68–72
Workman, Christ the, 111

Zachary, 39, 47 ff, 57 ff, 60 ff
Zeal, 83, 89 ff, 132, 184